CALIFORNIA GOLD-RUSH PLAYS

THE AMERICAN DRAMA LIBRARY

The American Drama Library is an ongoing series of American plays in anthology format, in which we plan to emphasize nineteenth and early twentieth century plays. Each volume will be edited by a specialist in the field, with the purpose of revisioning a particular genre, historical perspective, or individual playwright. The greater portion of the plays will be those which are previously unpublished, out-of-print, or difficult to find.

Much of our dramatic past has been ignored, belittled, or misunderstood, with the result that dramatic literature as a genre has not taken its rightful place in American letters. A serious loss in the study of American drama is the unavailability of published plays, and the commentary on them by which an art form and its audience interrogates itself and its responses to social and artistic change, from an historical point of view. This is the all-important process by which a field of study matures in relationship to the new ideas of any age. It is also the basis from which a dramatic repertoire grows.

The American Drama Library will, we believe, bring many more plays, new interpretations of dramatic form and cultural history, and reconsideration of literary reputations to our readers. Perhaps in the reflection of American experience this new material gives back to us, we may see in greater detail how, as a society, we give form to our feelings in the art of drama.

The Publishers

Other books in the American Drama Library Series:

American Melodrama / Edited by Daniel C. Gerould

American Popular Entertainments / Edited by Brooks McNamara

CALIFORNIA GOLD-RUSH PLAYS

JOAQUIN MURIETA DE CASTILLO
Charles E. B. Howe

A LIVE WOMAN IN THE MINES
Alonzo Delano

TWO MEN OF SANDY BAR
Bret Harte

Edited, with an Introduction, by
GLENN LONEY

PERFORMING ARTS JOURNAL PUBLICATIONS
NEW YORK

General Editors of The American Drama Library series:

Bonnie Marranca and Gautam Dasgupta

© 1983 Copyright by Performing Arts Journal Publications

Library of Congress Cataloging in Publication Data
California Gold-Rush Plays
CONTENTS: *Joaquin Murieta de Castillo, A Live Woman in the Mines, Two Men of Sandy Bar.*
Library of Congress Catalog Card No.: 83-61191
ISBN: 0-933826-34-6 (cloth)
ISBN: 0-933826-35-4 (paper)

Graphic Design: Gautam Dasgupta

Printed in the United States of America

Publication of this book has been made possible in part by grants received from the National Endowment for the Arts, Washington, D.C., a federal agency, and the New York State Council on the Arts.

CONTENTS

ACKNOWLEDGEMENTS

This edition of these forgotten plays, depicting an exciting, troubling, and mercurial time in California's transformation from a Spanish-Mexican territory into an American State, is affectionately dedicated to Celeste Ashley, who did much of the initial research on this project—which once was to have been an anthology of Pioneer Drama of the West.

The editor is deeply grateful to the curators and research librarians who have made reference materials, originals and copies of the plays, and other valuable documentation available. Among the libraries, collections, and organizations which have helped are the California Historical Society, the San Francisco Public Library, and the San Francisco Archives of the Performing Arts, all in San Francisco; the Bancroft Library of the University of California, Berkeley; the Stanford University Libraries, Stanford; the California State Library, Sacramento; the Henry E. Huntington Library, San Marino; the New York Public Library, and the Billy Rose Theatre Collection of the Lincoln Center Library of the Performing Arts in Manhattan.

INTRODUCTION

"Westward the course of empire takes its way," wrote Bishop Berkeley, in tracing the development of the American nation. Today, some are pained to think of the conquest of Western America as empire-building, but now that's very much what it seems to have been. Just over a week before Mexico was to cede the territory to the United States, in the aftermath of the lost Mexican War, gold was discovered in California. That was in 1848, and it sparked one of the greatest human migrations the world has ever seen. Not only by Americans from the East, the South, and the Midwest, but also by fortune-seekers from the British Isles, from France, Germany, and Sweden, from South America, and even from China. The Irish fled a fatal famine. Germans ran from poverty and a failed revolution. Between 1848 and 1852, in fact, the population of California—which was primarily Indian and Mexican before the influx of Forty-Niners—rose dramatically from 15,000 to 250,000.

In that brief period, some $200 million in gold was found in the placer mines, by digging, panning, and sluicing brown California dirt for nuggets and gold-flakes. These were indeed exciting times, stirring the imaginations of journalists, novelists, and dramatists, both at home and abroad. One of the first plays which purported to deal with life in the mines, *Cockneys in California*, was merely an exercise in fantasy, however. It was written in distant England by J. Stirling Coyne, an adept creator of farces, for a London production of 1849. Considering the numbers of highly educated men—doctors, lawyers, teachers—who rushed to the goldfields, hoping to make a strike which would transform them into millionaires, it is surprising that the great California Gold Rush didn't spawn more impressive and authentic dramas than this awkward, trivial piece and similar efforts seen on Eastern American and British stages. Even with writers of the stature of Bret Harte and Mark Twain honing their skills in the West as journalists, the San Francisco stage of the 1850s had no premieres of western dramas by these observant, witty men. Those were to come later, when both Harte and Twain had been lionized in the

East—and not without a real loss in force and verity.

As George MacMinn wrote in his 1941 study, *The Theatre in the Golden Era in California*: "It might be expected, however, that before long the argonauts [the goldseekers were popularly equated with Jason and his followers, seeking the Golden Fleece] themselves would produce a playwright, a competent amateur if not a professional, whose sense of comedy—or of serious drama—would not preposterously distort the truth about life on the Gold Coast. The fact is that such talent was exceedingly scarce. Nothing in the form of a regular, full-length play was actually printed in the new state until 1856."

Completing my doctorate at Stanford University, I did research in American theatre history and dramatic literature which aroused my interest in forgotten plays, especially those of the Old West, written by people who were actually in the places depicted in the plays at the time of their actions. A student colleague, Celeste Ashley, who was to help develop an impressive Theatre Collection—unfortunately later dispersed—for the Stanford Library, shared my interest. We planned to prepare an edition of Western or Pioneer Dramas, especially of those dealing with the California experience. [Celeste Ashley has since retired from her Stanford University post, but she has continued to support my efforts to publish at least some of the plays we located—so this is also her book.]

My first exposure to such works had been sparked by my discovery, as a UC/Berkeley undergraduate, of a forgotten Gold Rush play by one of the founders of my hometown in the Sierra foothills. The town is Grass Valley, which has a twin-city, Nevada City, home of the 1865 Nevada Theatre. This playhouse is considered by its valiant preservers as the oldest California theatre still being used for that purpose. Grass Valley's founder-playwright was Alonzo Delano. Since theatre activity began in Nevada City as early as 1850, Delano had professional models close at hand. An experienced writer, he was also a correspondent from the Far West for newspapers in the Midwest, the South, and the East. He wittily reported on life in the mines. Delano was familiar with the theatre of the East, as well as with that which was just getting started in Sacramento and in San Francisco— which was to become and remain for many, many years a thriving theatre center.

Alonzo Delano's *A Live Woman in the Mines; or, Pike County Ahead!* seemed not only an interesting picture of the rough-and-ready Forty-Niners—especially with its novelty of the arrival of the first woman in the mines, among a host of lonely men—but it also appeared to be a stage-worthy comedy-melodrama. Undaunted by my lack of directorial experience, I staged this unknown, forgotten work in William Randolph Hearst's Greek Theatre on the Berkeley campus as one of the annual "Sophomore Farces" of the late 1940s. It's all a bit hazy now, but I do recall our efforts to confine the performance of the relatively small cast to the central portion of that vast stage, which once had resounded to the art of Bernhardt and Pavlova. We did burst out, however, in a "Dream Sequence" of Mary arriving in the mines, to the unconfined joy of the eager miners. The immediate inspiration was Agnes de Mille's dream ballet in *Oklahoma!*, of course, but the actual choreography was devised by Durevol Quitzow, who derived his skills—also as leading dancer—from his family, who were disciples and students of San Francisco's own Isadora Duncan. The production was aptly labeled the "Sophomore Farce," for that's more or less how it turned out. Nonetheless, it was fun to do, and I still long to see this unusual historical-dramatic artifact given a really imaginative professional production.

Another fellow-student of theatre at Stanford, Stuart Wallace Hyde, completed an impressive Ph.D. dissertation, *The Representation of the West in American Drama from 1849 to 1917*, with an accompanying playlist of equally impressive length. Using this and other sources, Celeste Ashley and I began to draw up rosters of possible plays for an anthology of Western Drama. We soon found out that, for some earlier American historians and playwrights, the West seemed to have begun just across the Hudson River from New York City. There was a time, of course, when Kentucky and Ohio were really pioneer territory, areas of westward expansion. Such dramas as *Davy Crockett* and *The Lion of the West*, which drew their inspirations from bold personalities or vital events in the taming of the Midwest and the South, had already been rescued from obscurity by the *America's Lost Plays* series. So Ashley and I decided to focus on dramas of the Far West, especially those dealing with the Gold Rush in California and its immediate aftermath. We made lists. We crossed off those plays which had vanished without a trace. We eliminated those scripts which were really London or New York plots, reworked with a western setting. We also avoided those melodramas and farces about the Far West which seemed to have been written by bored actors during a tour of the English Midlands. An unusual number of these, as it happened, were concerned with the marital affairs of the Mormons in Salt Lake City, a subject which apparently both appalled and intrigued theatre-goers in Queen Victoria's England.

It used to be a commonplace of Hollywood Westerns that, possibly by right of Eminent Domain, the American West was there only waiting to be "won" by the hardy overland pioneers. Indeed, one U.S. Army World War II training-film—a patchwork of great film-clips—showed pioneers, cowboys, and U.S. Cavalrymen energetically slaughtering Indians to the accompaniment of a fruity narration along these lines: "And so, Americans moved constantly Westward, conscious that a Nation *had* to be born!" This was obviously not a consciousness shared by the Indians. In California, the scene of all three plays in this collection, not only the native Indians, but also the Spanish and Mexican settlers had to give way to the masses of Americans and other foreigners who came flooding into California. By the thousands, they were bound for the goldfields of the Mother Lode—in the Southern Mines—and for the riches of the Northern Mines. Unfortunately, many earlier settlers, who held large Mexican land grants, rapidly found themselves displaced by these emigrants. They often acted as "squatters," but they were protected by new American laws and property deeds. Captain John Sutter, builder of Sutter's Fort in Sacramento, saw his large landholdings overrun and seized by prospectors, staking their claims for the golden riches. On 24 January 1848, gold had been discovered at Sutter's Mill, in Coloma, news of which launched the Gold Rush. Sutter was driven out of California—a son murdered by a mob—to die in poverty and bitterness in the East. For those readers unfamiliar with the saga of the Conquest of California, there is a chronology of major events, from 1542 to 1882, in the Appendix. This not only provides a brief survey of the history of what came to be called "The Golden State," but it also can be useful in reading the plays. It helps explain the attitudes and actions—depicted in the dramas—of the new American settlers and prospectors regarding the Californians they found already on the land.

With the first stirrings of the Gold Rush, San Francisco became California's theatre center, a hub of producing activity, thanks both to relocated Easterners and to touring players—such as the aging Junius Brutus Booth, Sr., and his solicitous teenage son, Edwin Booth. One of his other sons, Junius Brutus, Jr., was to be a San Francisco regular in the theatre of the 1850s. One of the most interesting pioneers of San Francisco Gold Rush theatre, however, was David G. ("Doc" or "Yankee") Robinson. He was born in East Monmouth, Maine, and was, it was said, associated for a time with the great Phineas Taylor Barnum. Robinson's *The Life and Adventures of the Reformed Inebriate* was published in 1846 in Boston. The following year he opened a drugstore in San Francisco's Portsmouth Square, giving added import to the name of "Doc" Robinson. The stage soon lured him. His first drop-curtain was painted with curry and mustard powder, so primitive then were circumstances and supplies. His second stage was the Robinson and Everard Dramatic Museum—a name possibly borrowed from Barnum—on California Street, below Kearny.

Among the San Francisco-oriented plays credited to Doc Robinson in the early 1850s are *The Dashaways, Seeing the Elephant,* and *The Past, Present, and Future of San Francisco.* Even in its early days, San Francisco offered scope for the socially active; *The Dashaways* satirized this. (Its title is similar to that of a Victorian social spoof, *The Never-at-homes.*) "Seeing the elephant" apparently derived its initial currency from the curiosity and excitement generated by the exhibition of a large pachyderm. Some relate it to Barnum's ballyhoo for his specimen; others give it an earlier London origin. In the West, however, it took on more bitter overtones. Going to the mines with high expectations and having them harshly dashed was also described as "seeing the elephant." Later, jocular San Franciscans would use the phrase to indicate a projected tour of local landmarks, wonders, and night-spots.

Unfortunately, none of Doc Robinson's San Francisco play-manuscripts has survived. In an unpublished 1937 Federal Theatre study by Lois Foster, *Annals of the San Francisco Stage, 1850-1880,* Robinson's San Francisco career is reviewed. Apparently, he thought there might be interested audiences on the East Coast for his Gold Rush dramas, so he set out, leaving behind his wife and his son, Charles Dorman Robinson, later to become a noted painter of western scenes. He became gravely ill on shipboard and died in port in Alabama. It's reported that all his plays were stolen, including his epic survey of San Francisco history and his script of *The Reformed Drunkard,* which was, it has been alleged, stolen and rewritten as the enduringly successful temperance melodrama, *Ten Nights in a Barroom.* Since the Boston version of this Doc Robinson fable was already in print as a novel, this explanation of the origin of *Ten Nights in a Barroom,* while intriguing, may not be correct.

What did survive of Doc Robinson's antic stage humor and satiric wit are a number of his "Comic Songs," used in his various plays about San Francisco. They were published in that city in 1853, with the subtitle of *Hits at San Francisco,* "sung by him at the San Francisco Theatre." This is a pun, for they were, as reviewed by local newspapers, certainly hits with Doc Robinson's audiences, but they also were often sharply critical "hits" at corrupt local politicians and entrepreneurs, with their many odd or devious schemes. Pretensions of notable San

Franciscans and their distinguished visitors were mocked as well. One visitor to San Francisco who did not escape was the notorious European adventuress, Lola Montez. It has been said that she initially lodged with the Robinson family, and Mrs. Robinson sewed the spiders on her costume for her celebrated "Spider Dance." Lola Montez, who had been the mistress of King Ludwig I of Bavaria—not to mention Franz Liszt and others—had been created Countess of Landsfeld by the aged monarch. Robinson wrote a burlesque—*Who's Got the Countess?*—about Lola and her dance, which was performed with great success by a local comedienne, Caroline Chapman. The highlight was Chapman as Montez in the "Spy-Dear Dance." Tom Maguire, who was to be a major theatre-builder and producer in San Francisco for years, had bid for Montez's talents, but John Lewis Baker bid higher, so she opened 26 May 1853 at Baker's American Theatre. Her first-night box-office was reported at $4,500, but knowing local critics scoffed at her dancing. There were some San Franciscans, however, who were entranced by Montez and wrote poems about her to the newspapers.

Doc Robinson wrote his own poem about Lola Montez and set it to music for his audiences. It gives an idea of the topics and treatment favored by this early San Francisco playwright-satirist—as well as the tastes of Gold Rush theatre-goers. There are some references in the song which may be unclear today—these are footnoted immediately below the text:

Oh, have you heard the news of late
Of what happened in our State?—
There has arrived a monarch[1] mate,
   Imported from Bavaria!
If you would like to see the sight,
And aint afraid the crittur'll bite,
Just pay five dollars any night,
And Baker'll[2] get the show up right!
She'll glance you with those sparkling eyes,
And other means she will devise
To make you puff her to the skies,
While she the spiders will surprise!
And all the Bakers in the town
Will find the Countess does it Brown,
When with the dust[3] they must come down—
   To the Countess of Bavaria!

A Baker once, as I am told,
Became so fond of shining gold
That he at public auction sold—[4]
   The Countess of Bavaria!
Altho' he got but small advance,
Yet he went in and stood his chance,
Relying on that Spider Dance[5]
To put the public in a trance;

But when to see her they did go
The ladies thought, but didn't know,
The Countess lacked some calico,[6]
Which would improve the classic show!
Altho' some men were fairly sold,[7]
Yet Lola thanks them for their gold;
Her dancing knocks all dancing cold—
    She learned it in Bavaria!

That classic play-house[8] down below,
To which all moral people go,
Requires no trump of fame to blow—
    The Countess of Bavaria!
Altho' her fame was often told,
The morning that her tickets sold
She did poor Baker curse and scold
Because they brought so little gold!
While frightened Lewis[9] did protest
That with them he had done his best,
For all his soups he had well dress'd,
And they had each out-bid the rest!
But all his efforts were in vain,
And as his nose, to him 'twas plain,
That gold would not be showered like rain—
    On the Countess of Bavaria!

But people's tastes so disagree,
That what suits one may not suit me,
So you had better go and see—
    The Countess of Bavaria!
And if she deigns to you a chance
To see her classic Spider Dance,
Which did that Alta[10] man entrance
And fixed him with that killing glance!
But what increases our surprise
Is that our heroes, who despise
To shoot, yet like a martyr dies
A victim to a lady's eyes!
And thus in life 'twill ever be
We always find some foolish plea,
And you'll find one to go and see
    The Countess of Bavaria!

---

1. Ludwig I of Bavaria. 2. Theatre-manager John Lewis Baker. 3. Gold dust. 4. Opening-night tickets were auctioned. 5. Montez's specialty, in which spiders seemed to infest her costume. 6. Her costume was too scanty. 7. Cheated; "sold a bill of goods." 8. The American Theatre was a rival to Robinson's playhouse. 9. Manager Baker. 10. One of Montez's conquests.

Despite some hostile reviews and Doc Robinson's mockery, Lola Montez continued playing her repertory until the end of June. Her most popular attraction was a dramatic survey of her life and loves. After her San Francisco engagement, she retired for some months to that Sierra mining-town Alonzo Delano helped found—Grass Valley. She had taken and discarded a husband; she'd also acquired a pet bear, which she led around on a silver chain to the astonishment of the locals. It was said she had horsewhipped an editor who derided her talents. In short, she was a woman of some interest to the miners, whom she complimented on occasion by herself wearing miner's garb. During her stay in Grass Valley, tradition has it that Montez taught the little girl next door to dance. That child was Lotta Crabtree, who is reputed to have danced for the miners on a blacksmith's anvil, earning "pokes" or bags of gold dust. Later, as "The Darling of the Forty-Niners," she went on to a long career as one of America's first musical theatre stars. Grass Valley was also the birthplace of the distinguished Harvard philosopher, Josiah Royce, so the historic old town had an affinity for the arts and humanities in its earliest days. For Lola Montez, after Grass Valley her career was a downhill slide. She died in poverty and obscurity—an almost obligatory end for notorious women in the moral fiction of the time—and she lies buried in Brooklyn's Green Wood Cemetery as "Mrs. Eliza Gilbert." *Sic transit Lola.*

Doc Robinson obviously was no respecter of persons. If Montez was annoyed, that was as nothing to the anger of city councilmen and others who were his regular satiric targets. One of Doc Robinson's most popular numbers was a forlorn ditty to the tune of "A Used-Up Man." He called the song "Life in California," but he retained the "used-up man" phrase in all the refrains. Here are two verses to provide a sample of this early San Francisco entertainment:

I lives 'way down in Maine, where I heard about the diggings;
So I shipped aboard a darned old barque, commanded by Joe Higgins;
I sold my little farm, and from wife and children parted,
And off to California sailed, and left 'em broken-hearted.
   But here's a used-up man, a perfect used-up man,
   And if I ever get home again, I'll stay there if I can.
O I han't got no home, nor nothing else, I 'spose;
Misfortune seems to follow me wherever I goes;
I come to California with a heart both stout and bold,
And have been up to the diggings, there to get some lumps of gold.
   But I'm a used-up man, etc.

Doc Robinson delighted his audiences with this—updated from time to time with references to new San Francisco scandals and events—appearing in his Yankee guise, sporting a broken umbrella. A resourceful theatre-man, Doc Robinson instituted an early form of "Bank Night," with prizes for the audience. He also favored that popular nineteenth century stage attraction, the gradually unrolling scenic-panorama. His *Panorama of Venice* was a 2,956-foot wonder, costing $10,000 to construct and paint. He also showed a panorama of the "Antediluvian World," that is, the earth before the biblical flood. Someday, perhaps, Doc Robinson's stolen San Francisco plays will be found again. In the meantime, we have some musical specimens of his humor, this Yankee comedian, touched with Gold Rush brashness.

Two California plays from the 1850s are included in this volume, along with one from the 1870s, which recreates its author's own experiences and observations of the 1850s. The three plays are Charles E. B. Howe's romantic melodrama, *Joaquin Murieta de Castillo, the Celebrated California Bandit* (1858); Alonzo "Old Block" Delano's sentimental melodrama *A Live Woman in the Mines; or, Pike County Ahead!* (1857), and Bret Harte's adventure melodrama, *Two Men of Sandy Bar*, which was premiered in New York in 1876, and in San Francisco in 1878, following a national tour. It is unfortunate that there's no room in this volume for Warren Baer's jolly musical satire on Gold Rush mining swindlers, *The Duke of California* (1856). Or for Joseph Nunes's *Fast Folks; or The Early Days of California*—with a dedication to William H. Seward, the man who later bought Alaska for the United States. Nunes's comedy-melodrama was produced in 1858, at San Francisco's American Theatre. It's a West Coast equivalent to Anna Cora Mowatt's *Fashion* and owes its inspiration to the same playwright Mowatt echoed—Richard Brinsley Sheridan. Nor has it been possible to include either of Joaquin Miller's most interesting dramas of the West: *The Danites* and *Forty-Nine—An Idyll Drama of the Sierras*. Both were effective staples of the repertory of McKee Rankin and his wife, Kitty Blanchard, popular nineteenth century American touring players. Levi Damon Phillips has written a definitive doctoral dissertation on Rankin's *Danites* production for UC/Davis, where he is a Special Collections librarian. Perhaps the most famous of all melodramas about the Far West and the Gold Rush is David Belasco's *The Girl of the Golden West*. San Francisco-born in the midst of the Golden Era in 1853, Belasco experienced at first-hand what he put on stage so many years later, in 1905. Early involved in theatre, Belasco was once nearly hanged by vigilantes when he was mistaken for a horse-thief in Virginia City, Nevada. He was acting at Piper's Opera House during the great Comstock Lode boom. There are two reasons his notable melodrama is not in this volume: 1) its 1905 date, despite its authentic sources, puts it too far beyond the period of the Gold Rush, and, 2) it is already included in *American Melodrama* which Daniel Gerould edited for The American Drama Library Series of which this volume is part.

After a thorough search of the annals compiled in San Francisco under WPA auspices by Federal Theatre researchers and writers in 1937-38, there appeared to be no record of a professional production of either of the first two plays chosen for this collection. This, even though Alonzo Delano was a well-known personality and a respected writer. That doesn't rule out forgotten amateur productions. One volume of the Federal Theatre San Francisco histories is even devoted to records of amateur stagings, but neither *Joaquin Murieta de Castillo* or *A Live Woman in the Mines* is listed. It's entirely possible that the Federal Theatre researchers may have overlooked some newspaper reports of amateur shows in the late 1850s or in the 1860s. Or that amateur mountings of these plays occurred but were not, in fact, reported at all. In any case, Delano's affectionate, slightly comic exercise in nostalgia for the goldfields of 1849 was not published in San Francisco, but in New York, by Samuel French, as part of its popular series of "Minor Drama." These were plays sold for productions by stock-companies, amateur troupes, and schools, so it is likely that *A Live Woman in the Mines* in its day had its share of non-professional stagings.

It would be tempting to link Charles E. B. Howe, the dramatist of *Joaquin Murieta de Castillo*, with Julia Ward Howe, poet of "The Battle Hymn of the Republic," both because of their last names and their pronounced Union sentiments. Thus far, no relationship can be verified. In fact, aside from listings in local records as a resident of San Francisco, no important biographical information about Charles Howe has come to light. Possibly he intended his play for reading only, as a closet-drama. It was published in San Francisco in 1858, by the Commercial Book and Job Steam Printing Establishment. There are no records of productions or reprintings. But Howe did write some other plays, shorter and less ambitious. One of these, *Signing the Declaration of Independence; or, Scenes in Congress, July 4th, 1776*, was published by Samuel French, circa 1887. It was actually produced in San Francisco much earlier—in 1863, and, appropriately enough, in July at Maguire's Opera House. Living in the Far West had obviously left its mark on playwright Howe. Outside Independence Hall in Philadelphia, a patriot is made to say by the dramatist: ". . . you are a cowboy and a traitor. Such as you are as unfit for freedom as a rattlesnake would be to play with children. A tory and a cowboy!" Charles E. B. Howe's play about the notorious California bandit, Joaquin Murieta, depicts this legendary scourge of the West from Spring 1851 to 24 July 1853, when he was captured and killed by a posse led by Captain Harry Love, just as recorded in the drama. That the play is partly based on history is not so remarkable. There are, according to Francis Farquhar, who has made an extensive study of the Murieta literature, at least 20 versions of the Joaquin Murieta story. It has been retold in verse, reportage, drama, and fiction. Howe's version is especially interesting because it comes so soon—only five years—after the bandit's death. It is, in fact, one of the earliest attempts to characterize this daring bandit. The play appeared not long after the 1854 account by "Yellow Bird," or John David Ridge. This was the first version of Murieta's tale, part fact, part fiction, called *The Life and Adventures of Joaquin Murieta, the Celebrated California Bandit*. It had its first installment in May 1854, in the *Pacific Police Gazette*, but that first issue was also the last. A full ten installments appeared later in 1859, the year after Howe's play was published, in the *California Police Gazette*.

Since that time, versions have appeared in English and in Spanish. Joaquin Murieta has passed over into California legend; from a murderous desperado, he has been transformed into an Hispanic Robin Hood. The historian Joseph Henry Jackson, although he has admitted that there was a Murieta, doubted the many exploits attributed to him. Legend or truth, Murieta's image was and is a potent one. In the 1930s, near Grass Valley no less, people still pointed out the cave on Pilot's Peak, where Murieta was said to have hidden out after a foray in a Sacramento Valley town. Murieta's nemesis, Captain Harry Love, proved that the bandit had breathed his last. After the capture, Murieta's severed head and the pickled hand of his lieutenant, Three-Fingered Jack, were publicly exhibited. Indeed, many years later, the grisly trophies were still to be seen in carnival sideshows; at least the pitchmen assured customers that they were authentic. Nonetheless, there were those who said that Joaquin Murieta had escaped, a romantic but lethal Mexican anti-hero, who lived on to enjoy his ill-gotten gains far from California. The legend has been artistically enhanced by no less a modern talent than Chile's Nobel Prize-winner, Pablo Neruda. His poetic fantasy-drama, *Splendor and Death of Joaquin Murieta* (1966), insists often that Murieta was a Chilean. It also shows him as a man outraged by the Americanos who look down on him and mistreat his people. In the light of developing attitudes about the historic relationships between Americans and Hispanics, Neruda's vision of Murieta and his opponents could be viewed as a seminal literary comment.

And yet consider how much Charles E. B. Howe anticipated this time of polarization of attitudes. When Howe wrote his play, Murieta was widely considered a bloodthirsty Mexican thief, a dangerous, thoughtless murderer. His supposed Mexican origins certainly did not enhance him in the eyes of those immigrant Americans who feared him alive and could not forget him dead. He became a legend for his fearlessness, his daring. If murderous, he was still a brave desperado, one who was, however grudgingly, admired. But Charles Howe didn't depict a vicious, blood-crazed Mexican monster in his play at all. He created a poetic Joaquin Murieta, a real aristocrat, a natural leader, robbed of his patrimony—as were his fellow Mexicans of their lands and goods by the incoming Americans, who treated California as though it were their own and not a Mexican territory. Considering the condescension and often outright hostility with which the Eastern emigrant settlers treated the native Mexicans, Howe's portrait of Murieta as a valiant, intelligent, sensitive man, driven to a life of vengeful crime by deep wrongs done him, may be something of an American *mea culpa*. It is most unusual to find it so early in California history, not to mention American drama. Howe even allows Murieta moments of Robin Hood bravado and courtesy, when he protects some decent American settlers. Howe's play, no matter how high-flown its language or how devious the villainous plots of the bad priest, Gonzalles, is still an interesting testimony and document of life and attitudes in California in the 1850s.

That is even more the case with Alonzo Delano's *A Live Woman in the Mines*, published in 1858 in New York by Samuel French. Born in 1802 or 1806 in Aurora, New York, a third cousin twice removed from Franklin Delano Roosevelt, Delano (d. 1874) moved to the Midwest at 15, eventually dealing in drygoods and produce in South Bend, Indiana. On 19 April 1849, he and a small party of migrants began the 2,000-mile overland trek from St. Joseph, Missouri, to the California goldfields. Delano, it has been said, earned his living more with his pen than with his pan—that is, his mining pan. As "Old Block," he was soon providing newspapers such as the *New Orleans True Delta* and even the *New York Times* with his witty, but occasionally pathetic, accounts of life in California. Among his books are: *Pen—Knife Sketches; or, Chips of the Old Block* (1853), *Life in the Plains and Among the Diggings* (1854), *Old Block's Sketch-Book* (1856), and *A Sojourn With Royalty*, reprinted in 1936. In San Francisco, he had a produce business, but one of that city's disastrous fires incinerated that. Some measure of the man may be taken from the fact that, in the Panic of 1855, he permitted depositors of the bank he ran in Grass Valley to take their money out, even though he had telegraphic orders to close the bank and seal the safe.

Alonzo Delano was a remarkable man, and it shows in his unusual play. As George MacMinn says, in *The Theatre of the Golden Era in California*: "It came from the pen of a genuine California pioneer; it presented authentic and significant characters; its dialogue, full of flavor, was consistently realistic, and the whole was suffused with true atmosphere. That it failed to be adequately appreciated in California itself may be attributable to the fact that the local critics were generally disposed, by 1857, to assume the airs of sophisticates in all matters." One San Francisco book reviewer recommended it to miners. MacMinn admits that the play has never been accepted as a "possible contribution to American literature," yet he views it as "the most distinctively Californian of the plays produced by the golden era." Despite its formulary debts to standard stage melodrama of the day, Delano's play is amazingly fresh and direct, nowhere more so than in its portraits of the rough but good-natured prospectors of the goldfields, longing for homes and families left behind in the East, or even farther away, in England and in Europe.

Of the three plays in this collection, *Two Men of Sandy Bar* is the only one known to have professional productions of record. The drama's New York City premiere took place at the Union Square Theatre on 28 August 1876. Francis Bret Harte (1836-1902), its author, had made his name in the Far West as an especially apt observer of life in the mines, with a gift for translating those unusual scenes and characters into fiction. Actually, the name he made was his pen-name: Bret Harte. As editor of the *Overland Monthly*, he was able to share his own tales and those of other western writers with a fascinated, discriminating eastern audience, eager for insights into the life of adventure in the West. A number of his stories and poems, such as *The Outcasts of Poker Flat*, *Tennessee's Partner*, *The Luck of Roaring Camp*, *The Heathen Chinese*, *Salomey Jane's Kiss*, and *M'liss* became classics in their own time. Well into the twentieth century, they were still required reading for high school students of American literature. Born, like Delano, in New York State, Harte moved from Brooklyn to San Francisco in 1854. He learned the trades of printer, journalist, and editor, and later schooled his sometime colleague and friend, Samuel Clemens (Mark Twain). Although Harte held the sinecure of Secretary of the California Mint and, later, a professorship in "recent literature" at the University of California at Berkeley, as well as editorship of the *Overland Monthly*, he ran up debts and incurred other obligations. So he decided to move East, where his writings had already conquered—as they also had abroad, as far afield as Britain, France, and Germany. Unfortunately, also in the East, he was careless about repaying what he owed and awkward in dealing with others—even abrasive. Removed from the land and people which had given him his initial inspiration, his later work was either unconvincing invention or a faded reworking of his California triumphs.

Bret Harte's *M'liss*, adapted in San Francisco by Clay M. Greene, with Katy Mahew in the title role, at the California Theatre on 6 August 1877, had been well received. It would be again adapted, next time by John E. McDonough, as *M'liss, an Idyll of Red Mountain*. (As recently as 1976, it was seen off-Broadway in Manhattan as a musical.) Considering the great and continuing popularity of his California short-stories, Harte must have thought he was well advised to take some characters and situations from several of those classics, such as *Tennessee's Partner* and *The Outcasts of Poker Flat*, and rework them into a romantic melodrama of the Old West. The more serious aspects would be lightened with comic moments, partly supplied by a Chinese character, Hop Sing, played by C. T. Parsloe. Parsloe was to be much admired for his Oriental stereotypes, even in the subsequent—and disastrous—Bret Harte and Mark Twain collaboration, the western comedy-melodrama, *Ah Sin*, which premiered in New York on 31 July 1877. That play was the cause of an irrevocable break between the two writers.

It's curious that other writers have been, at least in terms of crafting acceptable stage-vehicles, far more successful with Harte's tales than he himself was. One interesting example is *Salomey Jane*, made into a popular play by Paul Armstrong, and later into a 1914 film, featuring Beatriz Michelena. And there were other Harte adaptations which pleased the audiences of their day. In *Two Men of Sandy Bar*, Harte preserved some of his most admired characters from various tales, but at the cost of distorting their initial freshness and reality. This he did by forcing them into a melodramatic plot of romance, mistaken identity, dubious relationships, gratuitous comedy, exotic locales, manipulated suspense, fortuitous actions inconsistent with character, and other devices dear to the nineteenth century melodramatist. Inexperienced playwright that he was, Harte didn't bring it off as well as the professionals. Nonetheless, there are in the play distinctive vestiges of Harte's vision of the Old West which are rewarding, if not especially demanding of stage-production. Despite its poor reviews in performance, the play pleased Harte well enough for him to include it in his *Collected Works*.

Perhaps it should be remembered that 1876 was America's Centennial Year. At the great Exhibition in Philadelphia, the huge Corliss Steam-Engine was on display; in New York, the Rev. Henry Ward Beecher was embarrassingly in court, and, in the West, General George Custer was making forays against the Sioux. Harte's westerners of the 1850s were by that time no novelty to eastern audiences. Harte didn't yet realize it, but his time had passed. The actor Stuart Robson had paid him $3,000—plus a $20 royalty each night until the sum reached an additional $3,000—to craft this drama from his famous stories. Opening-night critics in New York were not kind. The anonymous reviewer from the *Herald* was excoriating: "As an 'American drama,' it is an absolute outrage upon the intellectual reputation of the country." This judgment was modified by the critic's admission that there were, in fact, worse dramas than *Two Men of Sandy Bar* currently on the boards, but, in his opinion, none of them had such distinguished origin. Perusal of other plays then popular shows them not much of an improvement over Harte's play, in terms of reality of character, plausibility of action, and inventiveness of dialogue. But other writers raised fewer expectations than Harte had—and they managed the melodrama formulas better. There was more to this hostile critical reaction than cavils about Harte's craftsmanship. Other New York critics echoed the reservations of the *Herald*'s reviewer, but he said it more forcefully: "Ever since he left California, Mr. Harte has lived on his reputation and failed in his performances." A celestial metaphor was invoked: "He has reversed the path of the sun. He rose splendidly in the West and has set in darkness in the East."

The play had been tried out in Chicago by Stuart Robson, who initially played Harte's swaggering, pretentious Col. Starbottle. In New York, this was considered a minor, even unnecessary, role and an odd choice for the actor who had commissioned the play. Over a year later, having toured this play and others in his repertory across the country, Robson and his troupe opened *Two Men of Sandy Bar* in San Francisco. By this time, Robson had given up the colonel for the central role of

Sandy. After the 23 September 1878 opening, the *San Francisco Bulletin*'s critic thought the part was "quite out of his line, but not a bad performance." Bret Harte apparently still had some friends in San Francisco, if not in New York, for the *Bulletin*'s nameless reviewer suggested that the play's mechanical faults weren't entirely the playwright's. The play, he noted, had been undergoing changes at the hands of Robson and his troupe for two years. The critic from the *San Francisco Chronicle* preferred Harte's play as a closet-drama, to be read, as he said, with frequent pleasure. On stage, the play had, in his opinion, "a certain idyllic grace, a quiet pictorial quality, and an unobtrusive study of character." Unfortunately, those fine qualities were not enough, he said, to "violently stimulate the imagination or satisfy the dramatic desire." Fortunately, on both coasts, the scenery was found to be natural and pleasing. Thus, *Two Men of Sandy Bar* was seen as an ineffective stage work.

When one reads the play now, it's easy to see Harte's technical awkwardnesses as a dramatist, but it isn't so very much different in quality from Joaquin Miller's *The Danites*, which was generally approved by the critics of that time. Perhaps, as has been suggested, so very much more was expected of Bret Harte than of the run-of-the-mill melodramatists. One reviewer even negatively compared Harte's plotting with that of the ever popular Dion Boucicault—but Boucicault was a seasoned playwright-actor-manager. Bret Harte was a beginner in the theatre. Accounts of actual performances in New York make it clear that the Manhattan cast was inexperienced, awkward, uneven, and in some cases untalented. Tasteless minstrelsy was interpolated in the last act to get laughs. A Spanish dance by supers was critically derided. Later, in San Francisco, the dance was found "very pretty," but reviews indicate that the ensemble's performances on the long tour had become even more farcical and coarse. Bret Harte's drama was a novice's effort; his misfortune as a playwright was to give it to a company which could only cheapen it, rather than develop it and emphasize its special appeal as Harte's picture of the Far West in the Gold Rush era. Now, perhaps, readers can savor its nostalgia more indulgently.

Glenn Loney

A DRAMATIC PLAY

ENTITLED

JOAQUIN MURIETA DE CASTILLO

THE CELEBRATED
CALIFORNIA BANDIT

IN FIVE ACTS

BY

CHARLES E. B. HOWE

Dedicated to
P. Q. VROOM, Esq.
of Monroe County, New York,
for His Gentlemanly Worth
and Scholastic Attainments,
by His Friend,
The Author

CHARACTERS

Joaquin Murieta de Castillo
Garcia, Three-Fingered Jack
Gonzalles, a priest
Ignacious, a monastic scholar
Roderiguez, a renegade priest
Pedro, Jose, Juan,
Gale, Knox, Bill Harvey,
Jo, Missouri, San Antone,
Texas Bill, Zeke, Harry Love,
Henderson, Bill Byrnes, White,
Bill, Mike, Squire Brown,
Tennessee, Jack, Pitch,

WOMEN

Belloro
Rosa
Bonita
Mrs. Gale
Mary Gale

ACT I

SCENE I: *Two Priests conversing under the walls of a monastery. Time—Evening.*

(Enter Gonzalles and Ignacious.)

GONZALLES: 'Tis well we have met here, for those rude walls have ears within that might cause us to lose our own, if they should hear what I have to say; therefore this appointment, but the sound of our voices dies ere it reaches yonder grating, and the fire-fly's lamp is far preferable to the oil sconce light of the monastery's aisles, for the utterance of my thoughts.

IGNACIOUS: Most true, reverend father—the free air of heaven for conversing on worldly matters, while the monastery's cells, with beads and rosary, or the altar and shrine, are the only fitting places for silent worship. Yet of late I have often been lost in revery on wickedness—worldly wickedness; for your language has recalled to memory scenes long since forgotten. Mountains, brooks, trees and extensive plains, once familiar to my eyes, have again passed in panorama form athwart my dreamy vision, and voluntarily I have bowed my knees in prayer, saying, At last I have found the true spot to worship the true God. I fear it was sinful, reverend father.

GONZALLES: What the heart wishes for, the waking or dreaming thoughts will seek. Now I have a view of worldly scenes that I wish to lay before you, but listen, and you may profit by the result. By disposition you are romantic, and young blood heeds its soothings. Yet how could it be otherwise? for the hot Moorish blood of old Castile in your veins has not lost ardor by long study and close confinement within Santa Cruz Monastery, and you, sir, are prone to lean towards its promptings. *(Aside.)*—Ignacious is clay, and I will mould him to my purpose as the potter moulds the tile to shed winter rains. *(To Ignacious.)*—Ignacious, dost thou ever dream of thy boyhood home 'mid the hills of dear old Spain? and how more fair is their sweet verdure than in this land of the wiley

Aztec. In Spain the vine-clad hills o'ertop the romantic villages, in which there are many romantic homes; the trees wear a greener dress; the sky is more serene in its loveliness; the people are more happy, and the voluptuous swell of music rises on the soft twilight of the evening air, echoed by the lips of beauties, whose blood shines through their transparent skin with a rosy tinge; and the warm hearted Spaniard will ever bid a welcome. Unlike all we meet here. What a pity!

IGNACIOUS: What a pity! Reverend father, I am no voluptuary; yet, Spain, dear old Spain; how I long to see it once more, as I saw it in childhood, but—(A noise.)

GONZALLES: But—Speak out, Ignacious; we are all confidence.

IGNACIOUS: I heard a noise; I fear a listener.

GONZALLES: It was but an owl or bat leaving its nest in yonder eaves; and the stones are loose from decay and are easily displaced. Speak on.

IGNACIOUS: But, I am poor, and a novice in a monastery is seldom rich.

GONZALLES: It is what I would have said. We are poor; therefore, what a pity!

IGNACIOUS: Then you, too, reverend father, have dreamed of—of travelling.

GONZALLES: Yes, and if I had wealth, I would renounce my vows. At least I will get a dispensation to travel.

IGNACIOUS: Reverend father! holy horror! Sante Christo protect us. Sacrilege! (Crosses himself.) Renounce your vows? oh, no! A dispensation would be far better.

GONZALLES: Yes, I think it would be. I still retain a dispensation. I obtained it through the Bishop of Mexico and used it during the American war,[1] where I earned the soubriquet of "the fighting priest"; I roamed with as brave a guerrilla band as ever harassed Los Americanos. Caramba! I can fight, swear, or serve at high mass. Ignacious, would you become rich, powerful, adored—and that, too, in thy own native land, beneath the lovely ethereal skies of thy own dear native Spain?

IGNACIOUS: Why should I ask, how is this to be? For it is impossible. You do but tempt me through my wishes.

GONZALLES: No, I do not wish to tempt you—I swear it; yet I will tell you all. Within yonder walls there is a young man, who was reared and fostered there. He is thy senior classmate, and he is heir, sole heir, to titles and wealth, broad lands, and villages, and vine-clad hills that are in old Spain, besides plantations in Cuba. I alone possess the secret and proofs of his birth and heirship. I want one to personate him and divide with me the wealth. The one who so personates him shall have the titles for so doing. Is it worth the trial? Do you understand me?

IGNACIOUS: My head is in a blaze; all the blood in my body has rushed there. Reverend father, this is so new to me that I know not what to say. But yet—what of him? who is he?

GONZALLES: He is a forward, impetuous devil; one, I think, you like not; dictatorial in his ways and haughty in his manners. He was left on the roads when an infant, by an aged servitor, who died from inhaling, on a warm day, the dead winds of the Sierra Madre. I discovered him and possessed myself of the old man's papers, and they shall now become of some value, by being used.

IGNACIOUS: It is Joaquin.

GONZALLES: Yes, "Joaquin Murieta de Castillo," son of the former Governor-General of Cuba, and now within yonder walls of Santa Cruz Monastery, and the only heir to a dukedom.

IGNACIOUS: Ah, 'tis now I see the cause of his proud overbearing assumption. 'Twas born with him, and for it I like him less. Thou art very shrewd, Father Gonzalles; how shall we proceed? And what of Joaquin?

GONZALLES: Leave that to me. Keep your own counsel; be secret, and abide my time. He will probably die; he is too good to live.

IGNACIOUS: How terrible you look! You would not—(*An owl screams; Ignacious starts.*)

GONZALLES: Never mind, 'tis but an owl. Now to prayers, for there's the vesper bell. (*Bell sounds.*) Of this we will speak anon. To prayers for our success.

IGNACIOUS: To prayers! (*Exit.*)

GONZALLES: Ignacious, I fear, is too honest; yet he seems inclined to favor this. Why not? Who ever knew honesty or virtue to stand a severer temptation, when the body that inherits it leans incliningly towards the seduction; and this is pictured to his imagination by a descriptive mind. Religion is also a component of his disposition; yet I shall entirely destroy the promptings of his heart and turn him to my will, and until all my desires are gained, I say, conscience, lie thee still! (*Exit.*)

SCENE II: *A Guerrilla Camp in sight at the walls of a Monastery; saddles, men, and women lying on serapes;*[2] *camp-fire; kettles, etc. strewed around. Garcia walking uneasily about; Pedro looking at him; Juan, Roderiguez, Belloro, Bonita, Rosa, etc.*

GARCIA: *Caramba! Maldeta; Ladrones,*[3] *Los Americanos!*

PEDRO: In one of your old moods, Senor Garcia. What is to come next? Silver trains are scarce, and the rancheros are as poor as a friar's dog; for this damned American war, just ended, has shut up the mines, impoverished the people, and our trade has gone to the devil.

GARCIA: Our trade has gone to the devil, and there we shall have to go and find it; and if our luck lies next to the gates of hell's dominions, we must make an onset to pay for this delay. Since that last affray near the City of Mexico, where I received this (*holds up his hand with thumb and forefinger gone*[4]) from that cursed American officer, we have not had a single peso to turn a card for. *Caramba! Maldeta, Los Americanos!*

PEDRO: What say you, Garcia, to a church or two, and then for California; there are churches on the way that have escaped the war and are yet rich.

GARCIA: Any deed to get hold of gold. A good idea! California is a new field, and the Americans are flocking there by thousands; gold has been found in abundance, and if the Americans work as well as they fight, they will be angels of gold, and we will be the devils to take it from them.

PEDRO: We will pay a visit to the Church of Dolores in Sonora, which is on the way to California, and there is plenty of silver in vessels, altar railings, images, and money, to load five of our stoutest mules, besides gold enough to load another; and Father Novo I hate, as the devil hates holy water. I'll take his gown for my pay, and the spoils shall be divided among the band.

GARCIA: One less leaves ten; and your share as informer would be three times as much as either of the boys would receive. Now that's liberal; let's hear what the boys have to say. Ho, you lazy ladrones, leave the women to their cigaritos; a word with you all! (*Band gathers around Garcia.*) Boys, Mexico, Chihuahua [Che-wa-wa], Sinaloa, Guadalajara [Gau-da-la-hair-ah],[5] and almost the whole republic has been travelled over in vain. We have not found one, from bullion dealer to peon, worth lassooing; not a paso have we had for months, and now I say it is time we used our escopets [shotguns] and knives. What say you all for California; there is plenty of gold to be had and there is a church on the road that Pedro has put a red cross on, which he says is rich. What say you all?

GUERRILLAS ALL: For the church—lead us on! Yes, yes, lead us on!

JUAN: Lead us on! has been the cry too long already. Since you, Senor Garcia, saw the color of your own blood, you have quit your actions and drooped your head like a sick paroquet.

GARCIA: Hound of an exiled family, dare you taunt me?

JUAN: Taunt you! Why you have become a cheto[6] in camp at day, and at night steal cattle, for fear you'll forget your old trade. An honorable guerrilla would look only to the road for pay at daylight, and at night the shade of the Sierras would be his spot of safety, in place of playing gipsy under the walls of a monastery.

GARCIA: Hell![7] Have I not led where no one of you would follow? Have I not made streams of blood that sickened you all? Have I not killed more in one night than all the band have since you joined us? Have I not brought more booty into camp than any other guerrilla in the Sierra Madre? Have you forgotten all?

JUAN: Forgotten all? No! We all remember one brave act of Three-Fingered Jack's.

GARCIA: Where and when? if you remember so well.

JUAN: The time you killed your former master's only child, down in Chihuahua, to reach her patron the bullion dealer. She was a lovely girl; Cary was a playmate of mine; and damned foul work you made.

GARCIA: (*Draws his pistol.*) Hell and hell's furies! Take this and follow her! (*Fires at Juan.*) Curse the hand that served my fingers such a trick. I never missed before.

JUAN: (*Pulls his pistol and aims at Garcia.*) 'Twas well meant, but badly directed; the ball grazed my locks. No more shooting, Three-Fingered Jack, or I'll make sure work of you if I commence.

GARCIA: No more taunts about dead ones, or by the eternal shades, you'll wake such a hell in me that every saint in the calendar will swear that I am ten Judases thrice damned.

RODERIGUEZ: (*A renegade priest.*) Put up your pistols! Fools, is it your trade to kill each other? Talk business, not fight among yourselves, like a pack of hungry wolves; for the flesh of neither would make a meal, nor buy a bottle of aguadiente [whiskey]. (*They put up their pistols.*)

PEDRO: Father Roderiguez, Senor Garcia and myself were speaking of California. Los Americanos are filling every canyon, ravine, and river in that State in search of gold; and we would be in damned bad luck if we, as proud a guerrilla band as ever straddled mustangs, could not lessen their numbers, and load our purses with oro.[8]

RODERIGUEZ: True, my children; those cursed heretics of Americans have robbed poor Mexico by the war, and now there is a chance to regain at least part of what we have lost. My blessing on your undertaking.

ALL: Ho for California!

JUAN: I also say, For California!

BAND: And I, and I, etc.

GARCIA: Pass the gourd bags; then, Juan, your pretty sister can sing us our evening song, which will be sweeter than the music of a pistol-shot.

JUAN: No more shooting, Garcia.

GARCIA: No more taunts, Juan. Let us drink. (*Drinks.*) Pass the gourd, boys. (*Hands it to Juan. All drink.*)

JUAN: Bell, will you sing us "Our Home is Mexico"; and then we will retire; for we want to be on our journey before the sun rises.—Boys, join the chorus.

BELLORO: (*Takes a guitar and sings.*)

OUR HOME IS MEXICO

Air—"The Watcher"

We're a brave guerrilla band, as free as light we are,
And take our tribute on the land wherever we may be;
Our homes are the Sierras' shade, 'mid the chapparel so wild;
No wealth have we to boast of, like the lordly pampered child.

Chorus
We roam from summer vales to hills of eternal snow;
Whate'er the change may be, our home is Mexico! (*Repeat.*)

We levy tribute on the rich, and make them pay it down;
And good fare we receive from them of the litany and gown;[9]
And when the fray and prayer is o'er, we seek a quiet vale,
As to God above, to the maid we love we repeat th' exciting tale.

Chorus
We roam from summer vales to hills of eternal snow;
Whate'er the change may be, our home is Mexico! (*Repeat.*)

When the golden sun is shining from out the distant west,
And the humming-bird is seeking its downy pendant nest,
And the vesper bells are sounding on the mellow evening air,
Our hearts grow light with music and dancing with the fair.

Chorus
We roam from summer vales to hills of eternal snow;
Whate'er the change may be, our home is Mexico! (*Repeat.*)

SCENE III: *A Road.*

(*Enter Garcia.*)

GARCIA: This is lonely work. There is nothing but peones[10] out as late as this, and I have not met one that's worth a peso; ah! here comes a priest, and I will try the butt of my pistol on his head and see if that will make him remember where he left his last winnings at monte; for who ever knew a priest to lose. No! it's worth as much as the winner's soul to cheat a priest at cards. (*Enter Gonzalles, with a cowl over his face.*) Stop, Reverend Father! I want your purse; I care not how few ounces it contains, but the more the better, for my conscience's sake.

GONZALLES: Yes, Senor Garcia, a purse full, if you will earn them.

GARCIA: (*Draws his pistol.*) Off with your cowl, or I'll blow it from your face; who are you that knows me in the dark. (*Cocks his pistol; priest throws back his cowl.*) Gonzalles! the fighting priest! Ha, ha, ha. (*Laughs, and puts up his pistol.*) A very nice hombre to get money from particularly on the road; I would stand a better show to get it from a stone. Well, tradesmen often meet, for their wares bring them in contact. On the same errand? ah, you old hell-hound.

GONZALLES: No, you thrible-headed dog of the devil; but I have a job that will suit you, there being a purse of gold for every thrust of your dagger.

GARCIA: Then you must want only one blow to be struck, or your cell must contain at least a mule load of onzas;[11] for I would fill the skin of Santa Anna[12] in the president's chair so full of holes at that price, that there would not be room for another. What work is it?

GONZALLES: Strike as often as you think necessary to do the work. It's only a boy; he is in yonder monastery, and I want you to spirit him away. Leave his body outside the walls, so that it will seem as if it was the work of woman's jealousy.

GARCIA: Lead on! I know you; your word is good for the job. Show me his cell, and I will send his soul to heaven or hell! (*Exit both.*)

SCENE IV: *A room in a monastery; chair, table and lamp. Joaquin sitting at the table reading; rises and walks.*

JOAQUIN: Oh, how gloomy these walls have become. They are hateful to my sight; for their darksome shadow finds a reflection in my thoughts, and makes me sick at heart. What is there to cure this despondency? What thought, of all I have read, will aid to dispel these fancies of a home and a mother? I never knew what it was to have maternal care; yet how precious is the very sound of such a name as mother; and when connected with the name of home, oh how much more dear it sounds! There's a charm in the words that thrills through me as if they were electricity. Mother and Home! From all that I have heard of them, I have learned to long for their existence; yet I know them only by name. The blessed of this world are those who have a mother to counsel with and guide them, and the roof-tree to shelter them in hours as dark as mine. Mother and Home! I never tire repeating them. Then again, in my dark visions I see a fairy form that lights up and adds the glory of loveliness to my musings. That could not be my mother, for I have watched the wild blast of the hurricane and trembled, and that same form would glide before me, and all seemed pleasant—even the dread havoc that the wild wind caused seemed less fearful in its destruction. I have watched the stars, until my eyes grew weary with grazing on their twinkling orbs, and this form has passed, and I have forgot myself in her invisible presence. I have walked amid the flowers, and their rich blossoms gave forth no perfume, until her image crossed my path, and then I bemoaned, because the humming bird intercepted their odor. What fairy can this be? Is there a reality for these wild fancies? Yes; it is possible there is some place in this world inhabited by my vision; then why not leave these walls and go forth into the world and seek her? But what do I know of the world or its people? for I have not seen much of its surface, or associated with them. Yet I wish I was free, to act, to do for myself. I will—yes, I will be free! I am a prisoner here. This night I will leave this cell, and forever! What words? I am surprised at the very thought, and more so at their utterance. But shall I endure this serfdom? tremble when the Superior comes, to show him that I am a peon—a slave? observe his humor, and play the puppet to conciliate his favor? Oh, I have crouched at his look as a sloth hound does under the lash of his master. And to continue thus for days, weeks, months to come; no! I would rather be transformed to a monkey, and play in freedom on the boughs of a tree, than submit to confinement within these walls another space marked by a day. I want freedom; yet I tremble at the uncertainty before me. But I will be free; and this night, though the venom of my dagger's sting pierces a body more precious than the Pope's. (*A noise without.*) Psst! What noise is that? Who should invade the secrecy of my cell at this hour of the night? I will extinguish the light and use my dark lantern[13] for I fear, I know not what; for this is an untimely visit.

(*Enter Garcia, groping about with a knife in his hand.*)

GARCIA: He said, "His bed is on the left as you enter the door." I will find it and ease the sleeper.
JOAQUIN: What does that man want here? I see the glitter of a dagger. It is my life he seeks. Heaven, who have I harmed? Courage; a little light will do. (*Sets the dark lantern open on the table, springs behind Garcia's back and draws his dagger, as Garcia leans over the bed, lays his hand on his neck and holds him down.*) Move and I will kill thee, vile reptile. What art thou doing within these walls at this hour? Dost thou know thy doom? It is death!
GARCIA: Are you Joaquin?
JOAQUIN: I am.
GARCIA: Spare me!
JOAQUIN: Who are you?
GARCIA: I am Garcia.
JOAQUIN: Garcia, the fiend, the terror of Mexico? Why are you here?
GARCIA: To kill you!
JOAQUIN: To kill me! What for? and who employed you?
GARCIA: I know not—I came for pay.
JOAQUIN: Give me your knife. (*He hands it to Joaquin and rises.*) Then you are

Garcia, the murderer of the innocent. To do Justice a kind act, I would kill you. (*Motions towards Garcia.*)

GARCIA: Spare me, Joaquin, and I will be your friend in all you may ask.

JOAQUIN: (*Aside.*) My hands shall never be stained with human blood. (*To Garcia.*) Lead me from this place; I wish to leave it.

GARCIA: I will, but where to, then?

JOAQUIN: Any place; for I am sick of this abode.

GARCIA: Follow us! To-night our band starts for California, and before the morning dawns, many leagues will be placed between us and this spot.

JOAQUIN: Will you swear to be my friend in all things?

GARCIA: Yes; if you will not see too much for our safety; for our band are guerrillas.

JOAQUIN: Agreed; if you will befriend me until I reach a place of safety.

GARCIA: I will! I never break a promise.

JOAQUIN: Kneel then, and swear on this cross as I dictate. (*Garcia kneels and repeats after Joaquin.*)—I solemnly swear that I will be the true friend to Joaquin Murieta, until he is safe from harm. As I fail to keep my vow, so punish me, my patron saint, in this world and in the world to come.

GARCIA: I swear! (*Kisses the cross.*)

END OF ACT I

ACT II

SCENE I: *Emigrant's camp; women cooking; men playing cards; cattle in the distance; wagons, etc.; river in sight.*

GALE: Knox, it's your night to stand guard, I reckon. We needn't be scared of the Injins, for we're out of their range; for at this season they don't come so low down on the Gila[14] as this. Bill Harvey, you and Jo, go and hobble old Brindle, and stake out the roan colt; for the mustang is wild yet, and this bottom looks like the Mosquito Creek, where he was foaled, and he may take a likeness to stray. Mary, what is you and Bill Harvey perting about? 'Tend to getting supper ready.

MRS. GALE: Daddy, Bill Harvey's getting right pert lately after Moll and putting darn queer notions into her head. She can't do anything now-a-days, unless Bill's somewars to watch her. Bill, I reckon you'd better look to Jim Simese's darter[15] that's ahead of us in old Ike's train.

BILL HARVEY: Look yer, mamme; I reckon I know what's what—Jim Simese's darter Sal is a good gal enough, but she's no more account to Mary than a calf is to old Brindle. Sal can't mend clo's; she can't make bread, ride a hoss, or shoot a rifle, like Mary can. I'll bet my rifle agin a jack-knife, I can whip any man that come from Texas, this year, that says she can; dog-on my skin, if I don't.

MRS. GALE: Yer dreadful bold when there's nothing to be afeared on. A yaller-skin or Greaser[16] would run a hull rigiment jest like you.

MARY: Dog-on it! Do let Bill alone; he's sorter snarly now. I've been pestering him most to death all day; and I reckon it's hard enough for one of the family to pester Bill at a time. (*Takes up a tea canister.*) Mamme, I reckon we'd better have sassafras teas to-night; the boys are all tuckered out, and drinking saline water makes them awful thirsty. Shall we have long sweetening or short sweetening?[17] (*Bill stands up behind and kisses her.*)

MRS. GALE: Long sweetening. Bill, jest let Mary alone, I tell yer.

GALE: Bill Harvey, why don't you and the boys go and tend to them cattle? I reckon by this time you'll find 'em way down the bottom. Case, you go along with the boys, too. Take along your rifles—you mount jump up[18] some game. (*Bill Harvey, Jo, and Case shoulder their rifles.*)

BILL HARVEY: Daddy Gale is right pert to-night. He's socked himself down on that old saddle reading the Bible agin. I swar I believe he'll take to preaching Methodism as he used to, when we git to California; dog-on my skin if I don't. Mamme, too, is cross as Satan. Them old buckskin breeches she's mending must be tough as a bull's hide to git a needle through. (*To Mary, patting her on the cheek.*)—You ain't cross, are you, honey?

MARY: Clear out, Bill, or I'll—

BILL: You bet; I'm going. Come boys! (*Exit Bill, Jo, and Case.*)

MRS. GALE: Daddy, how long do you reckon it will take us to git to the diggins?

GALE: Nigh on to two weeks; for when we reach the settlements, I reckon we'd better stop and recruit the cattle, for they're powerfully tuckered out; and a few day's delay, I take on, wouldn't injure any of us. Mamme, I thought we would done better to take the Salt Lake route, but the Lord seemed willing it should be otherwise; and as we are all well and safe, we needn't complain; for it was all for the best.

MRS. GALE: Thank the Lord; for this trip has been powerful weakening. Saline water and the hot sun pulls a mortal down powerful fast, I reckon.

MARY: Shall I git supper ready?

MRS. GALE: No; I reckon you'd better wait till the boys come back.

MARY: Then I wish they'd hurry. Bill Harvey is the slowest mortal in the world. (*Aside.*)—He's as slow as the laziest critter in the train; I b'lieve he'd court me till doomsday, unless I pop the question; and you bet I'll take the chances; dog-on me if I don't. (*Firing outside—Gale and Mrs. Gale arise.*) Oh, Lord! what is that?

GALE: There's something wrong; there was several shots fired in quick succession. What in the world can it be? I must go and see. (*Mrs. Gale and Mary hold him fast.*)

MRS. GALE: Don't go and leave us all alone.

(*Enter Bill Harvey, wounded, a pistol in his hand.*)

HARVEY: Jo and Case are shot by the Guerrillas! Oh, God! I am wounded. (*Falls insensible; Mary goes to him.*)

MARY: Water, water! Give me some water, mother! (*Mrs. Gale hands Mary some water.*)

(*Enter Garcia, with a knife in his hand.*)

GARCIA: Caramba! Los Americanos! Death to the Americans!

(*Enter Guerrilla Band; Joaquin follows with drawn pistol.*)

JOAQUIN: Back I say! Back, or death to some of you! I swear I will kill the first who raises a hand against these defenseless people. Remember, Garcia, remember your oath! Those people never harmed you or yours, and why should you murder them? I did not think you loved blood so well. Is the current of life's stream so cheap, that you must wash in it?

PEDRO: Heed him not, Garcia.

JOAQUIN: I warn you, another move, and some of you die! Have gray hairs on the brow of age no respect from your fiendish hearts? Have not youth and innocence a charm that would repel the dastard acts of a coward from your souls? Go, go to your camp; and if harm befall one of these that's here, I will murder you all; I swear it. (*Exit band.*)

GARCIA: Damn that oath! (*Exit.*)

GALE: How can we thank you, our noble preserver; and how can I repay you for your timely protection to my family? I know you are good as you are wildly beautiful. (*Joaquin puts up his pistol and takes off his hat.*) Honor and nobleness are stamped on thy brow.

JOAQUIN: I need no thanks—much less pay. How is our wounded friend?

HARVEY: The wound is painful, but I do not think it is serious.

MARY: I thank you, noble sir, for your protection, and Mary Gale will always remember you.

JOAQUIN: No thanks, lady. A dishonest act I never committed, much less a murder; to protect you with my life was but my duty as a man, and I follow its directions. The least of God's creatures should not receive harm if I could prevent it.

MARY: What is your name, kind sir? Tell us, so that we can remember you and pray for you.

GALE: And I will beseech the throne of grace, in my daily prayers, to spare and protect you.

JOAQUIN: Thank you, good friends; I may need your prayers, for this world is new to me. My name is Joaquin—Joaquin Murieta.

(*Gale extends his hand; Joaquin kneels on one knee.*)

GALE: May Heaven's blessings go and abide with thee, and may the blessing of a father and mother follow thee for this act, and goodness attend thee for ever and ever. Amen.

SCENE II: *A road; mountains; river.*

(*Enter Garcia.*)

GARCIA: Joaquin has dared to interfere between the wolf and its victims. Hell's curse! That I should hold that oath so binding, when to cut his throat would release me from all promises. What is one life? Have I not taken twenty—aye, fifty—better, far better than his; and for less gold than old Gonzalles offered? To say I will kill Joaquin is easier said than done. I have seen him asleep close by my side, as unconscious as if he were in no danger; yet it seemed to me that whenever I approached him, with that thought on my mind, he would move uneasily in his sleep, and his eyes would open, as if his very eyes and ears did nothing but spy my acts and learn the fall of my footsteps. I hate him! No; I do not love him; then by hell and its furies, I fear him. A boy! caramba! I may just as well say I have found a master; Curse the name! I once had a master. Hell! how my blood boils! That master was my father; my mother his slave, and I born his peon. How I have seen that man whip my mother. Large scars showed their hideousness all over her once beautiful face. She said she was once beautiful—and I believe her. That master whipped my mother once too often. It was in a by-place; I heard the lash falling on the back of one begging for mercy; I hurried to the spot—it was my mother, bleeding at every blow; I felled the hound of hell to the earth—my master, my father—I plucked his eyes out; and then he begged for what he had refused to give, Mercy. I cut limb from limb of his body; his heart I trampled under my feet. I was blood—all I saw was blood. And then my mother embraced me and called me her child—(*laughs*)—and I became a fiend. When I think of that first act, I could drink blood. The Past—the awful Past—I cannot think of it! What a hell is conscience!

(*Enter Pedro and Jose.*)

PEDRO: Why, Garcia, you look as if some devil had frightened you. What's the matter, man?

GARCIA: Hell and the devil, both! My bosom is the hell, and my conscience the devil.

PEDRO: Only one of your old moods. Garcia, we must leave here. The interference of Joaquin is liable to give us trouble; for if another train of emigrants should come up, our skins would have to be bullet-proof to escape the Americans.

JOSE: Jesus Christo! I want to kill that refuse of a priest. Let me once get the chance! (*Clutches his knife.*)

PEDRO: Well, well, some other time. Our safety first—Joaquin after.

GARCIA: No! hell! no, never! Harm a hair of Joaquin's head, and I'll cut you in pieces; and I'll make yard meat of your body if ever you speak of it again.

PEDRO: There, talk no more of Joaquin. Garcia, I say, let us move from this place. Yonder is their camp-fire; two of whom fell by our shots this night. (*Laughs.*) A bad place for them to camp in! Garcia, the church of Dolores is three leagues from here, and I feel as if to-night is the very time to settle with old Father Nivo.

GARCIA: We'll go, Jose. Tell the boys to bring up the mules. Let Juan and Joaquin follow with the women, and tell them to meet us at the mission of San Gabriel, in California. Go, Jose! Meet us at the spring, for I will not go to camp. (*Exit Jose.*) Pedro, if the church of Dolores is as rich as you say, we'll have no reason to complain of this night's work. Ho, for crime! My blood is up, and this night I am a fiend again!

PEDRO: You will find all as I tell you, Senor Garcia; and I feel eager for revenge; for my star is on the rise, and before to-morrow's dawn old Father Nivo dies. (*Exeunt.*)

SCENE III: *A river; train of wagons in the distance.*

(*Gale, Mrs. Gale, Mary, and Harvey discovered.*)

GALE: Death has entered our train and in a sudden manner. Coming so unexpected, the shock has fallen more severe. Yonder is two graves, and the cross we have
placed above them will soon decay, and their sleeping place will be forgotten.

MARY: Poor Jo and Case!

MRS. GALE: They'll never see California, I reckon.

GALE: God's judgment will overtake their murderers; for blood will cry from the
ground for revenge, and the judgment will be terrible. The wicked have their
day, but the works of the good endures forever.

HARVEY: It's right hard to think that these devils escaped so easy. If we'd kept with
any of the trains, Jo and Case would been alive now. I reckon these devils will
catch it yet for this. My side is right sore, and every stitch of pain they have put
on me shall be paid 'em some day or other.

GALE: We must say farewell to this spot and go on our way; but sad will be the remembrance of last night's work; yet as this noble poet says—(*reads from a
book*)—we should "So live, that when the summons comes to join the innumerable caravan that moves to the pale realms of shade, where each shall take his
chamber in the silent halls of death, thou go not like the quarry slave at night,
scourged to his dungeon, but sustained and soothed by an unfaltering trust, approach thy grave like one who wraps the drapery of his couch about him and lies
down to pleasant dreams."[19] (*Exeunt.*)

SCENE IV: *Room in a Mission.*

(*Joaquin and Belloro dressed for a bridal.*)

BELLORO: Dear Joaquin, think you that Garcia will not meet us here, as he appointed on the night of his sudden departure from the camp on the Gila River?

JOAQUIN: Yes, dearest, I think he will, and I suppose he will have a bloody tale to
tell; for I have no doubt that the massacre at Dolores Church was the work of
his mutilated hand. The old priest with his skull cleaved open and his gray locks
mingled with his gore; the woman, his servant, killed by a shot in the brain; the
two men-servants, cut in many places, lying dead beside the altar which the
profane hand of the robbers had despoiled—all was horrible. And I was happy
to think you, dear Belloro, escaped the sight of such a heart-rending scene. I felt
my blood running like hot lava through my veins, for revenge on the sacreligious
monster murderers, when I gazed on their victims.

BELLORO: Dear Joaquin, I shudder at the sight of that man Garcia; for his appearance recalls to my mind the hooded cobra. But let us forget the past—for
God will punish them for their wickedness; and now that we are in a land of ci-
vilization, we must part from their company. Brother Juan is heartily sick of
them, and, as it is your own wish and Juan's also, I feel that I will have a double
protection in a husband and a brother; and you that I love—oh, how dearly my
heart and God alone knows! (*Bows on Joaquin's breast.*)

JOAQUIN: Forgive me (*embraces her*), my own, my dear Belloro—my golden Bell —that I should recall the past, wherein lie sad memories, and on such a day as this, but the music of your voice echoes like the sound of a merry chime on my heart-strings and dispels all that's rude. To-day, dear Belloro, you become my wife; and oh, with what anticipated pleasure I have looked forward to the hour when the indissoluble knot will be tied that makes us one on earth; and in heaven I feel that we will not be parted. Oh, the ecstatic thrill of joy that bounds thro' every fibre of my body, as I repeat the words, *My own sweet wife!* Dearest, they hang on my lips and leave a taste almost as sweet as honey. Oh, the vast space that once was void in my heart is filled with thy presence, my wife. The love I bear thee will be shown while life holds its seat within my brain; and all will be paid me ten thousand fold by thy love, my own sweet wife. At midnight, when the silent earth was undisturbed by busy life, I have dreamed of thee. I have gazed on the starry dome in a mood which hung on my mind like a thundercloud in a summer sky; and thy lovely form would glide into my musings, and all the darkness was dispelled; the flowers that bloomed in my pathway seemed to inhale their fragrance from thy invisible presence. Thou art of myself a part. How else should I have known that you, my golden Bell, did exist before my eyes beheld thee? And now, to become my wife! My heart bounds with an ecstasy of joy it never knew before.

BELLORO: There is a fatality in this, dear Joaquin; an invisible direction of the Omnipotent for our good. The death of my father left my brother Juan and myself alone and friendless, and we joined that guerrilla band for protection, as they travelled in the direction of Sonora, where we expected to meet an uncle; but, alas, we were disappointed, and yet how happy will be the result. Your sudden resolve to leave that gloomy monastery—the entrance of Garcia to take your life, and your power to overcome him and make him befriend you—your joining us, and the preservation of that old man's family from Garcia's bloody hand—all, all was guided by invisible spirits that hover over us and guide us as they will. But Joaquin, I never thought that I could meet with one who would become so dear as thou art and take such complete mastery of my heart.

JOAQUIN: God bless thee, Bell; bless thee! (*Kisses her.*)

(*Enter Juan.*)

JUAN: Have you forgotten your brother? Come, love-makers, there is time enough to talk and act lovingly after an important ceremony has been gone through with. The priest awaits you.

BELLORO: Juan, you are cruel.

JUAN: Not half so cruel as you are, Miss Belloro—and this is the last chance I will have to call you Miss, for you have chosen another protector besides your dear brother. (*Aside.*)—And if I had my choice and Mexico's Republic to pick from among her people for a husband for my sister, I would have said, *Joaquin, take her!* Yet he cannot love her more than I do.

JOAQUIN: So soon! Well, Juan, Time is a rapid messenger when the heart is filled with joy.

JUAN: (*Taking Joaquin's hand.*)—But when the heart is parting with all it holds dear on earth, then minutes seem weeks, and hours centuries; 'twas thus we parted with our father. Love her, Joaquin, and protect her! But you will not watch her happiness with more vigilance than I. Come; the priest is at the altar, and Bonita, Rosa, and our friends, are waiting to accompany you to the church. Come! (*Exeunt.*)

SCENE V: *Altar in an old church; music playing; boy swinging a censer; priest dressed in wedding robes; music stops; priest chants from a book which he holds in his hand.*

PRIEST: Beatus Vir qui timet Dominum in mandatis ejus volet nimis. Potens in terra erit semen ejus: Generatio recotrum benedicetur. Gloria et divitia in domo ejus; et justicia ejus manet in saeculum saeculi. Jucundus homo qui miseretus et commodat, disponent sermones suos in judicio: quia in aeternum non commovebitur.[20]

(*Enter procession; music; stops in front of the altar; priest stoops and whispers; then speaks aloud.*)

PRIEST: And you take this woman to be your lawful wedded wife; to love, honor and obey; to cherish in sickness and in health.
JOAQUIN: I do!
PRIEST: And you take this man to be your husband; to love, honor and obey; to cherish in sickness and in health. (*Belloro bows.*) Then in the name of the Holy Church I pronounce you man and wife; and what God has joined together, let no man put asunder. (*Music plays; Priest chants.*) In memoria aeterna erit justus: ab auditione mala non timebit. Paratum est cor ejus sperare in Domino; confirmatum est cor ejus; non commovebitur donec despiciat inimicos suos. Dispersit, dedit pauperibus; justicia ejus manen in saeculum saeculi; cornu ejus exaltabitur in gloria. Peccator videbit, et irascetur; dentibus suis femet et tabescet; desiderium peccatorum peribit. Gloria Patri Deo.

(*Enter Garcia, followed by his band.*)

GARCIA: Stop, damned priest! Stop this mummery! Stop! Curse you, I forbid it!
PRIEST: Sacreligious dog! How dare you interfere in that which concerns you not?
GARCIA: It does; it does! Belloro shall be my wife.
PRIEST: You are too late; she is married.
GARCIA: Married! Oh, God! The only being I ever loved on earth! (*Staggers and falls to the floor.*)

END OF ACT II

ACT III

SCENE 1: *A creek. Arrival of Joaquin, Belloro, Juan, Bonita, Rosa, and others.*

JUAN: This tedious journey is ended, and I am glad. We have reached the placers[21] in health; the miners are all taking out plenty of oro, and this is the place to make the ounces; for our chances are as good as any. Why, this is a pleasant country!

BELLORO: Truly, this is a pleasant place, and I really love this kind of scenery; there is something so noble and grand in the tall pine, with its long arms projecting from its sides, and something that's homelike in the chirping of those little birds. Unlike Mexico, to be sure; there are no palms here, with their tall trunks and leaves like wings—no orange, with its fragrant blossoms—or lime trees, with their deep green shade—or birds of gay plumage—or other sights that resemble our native place; yet I feel a sense of contentment; for it will be our home, will it not, Joaquin? And here we will be free from troubles and turmoils, such as harrass our people.

JOAQUIN: True, dear wife; and I hope that among the Americans we will find friends; for all that I have seen of them has been noble, generous, and kind. At first, we will be obliged to stay with some of our country people; but as soon as I can find a vacant casa,[22] we will take possession of our first home.

ROSA: Did you notice how those men stared at us as we passed them?

JUAN: Who? what men?

ROSA: Those men that were mining, down yonder, on the creek.

BONITA: Why shouldn't they, pray? I suppose they were pleased to see us; for 'tis said there are not many women in the mines.

ROSA: A very good reason, and a very good chance to get an adorer. Oh, I like that!

JUAN: You minx, envious of Bell! I suppose you begin to think of getting married.

ROSA: Why should I not? for Bell is the happiest mortal alive; and so would I be, if I had just another such a man as Joaquin for a husband!

BELLORO: Pshaw, how many Joaquins would you have in this world? One is enough. (*Juan, Bonita, and Rosa laugh.*)

JUAN: Hold me up, Joaquin, for God's sake! Belloro is jealous because Rosa wants a man like you.

JOAQUIN: I am the more happy at this, for Love shows itself in a jealous out-burst. Oh, you elf! you could love me more than I adore thyself.

BONITA: Come, Juan; do not stand there teasing Bell, but seek some place where we can rest. We will have plenty of time to see all we wish after we get settled and rested from the fatigues of this journey.

JUAN: I see a Mexican flag on yonder house, and no doubt there we can get entertainment and find some of our people. Come! (*Exeunt.*)

(*Enter Garcia.*)

GARCIA: From my hiding-place in that clump of bushes, I heard and saw all. Jesus Christo! how my heart aches! I never knew that I possessed such a soft piece of stuff until I saw her, the golden Bell! Sacramento! I cannot live and see her in possession of Joaquin. Why didn't I kill him? What shall I do for revenge? Hell! that I had the devil for a counsellor! What, is it possible that there comes Gonzalles? He is after me and my spirited coarse Joaquin, whose body I was to have outside the walls of a monastery. (*Laughs.*) Well, a purse of onzas now will put me in a good humor and save a dead man or two.

(*Enter Gonzalles.*)

GARCIA: Good day, old renegade! Where to, so fast?

GONZALLES: Good day, imp of darkness! I have not far to go. I was in hopes you had gone home.

GARCIA: Home! Where is my home, good fighting priest?

GONZALLES: In hell! What other home do you expect to have?

GARCIA: Very kind of you, and that job of yours is not yet done.

GONZALLES: By my patron saint, you have caused me a long journey. Your word is not as good as a rotten pine-apple, for that at least keeps its perfume.

GARCIA: I have thought that you set a trap for my good cabeza.[23] In place of my making holes in his skin, if I had not begged and swore like a *commandante*, he would have made holes in mine.

GONZALLES: No doubt you swore and begged; for you never would forget that part of your trade.

GARCIA: Joaquin made me swear on the cross.

GONZALLES: On the cross! You can swear well. To what purpose?

GARCIA: Simply to see him safe out of Mexico.

GONZALLES: You promised, and you have done it.

GARCIA: Yes, damn him!

GONZALLES: Where is he now?

GARCIA: In that tent up yonder, I think, by this time.

GONZALLES: How, by this time?

GARCIA: Why he was married at San Gabriel Mission, two weeks ago, and has just arrived.

GONZALLES: I did not stop at San Gabriel, or I would have heard of this; for the love of God, who is he married to?

GARCIA: To—to Belloro—the sister of Juan.

GONZALLES: I have seen her. She's a beautiful girl, I believe. Ah! I see you like it not—this marriage?

GARCIA: No, no; I like—hell's fire! how my bosom burns!

GONZALLES: (Aside.) It is better than I thought. Garcia, does Joaquin love his wife?

GARCIA: Yes; why, by the eternal shades! shouldn't he? Is she not all that's good and pure? Curse it; yes, they only live for each other.

GONZALLES: Then kill him through her, and, if you succeed, I will double the pay I promised you; here's a purse of gold—this work is worth more to me than all the wealth of these gold mines. (Hands Garcia a purse, which he lets fall.)

GARCIA: What! kill Joaquin, and Belloro, too? Curse you, foul priest, curse you! I wished for the devil, and you came; your foul carcass is worse than mine; the very buzzards would be poisoned by eating your flesh.

GONZALLES: Bah! parricide and murderer of a priest, robber of emigrants and desecrator of churches, bah!

GARCIA: (Attempts to draw a knife.)—I'll—I'll cut you in pieces!

GONZALLES: Not quite so fast; this stings. (Exhibits a pistol.) Garcia, I want you to do as I tell you, or I will have you hung by the miners to the highest limb on these trees. Do you understand me?

GARCIA: I do.

GONZALLES: I want you to keep at your trade. Travel over the State, and at every place you get a chance, do some deed that will excite the people, and be sure to leave the name of Joaquin for the bounty; and, by the time you return, I will have the train so arranged that Joaquin will fall a victim. Take part of your guerrilla band with you, and occasionally leave the name of Three-Fingered Jack with Joaquin's and after a short space of time, your names will be a weapon to meet an army of Los Americanos. Get all the wealth you can, and I will double the sum when we return to Mexico.

GARCIA: Is that all, good master?

GONZALLES: No sneering at me, Garcia. I swear I will hang you if you do not do as I bid you. You will never follow any other trade but that of a guerrilla, and I am advising you for your own good; follow my directions, and all shall end well. Pick up that purse (picks up the purse) for I suppose you want money. I want you to start to-day, or, at least, as soon as possible, for if you remain where Belloro is, you will lose what little sense you have got left. I will keep track of you and send you word from time to time, as I want you to hear from me. Obey the directions I give you, and all will end well.

GARCIA: And every step I take carries me nearer hell; I'll go, for it suits me, but this plot of yours—

GONZALLES: You know; no matter, so you are well paid.

GARCIA: I would like to go to that fandango to-night, but—

GONZALLES: Joaquin, Juan, Rosa, Bonita, and—Belloro, will be there; I believe that is his party.

GARCIA: Curse it! yes. No, no; I'll not go; the dance would be worse than the wedding scene at church; such feelings are new to me.

GONZALLES: Well, do as I bid you, do not go to the dance. I see you are impatient to be off; you can easily find me; I want to see you to-night.

GARCIA: I will meet you. (*Exit.*)

GONZALLES: A dance to-night? I will attend; it's no strange sight to see a priest at a Spanish dance. (*Exit.*)

SCENE II: *Night; a room; men and women; Spanish gentleman playing music; men and women dancing a fandango. After the dance, enters a party of drunken miners: Texas Bill, Missouri, San Antone, and Zeke.*

MISSOURI: Go in, old gals; you're some on a break-down, ain't you, Dolly? (*Pulls Rosa.*)

TEXAS BILL: Rip it to 'em, old yaller skins! Come here, my greaser love; you're right pert, and the dogondest purtyest gal I've seen since I left Texas. (*Tries to kiss Belloro.*)

JOAQUIN: Back, sir! (*Throws Texas Bill away.*) That woman is my wife, sir. (*Miners laugh at Bill.*)

MISSOURI: Got hell that time, Texas Bill; try again; these greasers ain't worth much, any how.

SAN ANTONE: (*Slaps Gonzalles on the back.*) I say, old mutton taller, who ever heard of a greaser having a wife?

GONZALLES: If you mean a Mexican, I have, sir; and many of them. That woman is his wife. (*Miners laugh.*)

MISSOURI: What if she is, you old liar? To kiss her won't hurt her any.

GONZALLES: You're a disgrace to the name of Americans.

MISSOURI: Leave here, you old ghost of the devil! or I'll batter that head of yours to a jelly. Vamose[24] the ranch! (*Takes Gonzalles by the shoulders and puts him out of doors.*)

SAN ANTONE: Good for you, Missouri. Now, boys, let's put in for the gals! (*Women all run back in fear.*)

MISSOURI: Hold on, till I get the rest of the boys; they are close by. (*Exit Missouri.*)

ZEKE: Neow, I say, boys, these 'ere gals are fresh ones from Mexico; I swow we'll have a rousen time; won't we, San Antone? (*Slaps him familiarly.*) For this 'ere is something like it, I swow. Let's have some licker; come up, boys!

MISSOURI: (*Outside.*) Murder! Murder! (*Enters.*) Boys, I'm cut by a damned greaser; oh! God Almighty! he has killed me. (*Falls.*)

TEXAS BILL: Who cut you? (*Goes to Missouri.*) Missouri, who was he?

MISSOURI: Oh, Lord! he—said—"So much—for Joaquin"—as he—stabbed me. Oh, Lord! (*Dies. All stand astonished, as scene closes.*)

SCENE III: *A creek, day time.*

(*Enter Gonzalles.*)

GONZALLES: Last night Garcia made the first move towards the accomplishment of my designs on Joaquin. If I had not so large a fortune to use my wits for, I would put an end to this by killing Joaquin myself, but there is Father Roderiguez, who is suspicious of my actions, and he keeps a vigilant watch over all I do. I must be wary, for he may possibly know something of my object in coming here, and that prevents me from accomplishing my plans more speedily. What I do, must be done quietly, for Garcia will only act against Joaquin indirectly, and I cannot trust any of the others even for money. Ah! I have it; tell those of the Americans I come in contact with that Belloro is all right—that she is inclined to be a good soul—kind and easy—not adverse to strangers—and get rid of her, and Joaquin will be at my mercy. For with some men, the hopes of this life dies with the loss of their wives, and Joaquin is one of these. Even now, all Mexico is being searched for him, and that mark of the house of Castillo—a Maltese cross on his breast—might betray all. No matter at what cost, this prize shall be mine, and a Cardinal's hat I will buy—in time. (*Exit.*)

SCENE IV: *Interior of a rude house; chairs, table, picture of a saint over the fireplace; Joaquin and Belloro standing, Joaquin's arm around Belloro's waist.*

JOAQUIN: Why do you hang your head with such a sorrowful look, my own sweet wife? Why, your cheek is pale! Is it because I am going to be absent for a few days? Oh, my dearest Bell, cheer up; for a desponding look from you would unman and tie me for ever at home.

BELLORO: Has this not been a happy home?

JOAQUIN: Why, yes; to be sure it has; and may the merry voice of my Golden Bell be left for years to come and sound as merrily as in the few months that are past.

BELLORO: I find happiness in every thing with thee, Joaquin. The music of thy footsteps, when you return from your labor of the day, gives me happiness; this room seems more pleasant when you are here; the day begins with your presence and ends with your return, and then I forget the weary hours that have past.

JOAQUIN: I know it, and feel it in every act, that my presence is necessary to your happiness. But, my dear wife, I will not be away from you but a few days—three, at most. Juan and his partner are on the claim at the flat, and they are anxious that I should come over, for they say it is a rich one.

BELLORO: I know there is not an hour you would be absent, if it was not for our welfare, but, oh, dear Joaquin, the heart of your Golden Bell counts the hours of your absence, and the hours seem so long; I feel a sense of fear when you are away, for our love is too holy, too sincere to last.

JOAQUIN: 'Tis but the tone of an anxious heart, which would divert all evil from its idol. Dear wife, I must start if I would get there before sunset, for it's a long ride and the day is nearly over. One kiss for fortune's smiles (*kisses her*) so, and I'll not be long from thee. (*Exit.*)

BELLORO: He has gone. It is the first time he has left me to be absent for a day. (*Cries.*) 'Tis not that I think he loves me less, for that would kill me, but absence of those we love afflicts the heart. Am I not a woman? and the love I bear my husband will sustain me. But when he knows that I am to become a mother, his joy will be increased a thousand fold. (*Walks in front of the picture of a saint.*) Oh, thou Mother of Mercy! sustain me, and protect my husband with thy merciful hand. (*Kneels down, kissing a cross as if in prayer.*)

SCENE V: *Grocery on a road; notice on the tent.*

(*Enter San Antone and Texas Bill.*)

SAN ANTONE: Look 'ere, Bill; what this ere notice say? I hain't no book larning, and yer right pert at readin; come and diskiver what it ses.

TEXAS BILL: (*Looks at the notice.*) Well, I'll be cussed if there ain't a going to be a meeting; this 'ere what it ses. (*Spells.*) "N-O-T-I-C-E, Notice.—There will be a meeting of the Miners of Woods' Creek at this place, this evening, September 19th, for the purpose of taking measures to drive all the Spanish population out of the county. All favorable are requested to attend.—MANY MINERS." I'll be dog-oned if I ain't in, sure.

SAN ANTONE: Look 'ere, Bill, that just suits me; I'm in for that, certain. Bill, who do you suppose killed Missouri t'other night at the fandango?

TEXAS BILL: Why, Joaquin, to a dead certainty; didn't Missouri say so after he got cut?

SAN ANTONE: Who is Joaquin?

TEXAS BILL: Some of them greasers, you can just bet, and an ugly cuss he is, too, for he killed almost a dozen that I've heard of.

SAN ANTONE: Bill, let's take a taste at that bottle, I'm cussed dry. (*Both drink from a bottle.*) That's good old rye, you can jest bet your buttons.

TEXAS BILL: Yonder comes the boys! and we'll just see if them 'ere greasers is a going to have all the good diggins or not; and besides, they ought to be driven out cause they kill and steal every chance they get.

(*Enter Miners.*)

SAN ANTONE: A pretty big party! Now who's a going to be spokesman. Zeke, let's hear what you have got to say about these greasers.

ALL: Zeke! Zeke! Zeke!

ZEKE: (*Gets a chair, and gets upon it.*) Neow, folks, this 'ere meeting has been called to hear what you got to say about putting all the greaser folks out of the county. They're a darned infernal set, and that's so, by golly! There's no mining where they are, for they get all the good diggings, and we don't stand any more show than a chicken does in the claws of a hawk. (*Cries of Good!*) That's so too, by Perkins! If we get a claim and take out an ounce, they get one and take out pounds; but that ain't the worst on't, for they're all thieves, and just as lieves kill a feller as not, and more especially if he has any money. Hain't they killed lots of the boys, all around here? and didn't Joaquin kill Missouri t'other night. (*Cries of Hang the Greasers.*)[25] Boys, by Jehosaphat! I wish we could hang 'em all, but I swow there are too many of 'em. Let's drive 'em from the county, I calculate that would be a damned sight better, I do, by gewilikins!

TEXAS BILL: That's the way to do it, drive 'em out. Do as we have done in Texas. Put up notices for these 'ere greasers to vamose; and them as don't go, we'll hang.

ZEKE: And don't let us buy any thing of a store-keeper that'll sell to a greaser. (*We won't, we won't.*)

SAN ANTONE: Go in, Yank, you'll do to bet on, for you're a dog-on good talker.

ZEKE: Here's some resolutions I've drawn up (*takes out a paper*) for the considera-tion of the meeting. Neow, I'll read 'em—Resolved. That every greaser found in this county after ten days' notice, shall be hanged by Judge Lynch[26] as soon as found. Resolved. That we are Judge Lynch, and hold ourselves responsible to the Court. Resolved. That every murder, theft, and horse stealing, which has been done in this county, was done by greasers. Them is my sentiments, and I do believe they are good ones, I do, by gracious! (*Cries of Good, Good.*)

TEXAS BILL: I make a motion that the people of this 'ere meeting tell every greaser they see of our resolution, and that one post up notices on the trees, warning them to leave.

ZEKE: Boys! you heered the motion; all in favor of it, will say aye. (*All: Aye.*) Mag-nanimously carried! The meeting is adjourned.

TEXAS BILL: Now, them as don't go, I'll swear, we make go. Come, boys; let's all go and licker up. (*Cries of Good! Good! All enter the grocery.*)

(*Enter Gonzalles.*)

GONZALLES: How little kindles a fire, and what superhuman efforts it takes to subdue it! So with the human passions. That notice I posted upon the house, has kindled a flame that will help me to the accomplishment of my full designs. My plot is yet small, but deep; and it will cause many to mourn and weep. (*Exit.*)

SCENE VI: *Mining scene. Juan, Joaquin, and a friend at work.*

(*Enter several citizens.*)

JACK: Who claims that horse staked out down yonder?

JOAQUIN: I do, sir.

JACK: Where did you get him?

JOAQUIN: I bought him, at Woods' Creek.

JACK: You lie! You stole him, you damned greaser thief!

JOAQUIN: I have got a bill of sale from the person I purchased from.

PITCH: I'll bet you're a liar. Hang the damned thief!

JOAQUIN: Gentlemen, I can soon satisfy you that I am an honest man, and that I paid my money for that animal.

JACK: How much did you pay for him.

JOAQUIN: Six ounces.

PITCH: Now I know you lie! for that horse is worth twenty ounces, and he was stole from old Daylor's ranch.

JUAN: Gentlemen, I know that he purchased him, but of course he will have to give him up.

JACK: You shut up! Nobody is talking to you; 'tain't your put!

PITCH: Oh, you don't get off so easy. (*Two grab Joaquin, with cries of hang him!*) No, boys, whip the damned greaser!

JACK: Yes, give him a hundred lashes; that will cure him of horse stealing!

(*Enter Gale.*)

GALE: What is the matter here? (*They commence tying Joaquin to a tree.*)

JACK: We're going to whip this horse thief.

GALE: How do you come to know he stole a horse.

PITCH: Why, he says he owns old Daylor's horse, and Daylor has offered a reward for the horse.

GALE: He may be innocent; he don't look like yer thieves.

JUAN: I know he is innocent of theft.

GALE: Boys, don't be too hasty!

JACK: You're an old Methodist rascal, if you want to take a greaser's part.

GALE: I am an honest hard-working man, as you all know, I reckon; and look yer, I say, find out if he stole the horse first, before you whip him!

JOAQUIN: Gentlemen, I am innocent!

JACK: You're a liar! Give it to him good. (*Commence to whip him.*)

GALE: For God's sake, are you men? Stop whipping him!

JACK: Shut up, you old rascal (*pulls his pistol*), or I'll blow the top of your head off. (*They continue to whip Joaquin, and count the blows.*)

PITCH: 95, 96, 97, 98, 99, 100. One more for full count! There, that will do for his meat; let him down. (*They loose Joaquin, who falls insensible at the foot of the tree.*) Now you and your tribe leave here by dark, or, damn you, we'll hang you all. (*Gale goes to Joaquin, and supports his head.*)

JACK: Who is he, anyway?

GALE: Oh, God! this man saved me and my family from being murdered on the Gila River. Noble, generous boy! What an outrage is this? Poor Joaquin! (*Supports his head.*)

ALL: Joaquin!

PITCH: Boys, we ought to hung him!

END OF ACT III

ACT IV

SCENE I: *Joaquin in front of his home, pale, haggard, and fatigued.*

JOAQUIN: Is it possible I am still alive, and before the door of the only home I ever possessed, with a heart degraded by unjust punishment? A home, oh, God! where I expected to find so much of this world's happiness; a home where I have experienced all the joys of heaven. Now, now degraded by the lash of unfeeling men; oh, what tale shall I tell to conceal the depth of my misery from my dear wife? What shall I say to her? That I have received a hundred lashes? Ah, no; for they would fall more heavily on her heart than on my innocent back. God! that man should have so little faith in man! Those men fell upon me and called me "thief" and lashed me as if I was some refractory peone. Why should I suffer this, without having revenge? I will—I will suffer all for thy dear sake, my wife; I will bear all and not complain. How will I break this sad news to her? God give thee, my wife, strength to bear this first sad affliction. That good old man paid me the ransom of a hundred lives by his kindness, and I feel that I yet have friends who will pity me. How I need thy consoling voice, dear wife, to heal the wounds which are on my heart and body; for thy sympathy is a balm, and thy voice is an antidote for all my sorrows. My own sweet wife, I come, and by thy side I will forget all harm that has been done. (*Enters the door.*)

SCENE II: *Joaquin's home. Rosa, Bonita, and Juan; Joaquin kneeling at the bedside of Belloro.*

BELLORO: Touch me not, Joaquin; I am polluted! Oh, the misery of this day!
JOAQUIN: What strange words! You are sick; I am by thy side, my own sweet wife. How dreadfully pale you are. (*Aside.*)—Oh God, can it be that the disgrace I have received has been told her, and has caused this? Dear wife, do not hate me, for it would kill me; I am innocent; I am yet thy Joaquin. Do not turn from me!

Ah, I know thy loving heart too well to think that you will not forgive me.

BELLORO: Touch me not, Joaquin! (*Rises in bed.*) I tell thee I am foul—polluted—a being not fit to live, nor yet prepared to die!

JOAQUIN: Say not so; talk not of dying; for my heart is bursting with its sorrow. You die? No, no!

BELLORO: Joaquin, the priest has been here. I am dying, and you heed not what I say!

JOAQUIN: Spare my wife, oh God! No, no, you will not die! Do not take to heart what punishment I received; it was nothing, for I am innocent.

BELLORO: I too am innocent! Joaquin, you are as dear to me as ever. But—I am dying!

JOAQUIN: No, no! oh, God, no!

BELLORO: Hear me, Joaquin. But a few hours since, some men came rushing into this room and said you was hung—that you was dead. I fell in a swoon upon the floor, and when I awoke, Rosa stood over me—but I was your wife no more!

JOAQUIN: Am I not by thy side! Talk not thus; 'tis but a wild dream; you are only a little unwell, dear wife.

BELLORO: Dear Joaquin, listen to me for a few moments, for I feel that my life is ebbing fast. Listen, and forgive me.

JOAQUIN: I will—I will!

BELLORO: Dear Joaquin, I am happy—you are here. Those men took more than my life—they destroyed my virtue! My heart is broken! Bless your Bell, Joaquin; think of Bell sometimes! My husband—my Joaq——. (*Falls back dead; Juan and women kneel.*)

JOAQUIN: (*Takes her hand.*) Dead! (*Gives a scream and falls to the floor. Scene slowly closes.*)

SCENE III: *A forest scene. Enter Gonzalles.*

GONZALLES: Garcia, the three-fingered devil, has exceeded my expectations, from what I hear of his exploits, and even my own acts have produced effects I did not anticipate. It is over a year since Garcia started, and well has he followed my directions. From Los Angeles to Mount Shasta, the name of Joaquin and Three-Fingered Jack ring like a death-knell on the ears of the traveler. Seven men were killed in four days at Marysville; five killed and robbed at Bidwell's Bar; besides many others; and the northern country may well be in arms. Captain Wilson and General Bean were killed at Los Angeles; besides, cattle drovers, jew-peddlers, and Chinamen innumerable. It's time Garcia returned, for I wish to see him. After the use that mutilated hand has been put too, I think he will find a way to use it on Joaquin; and now that Belloro is dead, he will do so the more readily.

(*Enter Pedro.*)

PEDRO: Father Gonzalles—the very man I wanted to see.

GONZALLES: Welcome back, Pedro. (*Shakes hands.*) Where is Garcia?

PEDRO: Coming this way, for there was a house burnt in the lower country a few nights since, and every soul murdered as they came out—men, women, and children, and I think that must be Three-Fingered Jack's work, and no other's. (*Throws off his serape.*)

GONZALLES: I see you have made it pay; the richness of your clothing shows success.

PEDRO: Yes; our purses are not empty, but it has been hot work for our party.

GONZALLES: Why, how is that?

PEDRO: Harry Love, the Deputy Sheriff of Los Angeles, played the devil among us. He captured Claudio, and Mountain Jim started to overtake them, and Love, seeing that he could not escape with Claudio, and Claudio shouting for the boys to come on, Love drew his pistol and shot Claudio, leaving him on the road dead as a stone post. Harry Love is an awful man to contend against, for he does not fear the devil, and he is the worst enemy we have in the State.

GONZALLES: (*Aside.*) Claudio was a cowardly murderer, and Harry Love saved the county some trouble and money by shooting him. Pedro, peace to Claudio's soul; an *Ave* or two, and he will rest well, I hope—(*aside*) in hell.

PEDRO: Where is Juan and Joaquin?

GONZALLES: Come with me and learn all. How I pity Joaquin; his wife, Belloro, is dead.

PEDRO: Sacramento![27] Bell dead!

GONZALLES: Yes, and to-day we bury her. There will be many a sad tale told for this, but come and learn all. (*Exeunt.*)

SCENE IV: *Mountain scene, with forest. Music. Enter funeral procession, led by Priest Gonzalles. Boy swinging censer. Coffin with bearers. Joaquin and friends.*

GONZALLES: (*Chants, with open book in his hand.*)
Tantum ergo Sacramentum
Veneremur ceruni
Et antiquum documentum
Novo cedat ritue
Presatit fides supplementum
Sensuum defectue.

(*Priest swings censer in the grave; body is lowered; priest chants.*)

Mers stupebit et natural
Cum resurget oreatura
Judicanti respondura.
Index ergo cum sedebit
Quidquid latet apparebit
Nil inultum nemanebit
Pio Jesu domine
Dona eis requieum.

(*Music. Exit of Gonzalles; Priest and censer-boy swinging burning incense; Joaquin kneels at the grave; Enter Garcia, stands surprised.*)

JOAQUIN: The grave of my wife; Oh, God! (*Bows his head; rises.*) The grave of all my fond anticipations—the burial spot of all my hopes of joy in this life. The chamber where the good will rest; the grave the portal opening into Paradise. But why should thy form be laid within the mold, food for worms? Yet this heart will bend, like the cypress, forever over this hallowed spot, last resting place of thee, my wife. Oh, Death, unholy curse of mortality, why have you robbed me? God of heaven, and men of earth, what have I done that I should be used thus? And thus afflicted, oh, what have I to live for now?

GARCIA: Revenge!

JOAQUIN: Revenge—deep revenge! 'Twill help to cure the sorrow of my soul, and I will have it. (*Kneels at grave.*) Oh, by thy sainted soul, dear wife, by every spot hallowed to mortality, I swear I will revenge thee! With thy body has gone down into the grave all that is good on earth of me! Revenge, with its unholy light, takes possession of my soul! Oh, thou furies of the eternal shades, aid me, that I may wreck a vengeance on mankind that will make devils laugh. Hecate, embitter my soul! I will not believe in celestial heat; and my soul and body will I give to thee, oh hell, when my vengeance is complete!

JUAN: And I, too, will aid thee. I swear it, by the dead body of my sister, who lies beneath this sod; I will have revenge!

GARCIA: And I! Hell! I have something to kill for now.

JOAQUIN: A thousand lives will be but a just revenge for my golden Bell, my own sweet wife. (*Rosa and Bonita kneel at the grave; Joaquin, Juan, and Garcia clasp hands, with the left hand raised above their heads.*)

ALL: We swear to revenge Belloro!

SCENE V: *Mountain scenery; a cave; band comes out of the cave. Pedro, Jose, Roderiguez, Gonzalles, women, etc.*

GONZALLES: All here, but Juan, Garcia, and Joaquin.

PEDRO: And Claudio, who has gone to—to the other world.

RODERIGUEZ: God rest his soul.

PEDRO: God rest our bodies. Now that Joaquin joins us, we will have work enough to do.

BAND: Welcome to Joaquin!

(*Enter Garcia.*)

GARCIA: Boys, the work has commenced! I never saw anybody so cool.

PEDRO: What is it, Garcia? Spit it out.

GARCIA: Joaquin has got his first blood.

RODERIGUEZ: Who was it?

GARCIA: The one who helped to whip Joaquin. It was so coolly done, it makes me laugh. (*Laughs.*) Juan, Joaquin, and myself were coming down the hill, and ahead of us on the trail was a man whom Joaquin recognized as one who helped whip him. Joaquin tapped him on the shoulder and said, "Good day, my very good friend." The man turned, and yelled out, "Joaquin, by God!'" and fell on his knees, and Lord, how he begged. "Have you got done begging," said Joaquin. "For if you have, pray; for you're the first of the score that I'm going to kill." The man prayed for the Lord knows who all—wife, children, father, mother, and every relation in the world that he could think of; and as he said Amen, Joaquin blew his brains out. Joaquin then put his pistol in his belt, and walked on, whistling "The Devil's Farrier." I searched the man's pocket, and got a purse full of oro.

ALL: Good for Joaquin!

GONZALLES: Boys, he would make a good patron for the band.

GARCIA: The coolest in action I ever knew.

RODERIGUEZ: I love Joaquin, for he is brave. Let's make him our leader.

GARCIA: I am willing!

OTHERS: And I—and I—I—I!

GONZALLES: Yonder comes Joaquin and Juan down the rocks. (*Cries of welcome to Joaquin!*)

(*Enter Joaquin and Juan.*)

JOAQUIN: Boys, I have come to join you, and as I only want revenge, I suppose I will be more welcomed.

GONZALLES: I take it upon myself to say for the band here that you are welcome, and Garcia and the boys say that you must be patron and leader of them.

RODERIGUEZ: That is what we all say.

ALL: Yes, yes.

JOAQUIN: Companeros, I have a large job before me. There are men that I would not have killed by any other hand than mine for their weight in gold. I want but one month to do it in, and then you can kill who you please. I want them that whipped me, and I want the ravishers of my wife—her murderers! By the eternal shades! I will allow no man to kill them but myself. We have not always been guerrillas. There is one I would not see come to harm—an old man named Gale; you remember him on the Gila river. Boys, he is a good man. Spare him and his family, for my sake—for the sake of Belloro. And by the eternal shades of hell! I will kill the first man that injures them. If I am to lead you, you must obey.

PEDRO: Joaquin, we all swear to obey you.

GONZALLES: Revenge for Joaquin! Swear for revenge! (*Holds up a cross. Band raises their right hands.*) We all swear to be true to Joaquin and aid him in his revenge.

ALL: We swear! (*Scene closes.*)

END OF ACT IV

ACT V

SCENE I: *Forest scene—Love's band.*

HARRY LOVE: Gentlemen, at last I have received my commission. (*shows a paper.*) It is dated May 17th, 1853. The bill was passed by the Senate and Assembly, and signed by John Bigler, Governor of California, the same day. The longest term they would give us is three months to capture Joaquin and his band. The pay is one hundred and fifty dollars per month; the time is short, and the pay is small. As we are already organized, we need lose no time. You will hold yourselves subject to the order of Lieutenant Byrnes.

WHITE: Ah, Harry, the people of San Joaquin County have offered five-thousand for Joaquin, dead or alive; and the Governor offers one-thousand more. Now, if Joaquin is captured by us, are we in on the rewards?

HENDERSON: To be sure we are. Do you think Captain Harry Love wants to make money out of us? No, sir; Harry will give each man his share of the rewards, certain, sure.

BYRNES: What do the rewards amount to? I go in for the fight, for all depends on us now. Joaquin and his band are our game.

HENDERSON: Joaquin dead or alive, that's the programme. Hain't Joaquin blotted out some of my old friends, and some of the best men in the State? There's Captain Wilson, Ruddel, and Jo. Lake, boys, I'd go my bottom dollar on. I'll get even if I once get a bead on any of Joaquin's band. Damn the rewards!

HARRY LOVE: The rewards shall be shared equally, and if we get the rewards, and the pay allowed, it will not more than pay expenses. The rewards are poor stuff. I want to pay Joaquin and Three-Fingered Jack in their own coin for killing General Bean and Captain Wilson.

WHITE: When do we start? Three months ain't much time to work in.

HARRY LOVE: To-day. Byrnes, take the boys and go to San Jose, and I will meet you there in a few days. Scout over the mountains and keep watch of the roads and find out all you can about Joaquin, and we'll give his band the benefit of all the proclamations before three months pass.

BYRNES: I have a plan that I think will carry us through. Does Joaquin or his band know you?

HARRY LOVE: His band all know me—more especially Three-Fingered Jack, for I sent a ball so near his head one day that he ducked, and I have since heard that he said it made his head ache for a week, but I never saw Joaquin to know him.

BYRNES: I know that renegade priest, Gonzalles, and I know Joaquin. I think I can buy Gonzalles to betray Joaquin.

HARRY LOVE: I wish you would try it. Pshaw! you'd only lose your head.

BYRNES: I'll take the chances.

HARRY LOVE: Well, try; but if they blot you out, I will have a deeper reckoning against Joaquin and his band.

HENDERSON: Harry, Byrnes is heavy on a scent after greasers.

HARRY LOVE: Byrnes, I want to see you off for San Jose, and then I will try my plan, and if you go on the scout, Henderson will take charge of the men until I join them at San Jose.

HENDERSON: When will that be?

HARRY LOVE: In a few days at most.

ALL: Go in, Harry!

WHITE: Time will try our mettle.

HARRY LOVE: Come, boys, I want to see you started. (*Exeunt.*)

SCENE II: *Mountain scene.*

GARCIA: Ho! boys, Joaquin's month is up! Hell! isn't he the worst man you ever saw?

PEDRO: He beats the devil, and he takes the worst chances in the world to kill his man. He has killed fifteen between Wood's Creek and Murphy's Flat, and every one in the day-time. He's lightning; he shoots faster than any man can count.

ROSA: And every time he fires, he says: Another for murdering my wife. Joaquin has revenged Belloro in every man he has killed. Dear Bell, how well he loved her!

(*Enter Joaquin.*)

JOAQUIN: All here, Garcia?

GARCIA: Yes.

JOAQUIN: Boys, I have killed all but one of my enemies, and if I knew where he was, I would follow him even into the infernal regions of the devil; or if he was dead, I would dig him up to put a ball through his brain. I now take a new stand. Garcia, how many horses have we got?

GARICA: About fifteen-hundred.

JOAQUIN: Our organization will be two-thousand men when all is completed, and they are in Mexico, Lower California, and in this State. So, you see that I have not been idle. With the money you had when I joined you, and that I have taken since, we have money in abundance. I found twenty-thousand dollars in the saddle-bags of one, fifteen-thousand with another, and all is deposited in a safe place, and now I intend to send one-hundred-thousand dollars to Mexico, and then equip fifteen-hundred men, and sweep this State from Mokelumne Hill to the Colorado. "I intend also to kill the Americans by wholesale, burn their villages and ranches, and run off all their property so fast that they will not be able to collect an opposing force, and that will finish our work, and my revenge will be completed. And then, my brothers, we will be paid, too, for some of the wrongs of poor Mexico. This is the reason I have kept you so busy collecting horses. We will then divide our gains, and my career will then be ended, and may the rest of our days be spent in peace."[28] Gonzalles, you we want to send to Mexico. We have a remittance of one-hundred-thousand dollars to place in your hands for safe delivery to our bankers at Sonora. This is the commencement of all that ends, and I hope we will live to enjoy it with our friends.

ALL: Joaquin forever!

GONZALLES: I will accept of this trust, for my mission is peace, and I am tired of this warfare. (*Aside.*)—If that hombre keeps his appointment, I will set a trap that will snare the hunter and free the game; then Joaquin's time will end, for Joaquin, *he* is doomed. Joaquin, you can depend on me for its safe delivery.

JOAQUIN: Prepare, Gonzalles, for within a month you shall be upon your road.

GONZALLES: I shall prepare. (*Exit.*)

PEDRO: Ho! Joaquin, what is this?

JOAQUIN: Reayes, with armed men! Men, prepare!

(*Enter Reayes with four men.*)

JOAQUIN: Who are you, and what business brings you here?

FIRST HUNTER: We are hunters, in search of bear and deer.

JOAQUIN: We are hunters, also. You have found us here, and I have no guarantee that you will not tell you have seen us, and if I tell you who I am, you will tell it the first opportunity; therefore, you must die.

BILL HARVEY: (*Steps forward and fronts Joaquin.*) I suspect who you are. You are Joaquin Murieta, and, sir, I know you to be a gentleman in spite of all they've said against you. We are hunters, and I pledge you my word we will not speak of you or your company for one month, if you will allow us to go.

ROSA: (*Steps to Joaquin.*) Oh! Joaquin, spare them!

JOAQUIN: (*To Bill Harvey.*) I believe you, for I met with you a long, long time ago. (*Aside.*)—Oh, God! it was when I was innocent; what a change a few short years make for weal or woe! I believe you, sir.

BILL HARVEY: Is this the noble Joaquin I met on the Gila? I was wounded then, and you saved us.

JOAQUIN: Yes; go, you and your company! You are safe. Speak not of the past; Joaquin is not the being he was. Go! (*Party shoulder their rifles.*)

BILL HARVEY: 'Tis a pity for so good a man—

JOAQUIN: Go, sir, go! I am not over-patient. Go! (*Party exit.*)

ROSA: (*Claps her hands.*) Good, Joaquin, good!

ALL: Good for Joaquin!

ROSA, BONITA, BAND: (*Sing.*)

When the golden sun is shining from out the distant west,
And the humming-bird is seeking its downy pendant nest,
And the vesper bells are sounding on the mellow evening air,
Our hearts grow light with music and dancing with the fair.

(*Chorus*)
We roam from summer vales to hills of eternal snow;
Whate'er the change may be, our home is Mexico! (*Repeat*)

SCENE III: *A wood—Enter Gonzalles.*

GONZALLES: What, not yet come! The time was set precisely. I detest a laggard, a procrastinator, a thief of others' hours. There is no faith to be put in such men. In my anxiety to be here, I may be before the time; the sun is yet some hours high above the horizon, and I will wait. How assiduously I have tracked Joaquin and plotted for his fall; yet I have struck no blow. But now all of my schemes are ready to fall upon him with their fatality, for I must win. I am known far and near as the Fighting Priest, yet I have never taken life but in self-defense; therefore, my conscience is easy. It is only he that takes life for pay, or revenge for insult, that is a murderer; but he who strikes a life-taking blow in self-defense, and without malice aforethought, should not be held guilty. To strike when a hand is raised to kill thee, why, thy soul cries for revenge, and as the life-blood oozes from the veins of the victim, it rather cries for mercy than bears hatred. So, then, I strike no blow; yet they will fall, and others doing the deed leaves me free from guilt of conscience. Wealth I must have; I said it more than once; and that, too, before many months. Hist! a foot-fall, a shadow; he comes! (*Whistle blows; Gonzalles replies; enter Byrnes.*)

BYRNES: Here at last!
GONZALLES: I have been waiting.
BYRNES: I have but little time to spare. To business! What of Joaquin?
GONZALLES: As we agreed. I think you have forgotten something.
BYRNES: What, Sir Priest? Ah, yes! the ounces; here they are, (*hands the priest a purse*) and every one good Spanish ounces; (*aside*)—and every one will buy a Spanish head.
GONZALLES: Here I have written all that will interest you. (*Hands Byrnes a paper.*) I will leave in one month, and then the band will all be gathered; that will be a good time to strike.
BYRNES: (*Looks at the paper.*) What! is it possible! Priest, I believe you are in earnest in this.
GONZALLES: I am, and to the death.
BYRNES: Will you tell me why?
GONZALLES: No, not until the last ounce is paid, and I am sure there is no escape.
BYRNES: And then—
GONZALLES: I will tell you. Adios! Remember, our next meeting is on the hill. Adios! (*Exit.*)
BYRNES: There is a reason for this, and I *will* know what it is. (*Exit.*)

SCENE IV: *Room in a rude house; a prisoner chained, sitting in a chair; a Court of Justice; table with papers; men sitting, standing, smoking, etc.*

JUSTICE BROWN: Dick, I am going to swear you about this case. Hold up your right hand. You solemnly swear you will tell the truth touching the murder of a person known as Germany, and nothing but the truth, so help you God! And if the prisoner is guilty, he dies within one hour.

DICK: I will tell the truth just as sure as you are born. I had been down to the store getting some grub and fixin's, and was on the road home, and I heard old Germany cry murder three times as loud as he could yell, and I started for his tent, and the first thing I saw was Germany lying across the floor with his throat cut from ear to ear. Ugh! you bet it was an ugly sight.

JUSTICE BROWN: Who else saw him?

DICK: Jim, Big Mike, Bill, and some other boys but I got to the door first.

BILL: Yes, we come up, and I seed old Germany's pockets was turned inside out, and then I knew he had been robbed.

MIKE: Squire Brown, I stand forenenst ye's, and I swear by the holy cross I seen two Mexican greasers whip round the tent, and jest break for the chapparel, and this heathen I believe was one of them.

SQUIRE BROWN: We do not want your testimony until it is called for; we can't believe what you say now, but under oath we will.

MIKE: Who are ye's any way? Ye's are only the judge, and we's the jury, the constable, and sheriff, and yer after doubting an honest man's word. Vat the divil does your honor take me for?[29]

JUSTICE BROWN: I only meant that your testimony was not legal unless you were sworn.

BILL: Sworn be damned! After the boys said they had seen the two greasers, that was enough; we pitched into the chapparel after them; I took down the road and the boys went up the road, and when I got down to Tennessee's store, this greaser come riding up, and then the boys come up and arrested him.

TENNESSEE: Squire Brown, that is the truth; this greaser come out of the bushes and he seemed frightened, for I saw him.

ALL: He's the man! hang him! hang him!

JUSTICE BROWN: Prisoner, what have you got to say?

PRISONER: Mas, yo no sabe para que tengo esta cadena. (*Rattles his chain.*) Yo no hablo el Americano. En poco tiempo el muy amigo viendra aqui. Der Dios, yo no entender alguna cosa de esto.[30]

MIKE: You lie, you damned greaser thief; ye's can talk American, so ye's can.

JUSTICE BROWN: Boys, let's talk this over for half an hour.

(*Cries of—Hang him! string him up! no talk! hang him! Enter Joaquin, dressed as an American; looks at Pedro.*)

JOAQUIN: (*Aside.*)—I was right; the rascal! to get drunk and stray away from us.

PRISONER: Muy gracias! muy gracias! mi patron.[31]

JUSTICE BROWN: Who are you, sir?

JOAQUIN: "My name, your honor, is Samuel Harrington. I am a packer from the town of San Jose, and I am just now on my return from the northern mines, where I have been packing flour and other provisions. I am encamped within five miles of this place, and having heard from a citizen of your town this morning that a dark-skinned man, with gray eyes, was in custody on a charge of murder, and that, although there was no positive proof against him, yet there was so strong a prejudice against Mexicans that there was great danger of his being hung by the infuriated populace. It just struck me that the prisoner might be one of my hired men, a Mexican, whom I sent to town last night, and who, much to my astonishment, did not return. I find that it is indeed the case. Your prisnoer is none other than my packer and consequently cannot be connected with any robbing or thieving band around here. He has been with me for four years, and no man ever sustained a better character. I shall wish, your honor, to testify in his behalf; but before I take my oath, I would like to prove my identity as Mr. Harrington of San Jose. Please examine these letters."[32] (*Hands Justice Brown a package of letters.*)

JUSTICE BROWN: (*Reads.*)—Mr. Samuel Harrington, San Jose. Two letters from San Francisco; also, from Marysville, Nevada, Sacramento, Stockton, and from the Atlantic States. Mr. Harrington, you have a family I see, as your wife's sister speaks very affectionately.

JOAQUIN: No—yes—that is, I had a family, but they are all dead.

JUSTICE BROWN: That is sad. Mr. Harrington, we will swear you, and your evidence will be taken without any scruples. (*Holds up his hand.*) Hold up your hand. You solemnly swear the statement you have made is true in every particular, so help you God.

JOAQUIN: I do.

JUSTICE BROWN: Boys, I believe what Mr. Harrington has said is the truth. What do you say?

DICK: I believe him.

ALL: And I, and I, and I.

MIKE: By the powers of Saint Patrick, may the divil catch me if I do.

JOAQUIN: Dare you doubt my word, sir?

MIKE: I dare that. (*Aside.*)—May the divil catch me but yer one of his imps.

JOAQUIN: You're a fool.

MIKE: There are many of them fornenst ye.

JUSTICE BROWN: Mr. Harrington, there is but one opinion, and that is, the prisoner is not guilty. Bill, take off his chains. There, he is free, and we are sorry to have detained him. (*Bill sets him free.*)

JOAQUIN: Thank you, your honor; yet caution is necessary these dangerous times. Come, Pedro, we will go. Good day, gentlemen. (*Exit Joaquin and Pedro.*)

MIKE: The divil catch them, for 'pon my word as an Irish Count, I belave ye've let two of the damndest villains go that walks on the earth unhung, and so I do.

(*Enter a man.*)

MAN: Squire Brown, here's a letter for you.

JUSTICE BROWN: (*Reads.*)—"Your prisoner is Pedro, the worst thief and murderer in Joaquin's band. Hang him if you would save your own lives. In haste, from

ONE WHO KNOWS." "TO SQUIRE BROWN."

MIKE: Oh, musha worra! Mr. Harrington was Joaquin—the divil! Did ye's mind the look he gave me? Boys, we'll catch the spalpeens yet. (*Scene closes.*)

SCENE V: *A mountain road.*

PEDRO: How, by all the saints, Joaquin, did you happen to come in such a good time. Ugh! I expected to be hung.

JOAQUIN: Our proverb says, The devil takes care of his chickens. I came back to camp last night unexpectedly, and I found that you and Garcia had gone out to try your hands, and shortly after Garcia came back and said that he had killed a man in that little canvas town, and they had arrested you for the murder. "So, I then thought of several plans to save you. I had in my possession those letters of Harrington's which, thanks to my good sense, I had preserved, and I soon form-ed the plan of passing off for a respectable merchant, and it worked to a charm. I always save such papers, for sometimes they can be put to good use."[33]

PEDRO: How did you come to get them?

JOAQUIN: Easy enough; I killed a man on the road the other day, and I found them in his pocket, and but damned little else.

PEDRO: Joaquin, you ought to be a California judge, for you are heavy on papers. That Sunday ride into Stockton, where five-thousand dollars reward was posted on the court-house door for Joaquin, dead or alive, which you generously offer-ed to increase ten-thousand more by signing you name to the document; then your letter to Governor Bigler, asking him to increase the State's offering to ten-thousand dollars in place of the small sum of one-thousand, which he so begrudgingly offered.[34]

JOAQUIN: I had an idea of sending him nine-thousand dollars to make up the sum, for my head is worth more than they have offered yet.

PEDRO: (*Laughs.*) And they will have a merry time before they get it. I am in a hurry to get to camp.

JOAQUIN: And so am I, for I am as dry as a squirrel hole, and as hungry as a coyote. Our horses are at the foot of the hill, and they soon carry us to camp. Come. (*Exeunt.*)

(*Enter Byrnes.*)

BYRNES: I was too cautious, or I might have heard all they said. "Ten-thousand dollars," "Joaquin," "John Bigler," "killed a man on the road." I wonder who they are. I know their faces, but I do not remember where I saw them before. I swear I believe they are some of Joaquin's band. I will know very soon if that priest keeps his appointment.

(*Enter Gonzalles.*)

GONZALLES: Good day, Senor Captain.

BYRNES: (*Surprised.*) What! are you here? You came as still as a fox. Who are those two men?—here—going there down the hill—see!—there, those two.

GONZALLES: (*Looks.*) Ah! what! (*Laughs.*) Pedro and —and—

BYRNES: Who?

GONZALLES: Dressed as an American! Ah, so, Joaquin Murieta! He has got Pedro free, and how, by the saints, I do not know.

BYRNES: Joaquin! Had I been sure that he was Joaquin, I would have sent a ball through his heart. They stood on this very spot, and talked of their villainies. I lay concealed in yonder bushes waiting your arrival, and overheard part of their conversation. Now, I know the meaning of their words. I will know them when I see them again.

GONZALLES: It is just as well, for within one week the band will be on their road to San Juan Mission, there to collect their gold for me to carry to Mexico, and Joaquin will collect his forces to sweep the southern portion of this State, and when the band reaches the coast range, they will be easily exterminated by your party.

BYRNES: Is this the last news you have to tell me?

GONZALLES: It is; here are my last memoranda. (*Hands Byrnes a paper.*)

BYRNES: You have earned your gold. (*Hands him a purse.*)

GONZALLES: All is truth so far; the future for success lies with yourself.

BYRNES: Sir Priest, tell me why you have betrayed Joaquin.

GONZALLES: Revenge and gain; in another land—

BYRNES: For what, Sir Priest?

GONZALLES: To gain wealth—titles—a dukedom. Adios! farewell forever! adios!

BYRNES: Titles and wealth in another land! a dukedom (*laughs*) in the wilds of California! The best wealth in this world is a free man 'mid the mountains, with his rifle for a companion; the best title to a dukedom, an honest heart, firm in its honest purposes.[35]

SCENE VI: *A wood.*

HARRY LOVE: Sad, sad news we hear from every quarter of the southern mines[36] of Joaquin's band. The accounts of many murders have reached us since we started. If Byrnes does not return very soon, we shall be obliged to go on without him, which I would most sincerely hate to do.

HENDERSON: Yes, it is time we met Joaquin's band, and a few shots at their dark skins will pay off some of them for their dark deeds.

WHITE: Well, it is time Lieutenant Byrnes came back, and if he is alive, I'll swear he has some secret that will put us on the right track.

HARRY LOVE: Byrnes has got them, I am sure, but our time is almost up, and if we would meet them, we must seek their den. If I go among them, they know what I come for; they know me as well as a hunter knows his game, and the least suspicion that leads them to think that Byrnes is on their trail will cause him to lose his head, as sure as I can hit that clump of bushes. (*Pulls his pistol and fires.*)

WHITE: You hit the bush for I saw it move; yet Byrnes has a risky job, but he knows how to carry out every plan he sets himself to do.

HARRY LOVE: I would rather be put in a den with a she-bear and two cubs than to try and track these greasers alone and spy out their acts. Give me a fair field, and I will fight six of them any time.

HENDERSON: I'll bet we will have enough to do when Byrnes comes back. (*Looks out.*) What! Byrnes, I'll swear! for I know the height the heels of his horse throws the dust.

HARRY LOVE: Byrnes, by the Immortal! Here he comes.

(*Enter Byrnes.*)

HARRY LOVE: Welcome, old boy! (*Shakes hands.*) We were all anxious to see you. What success? Spit it out, for we have lain in camp so long that we have got rusty. Let's hear the news.

BYRNES: Captain, we have got one dead besides the others, sure.

HARRY LOVE: Got one dead? How is that?

BYRNES: Who fired that pistol at those bushes across the ravine.

HARRY LOVE: I did. Why?

BYRNES: You have killed one of Joaquin's band, the Priest Gonzalles, better known as the Fighting Priest, Joaquin Gonzalles, and the man of all others that wanted to live to see Joaquin killed, and the traitor of Joaquin Murieta's band.

WHITE: Good! a lucky shot!

HARRY LOVE: What was he doing there, for God's sake?

BYRNES: I think he saw you, and was trying to hide from sight. As I rode past some bushes, I saw his horse, and a few feet further on, I found him lying upon his face on the ground. I dismounted and went to him, and I found he was shot through the head.

HENDERSON: The priest had his head in a damned bad place, that's all I've got to say.

HARRY LOVE: I am sorry—for it was entirely accidental.

WHITE: You are sorry! What, to kill a darned snake, a traitor, a murderer, a—

HARRY LOVE: No, but I would like to have given him a fight for his chances.

BYRNES: Harry, we have got the best of Joaquin's band, sure! (*All give three cheers.*)

HARRY LOVE: Byrnes, let us hear what you have done; for we are anxious to hear what the prospect is.

BYRNES: I went to Mokelumne Hill, to Sonora, to Mariposa, and to every Spanish place in the Southern mines. At last I heard of Joaquin's band being at Chapparel Hill, near San Andreas, and I went there, and fell in with a Spanish priest, and I soon learned from him that he hated Joaquin. Then, by plying him with wine, he acknowledged that he was one of the band, or at least knew all their secrets, and I bribed him.

WHITE: Did he tell you?

BYRNES: Yes, and agreed that if we would kill Joaquin certain, and all of his band if possible, that he would put me on their track. I consented, and to make it certain on my part, he only wanted fify ounces for full information.

HARRY LOVE: What, did you have to pay the black rascal eight hundred dollars?

BYRNES: Yes, every cent of it, and I have got his receipt in my purse. I had several meetings with the priest, and he always met me at the appointed time, but I had to watch him very closely, until I was certain that he was in earnest, and then I followed him through ravines, gulches and canyons, where no one but the devil or Joaquin would go, unless on the same errand I was. But I found everything true he had said. Once Joaquin passed within a few feet of me, and I did not know him; Pedro, one of his satellites, was with him; Joaquin had been to a small place on the Mokelumne River, and got Pedro free from a charge of murder, just as the people were going to hang him. Joaquin played himself off for a respectable packer and trader of San Jose; and the result was, Pedro was let go. I saw them as they came down the hill, and I hid in the bushes near a flat piece of ground, the spot where I had agreed to meet the priest. Joaquin and Pedro stopped directly opposite me and commenced laughing and talking, so that I heard part of their conversation, which was about themselves and the rewards offered. Soon after, the priest came, and he told me who they were.

WHITE: Great God! What a chance you lost!

BYRNES: Just so, White; yet it is far better as it is, for now we will get the full band at one sweep. In a few days, they will be on their road to San Juan, and they will go through Pacheco's Pass; and when we once get them in this coast range of hills, they are ours, sure. But the priest Gonzalles, who informed, is dead.

HARRY LOVE: I am glad I shot the cur, for a traitor is the worst enemy to God or man on the earth. We will go and bury the poor devil, and then to the saddles, and as we ride we can hear all your adventures.

BYRNES: Gonzalles met his end in an unexpected manner. Joaquin's gold will do him no good, for he was to meet Joaquin at the Mission and carry their gold to Mexico, and I suspect he was on his way to the rendezvous.

HARRY LOVE: Byrnes, I hope your plans are all well taken. I heartily approve of them, thus far. Come, after this priest is disposed of, we will complete our plans, and when completed, Joaquin is ours, or I am damned. (*Exeunt.*)

SCENE VII: *Mountain scene; rocks; men and women lying about; Joaquin's band all present.*

JOAQUIN: We are well on our journey, and before the sun sets we will reach the pass; from thence a day's journey will carry us to the rendezvous. Padre Gonzalles will be there, and all ready to start for Mexico. One month will prepare us for our final exploit, and then for Mexico and peace; you boys, to enjoy your wealth, and I to mourn over the loss of her whose dear form is ever before me, to count over the stripes upon my back, and think over the deep and deadly revenge I have taken.

GARCIA: Joaquin, are you satisfied at what has been done?

JOAQUIN: Yes, so far. Why?

GARCIA: I will tell you. Curse it! I will tell you. (*Rises.*) I loved Belloro as dearly as you did. I, too, have been revenging her. Damn them! I have paid Los Americanos well. Hell! how I have killed them. Old Gonzalles wanted me to kill you long ago, and I would not on account of Belloro. Gonzalles says your name is Joaquin Murieta de Castillo, and that you belong in old Spain. So, you had no right to Belloro. If she had been my wife—

JOAQUIN: Belloro had been your wife! You're full with liquor, fool. My name is De Castillo! Fool! you are a liar and a devil that speaks of angels!

GARCIA: I've told you the truth. Yes, by God! and if Belloro had lived, I would have possessed her.

JOAQUIN: (*Jumps up and draws his pistol.*) Damn you! Dare you talk thus to me? I will send you to eternal hell if you breathe her name again. Why should I be angry with a fool? Ah, my sainted wife! Why should not all that saw thee love thee? for you were all that was good on earth. (*Cries.*) Oh, God! you were all that was good on earth of me.

JUAN: Garcia, you are a damned fool.

ROSA: Yes, to talk thus to Joaquin; he would have been justified if he had shot you, for you know how the mention of her name affects him.

JOAQUIN: Let it pass; her name is a worthy name for a saint.

PEDRO: Look, Joaquin, here come some men.

JOAQUIN: Who can they be? Get ready boys, (*all rise*) but be careful.

(*Enter Love, Henderson, White, and others.*)

HARRY LOVE: Which way is this party travelling?

RODERIGUEZ: We are going to Los Angeles.

WHITE: (*To Pedro.*) Where are you going?

PEDRO: To the Mariposa.

JOAQUIN: No, we are going to Los Angeles. (*To Love.*) Sir, if you have any questions to ask, address yourself to me; I am the leader of this company.

HARRY LOVE: I will address who I please, sir. Who are you? (*Joaquin starts to go, looks hard at Love, but keeps moving.*) Stop, sir, or I will blow the top of your head off.

JOAQUIN: Boys, every one for himself—go! (*Exit; Love fires at him; Henderson follows Joaquin.*)

(*Enter Byrnes.*)

BYRNES: Shoot him, Henderson; that is Joaquin.

GARCIA: Shoot, boys, shoot! (*Garcia and others fire; Love shoots Garcia; Garcia and others fall; women exit; four are taken prisoners; Joaquin enters, followed by Henderson, and staggers as Henderson fires.*)

JOAQUIN: Don't shoot any more. My work is done. (*Falls.*) My wife—my Belloro—I—come. (*Dies.*)

HARRY LOVE: Crime brings its own reward, and the stern hand of justice deals out the weight of its punishment.

END

FOOTNOTES

[1]*American war*: the same conflict described by Americans as The Mexican War, concluded by the Treaty of Guadelupe Hidalgo (2 February 1848), in which California was ceded to the United States, among other concessions, since Mexico lost.

[2]*Serapes*: often colorful blankets or cloaks, worn over the shoulder or shoulders, as well as being used as bedding and cover.

[3]*Maldeta; Ladrones*: a curse (on them); thieves.

[4]*Thumb and forefinger gone*: hence Garcia's nick-name, "Three-Fingered Jack," by which he was best known to fearful Californians.

[5]*Gua-da-la-hair-ah*: playwright Howe's attempt at phonetic spelling of these Mexican States; *hair* should be *har*, in Spanish, but this probably represents then current California American pronunciation.

[6]*Cheto*: obscure; possibly a pet, or paper-tiger.

[7]*Hell!*: a strong oath for the stage at that time.

[8]*Oro*: gold.

[9]*Litany and gown*: the clergy.

[10]*Peones*: peons, peasants.

[11]*Onzas*: Spanish for ounces, but actually a gold coin then worth about $16.

[12]*Santa Anna*: President of Mexico, defeated in the Mexican War.

[13]*Dark lantern*: a metal lantern with no glass; the candlelight is disclosed only when a hinged door is opened.

[14]*Gila*: Gila River.

[15]*Darter*: daughter.

[16]*Yaller-skin or Greaser*: Western American expressions for Mexicans, based on stereotypes about skin-color and oily complexion.

[17]*Short sweetening*: suggested meaning: a lot or a little sugar, but this may refer to different kinds of sweeteners.

[18]*Mount jump up*: you might scare up, or flush out, some game.

[19]*Pleasant dreams*: this quote is a prose restatement of the thought in William Cullen Bryant's much-admired poem, *Thanatopsis*, but its actual author is at present unknown.

[20]*Commovebitur*: from the Roman Catholic liturgy.

[21]*Placers*: the California placer mines, where gold was recovered by panning or washing in sluices.

[22]*Casa*: house.

[23]*Cabeza*: head.

[24]*Vamose*: corruption of *vamos*, or "Let's go," but meaning "Get out of here."

[25]*Hang the Greasers*: advocating vigilante measures, in which American emigrants took the law into their own hands, often acting as judge, jury, and executioners.

[26]*Judge Lynch*: "Lynch-Law," judgment by lynching, or hanging without a legal trial, conviction, and sentence.

[27]*Sacramento!*: this is an oath—"By the Holy Sacrament!"—not a salute to California's state-capital.

[28]*Peace*: supposedly a quote from Joaquin Murieta; possibly from a popular account.

[29]*Take me for?*: despite the hint of the Germanic in "Vat" for "What," this is supposed to suggest an Irish brogue.

[30]*Cosa de esto*: "But I don't know why I'm chained. I don't speak American. In a little while, my friend will be here. By God, I don't understand anything of this."

[31]*Mi patron*: "Many thanks! Many thanks! My leader!"

[32]*These letters*: supposedly a Murieta quote.

[33]*Good use*: supposedly a Murieta quote.

[34]*Offered*: Joaquin Murieta's bravado and sense of humor, in the tradition of Robin Hood, is demonstrated here.

[35]*Honest purposes*: typical American republican sentiments of the period.

[36]*Southern mines*: this was the "Mother Lode" country, site of early gold-strikes of great wealth, including El Dorado, Amador, Calaveras, Tuolumne, and Mariposa Counties; there was also a Northern Mines area, site of later riches in "hard-rock" quartz goldmining.

A
LIVE WOMAN IN THE MINES

OR
PIKE COUNTY AHEAD

A LOCAL PLAY IN TWO ACTS

BY

"OLD BLOCK"[1]
ALONZO DELANO

NOTE

The plot of this play is founded on fact. The history of John and Mary Wilson is that of hundreds who have come to California—and their misfortunes and ultimate success is a type of what many others have experienced within the author's knowledge.

Pike County Jess[2] is only a type of an open, generous, off-hand, uneducated, south and western man—copied from a character I met in crossing the Plains in '49.

High Betty Martin is a specimen of a back-woods, western Amazonian, such as I have seen, not only in the West, but upon the Plains—who is indomitably persevering and brave under difficulties, but withal with woman's feelings when difficulty is over.

Old Swamp, the Judge, Stokes, Ned, and Joe were my companions in the mines; and their disposition to make the best of bad circumstances is a truthful illustration of my messmates. The scene of the petticoat is true in the main, only that the author was the speaker on the occasion. Jones is a veritable character in name, adventures, and vocation. He is at this moment a citizen of San Francisco, and by his own permission I introduce him. His turkey dinner is copied mainly from his own letter to the author.

The other characters are introduced to carry on the plot, but are each as were daily seen in 1850, as well as at the present day.

THE AUTHOR

CHARACTERS

Pike County Jess, The Poet and Philanthropist
John Wilson
Cash
Dice ⟩ Gamblers
Sluice, the Plucked Pigeon
Judge
Stokes
Joe
Ned
Old Swamp, the Sermonizer
Doctor
Jones, the Printer Man
Express Rider
Watchman
Postmaster
Chinaman
Miners
Mary Wilson, the Live Woman
High Betty Martin (Betsey)

Costume—Modern and Mining[3]

ACT I

SCENE I: *J. Street in Sacramento. Time—about August, 1850.*

(*Enter John and Mary.*)

JOHN: (*Embracing her.*) Ah! Mary! Mary! Is it thus we meet again? No hope—no encouragement?

MARY: Oh, John, I am tired almost to death. I have been walking all day, inquiring for a situation at every respectable house, without success. I offered to do anything: to wash—scrub—in short, to do the most menial service; but every vacancy was filled.

JOHN: How were you received?

MARY: Generally with kindness. Some seemed to pity me, and encourage me with hope; some kindly advised me to go to the Mines and set up a boarding-house, while others looked coldly on me as a suspicious thing, and rudely answered to go somewhere else, they did not want my services, while I occasionally met one who crushed my heart by base insinuations, which, while it brought the blush of shame to my cheek, excited my indignation, that poverty and misfortune should be a mark for rudeness, and that wealth should be entitled to such license.

JOHN: O that I had been with you then! I too have been unsuccessful. I offered to perform any service, no matter how low, if it was honest. I felt willing to engage in any employment suited to my capacities, but I found every place occupied, from the boot-black to the merchant's clerk; and now, without a dime to buy a crust of bread, or provide a simple lodging for her I love better than my own life, I feel as if all hope had fled, and that here in the land of gold, and amidst the splendor of wealth, we are indeed beggars.

MARY: It is hard, John, but I feel it not for myself. When I see your anxious brow, your cheek pale with exertion, scarcely recovered from the debilitating effect of Panama fever,[4] yet struggling manfully to provide something for our subsistence, I forget my own weakness, my own helplessness, and gather fresh courage, and hope against hope and feel from my very soul that we must, we will yet succeed.

JOHN: O, Mary, Mary, why would you leave the comfort of your father's house to share my misery? When our hopes were blasted by the dubious turns of mercantile speculations: when it became necessary for me to try my fortune again in the world, why should you cling to me in the darkest hour, share the perils of the sea, risk the sickness of the tropics, and now be reduced to beggary by my misfortunes? O, Mary, Mary, why did you not let me suffer and die alone?

MARY: (*With fervor.*) You little know the strength of a woman's love. Where her heart is, there is her heaven on earth. I will never leave you till death throws its dark mantle round me; "wither thou goest I will go, thy people shall be my people, and thy God my God."[5]

JOHN: (*Clasping her in his arms passionately.*) You are my guardian spirit—my guiding star. As we have lived together, so will we die. Faint and weary as I am, your words have given me new courage, and with the morning sun we will make one more effort. Surely our countrymen will not let us starve!

MARY: No; a crust will not be refused to honest poverty, and I feel at this moment as if our darkest days had come, and a light must soon glimmer on us. Talk not of death, John, for, till the breath is out of the body, nobody in California dies. Courage then for another effort—aye, another and another, if need be—we will succeed.

JOHN: I never dreamed that you had such resolution.

MARY: And I never knew that I had it till necessity prompted it. I am only like thousands of others who have come to California; who knew not their own strength till occasion developed it.

JOHN: And now for a shelter to pass the night in. If we can only find an empty shed —a vacant tent—(*Crosses.*)

MARY: And if not, the blue vault of heaven beneath the spreading canopy of some friendly oak, with the twinkling stars for lamps will suffice.

JOHN: O, Mary! Has it come to this?

MARY: Hush! my husband. (*They retire up the stage as if in search of a lodging-place.*)

(*Enter Cash and Dice.*)

CASH: How much did you pluck that goose?

DICE: A cool five-thousand.

CASH: Five-thousand! you are in capital luck. How did you come it over the greenhorn so nicely?

DICE: Why, the moment he came in I had my eye on him. I saw he was a green 'un, just from the Mines, and therefore proper game. I carelessly began talking with him and found out that he was on his way home; told me a long yarn about his father and mother; old man was crippled, and the old woman supported the family by washing and all that nonsense, and how he should surprise them when he got home, and that they shouldn't work any more, and all that sort of thing; let out that he had dug a pile by hard labor, and had the money in his belt.

Well, of course I rejoiced with him, commended him as a dutiful son, and to show him my appreciation of so much virtue, insisted on his drinking with me.

CASH: Ha! ha! ha! You're a perfect philanthropist—well—

DICE: At first he rather backed water,[6] but I would take no denial, and I finally succeeded in getting the first dose down him. A little while after, not to be mean, he offered to treat me.

CASH: Of course you was dry.

DICE: Dry as a contribution box. I winked at Tom, so he made Sluice Forks'[7] smash good and strong and somehow forgot to put any liquor in mine.

CASH: What monstrous partiality!

DICE: Directly he began to feel the second dose and grew friendly and confidential. Well, I offered to show him around among the girls, in the evening, with all the sights in town, and at the same time cautioned him against falling into bad hands, for he might be swindled or robbed by strangers.

CASH: Good fatherly adviser—ha! ha! ha!

DICE: Yes, and he grew grateful fast, for he insisted on my drinking with him.

CASH: Ah! that hurt your feelings.

DICE: I told him I seldom drank anything—

CASH: Only when you could get it, I s'pose?

DICE: As he would take no denial I—hem!—reluctantly consented and nodded to Tom, who flavored his glass with morphine and mine, particularly, with cold water.

CASH: You're a practical illustration of a California temperance society.

DICE: It wasn't long before he was the richest man in California, and a damned sight the smartest. Of course he was, so I invited him up to the table to see the boys play. He asked me if I ever played. I told him I seldom staked anything, but what I did I was sure to win, so I threw a dollar on the red.

CASH: And won, of course.

DICE: Of course. And then I proposed that he should try it. He demurred some, but I told him a dollar was nothing—if he lost I would share the loss—so he finally let a dollar slip on the red.

CASH: And won, of course.

DICE: To be sure; our Jake knows what he's about. Sluice Box was absolutely surprised when two dollars were pushed back to him. He then doubled his stakes and went on winning till he thought he had Fortune by the wings, when suddenly his luck changed, and he began to lose and became excited. It was my treat now, and that settled the matter, for he swore he would not leave the table till he had won the money back. So he staked his pile, and we fleeced him out of every dime, and a happier man than Sluice Box at this moment does not exist.

CASH: How, at being robbed?

DICE: Not that exactly, but, by the time his money was gone he was so beastly drunk that Tim kicked him out of the Round Tent[8] into the gutter, where he now lays fast asleep, getting ready for another trip to the Mines, instead of helping his mother wash at home, and plastering up his father's sore shins.

CASH: Ha! ha! ha! the fools are not all dead. We'll go it while we're young. (*Sings.*) "O, Californy, the land for me."

DICE: Stay! look there; who are they? (*Pointing to John and Mary in the back-*

ground.)

CASH: A devilish fine woman! I say, Dice, there's game; I'm in.

DICE: Wonder who that feller is with her?

CASH: O, some fool of a husband, brother, or lover. What's the difference? It's game and we'll come down on the bank and take our chances.

DICE: Good; I go halves. (*John and Mary advance.*)

CASH: (*Inquiringly.*) Good evening. You are strangers?

JOHN: But recently arrived, sir.

DICE: Eh! looking for lodgings, perhaps?

JOHN: Rather in search of employment. Lodgings, however, are desirable at this hour.

CASH: What business do you wish to engage in?

JOHN: Any that is honorable. The truth is, my means are rather limited at present, and although I was bred a merchant, I am not above earning an honest living in any profitable way.

DICE: And the lady?

JOHN: Is my wife, sir.

CASH: Eh! oh! ah! I say, Mr. Dice, you want a clerk, and my family will afford asylum for the lady.

DICE: Exactly, I think you are just the man I want; good salary, no reference needed.

MARY: You are very kind, gentlemen. Certainly this is unexpected.

CASH: Tut! nothing for California, and—hark ye—there is something in a pretty face and bright eye that—

MARY: (*With reserve.*) Sir!

CASH: O, nothing, nothing—we make bargains in a hurry in Sacramento.

DICE: Well, sir—will you go with me? My business is urgent—I've no time to waste.

JOHN: Please give me your address; I will call in the morning.

DICE: Morning? No, my business is in the evening. Go with me now. Mr. Cash, take the lady to your family—*to your family*, Mr. Cash; I will conduct the gentleman to my office. Come, sir, (*to John*) my office is in the Round Tent.

CASH: Madam, I will conduct you.

JOHN: (*Aside to Mary.*) Mary, I don't half like these men; there is something strange in their manner.

MARY: And I don't like it at all. I will not go without you.

CASH: Come with me, Madam—I have no time to spare. (*Takes her rudely by the arm.*)

MARY: Let me go, sir! I shall not go without my husband.

DICE: He's engaged with me. Come, sir, this way! (*He endeavors to pull him along.*)

CASH: No ceremony in California. I shall introduce you to my family, and (*aside to her*) if a thousand dollars will make you happy, I am your man, my dear.

MARY: (*Struggles as he attempts to pull her along.*) Back, sir—you are a villain.

JOHN: (*Struggles to protect Mary.*) Stand off, sir! Villain, unhand my wife!

DICE: Go it, Cash—now's your time. Be quiet, fool (*to John*), it's a cool thousand; you'll never make money faster nor easier.

(Mary screams as Cash endeavors to force her off; John struggles to reach her, but is overthrown by Dice, who suddenly draws a pistol, and presents it at him. Enter Pike, running.)

PIKE: Hillo, mister! Whar ye gwine to with that ar' live woman? Open yer traps, I say, and let 'er go! no jumping another man's claim in these diggins.[9] You won't? *(Knocks Cash down and releases Mary.)* What a gang on 'em! I say, you varmint, pick up yer tools and *vamos*[10] these diggins. Don't undertake to jump a claim that's already prospected. *(Collars Dice and forces him off—Cash gets up and sneaks off.)* Thar, strangers, is a specimen of Pike county justice, and if I catch you in these diggins again, I'll grease yer ears and swaller you whole. *(To them as Cash goes off, left.)*

JOHN: My good fellow, we are under infinite obligations to you.

MARY: Those villains tried to entrap us.

PIKE: Tried to trap you, did they? Set their trap wrong there, for the spring caught their own fingers, anyhow. Who are ye? Whar d'ye come from? Whar ar ye gwine to? What ye doin here, strangers?

MARY: We have just come to California; my husband was sick on the Isthmus; we lost all our money; we have both been trying to get work, but without success. We do not know what to do, or where to go, and were wandering up and down in search of a shelter when those villains assailed us, and you came to our rescue.

PIKE: I hope I may never strike a lead ef you arn't the prettiest speciment of a live woman I've seen in Californy. Don't get mad; I'm only a rough miner, but my mother was a woman, my sister is a woman, Caroline Betsey is a woman, and the last letter she got writ she said she was comin to Californy on her own hook. Is that chap your husband?

MARY: Yes.

PIKE: Wal, old feller, I kind o' have a sneakin for you, jist for your gal's sake. Thar's my fist on it; what may I call your name, stranger?

JOHN: John Wilson, my good fellow.

PIKE: Wal, John Wilson, you're strapped, are you?

JOHN: It is too true; my cash account is rather easily balanced, just now.

PIKE: Don't know whar to roost, eh?

JOHN: Indeed I do not.

PIKE: Well, I live up in the mountains, where you have to dodge to keep out of the way of sunrise; so jist go with me to Stringtown,[11] and set up a boarding-house, or a store, with your gal thar—you'd make money.

JOHN: I really appreciate your kindness, but I have neither the means to get there, nor the money to begin with when I am there.

PIKE: Pshaw! I've got the dust. Say you'll go, and I'll plank down all you want till you can pay. Your gal will keep you honest. I drive three mules and a jackass; come down for supplies for the boys; take the back track to-morrow. Gal, what's your name?

MARY: Mary Wilson, sir. Ha! ha! something of an original.[12] *(To John.)*

PIKE: Wal, Mary Wilson, my gal's name is Carolina Betsey,[13] known at home as High Betty Martin. What do you say—will you go to Stringtown and prospect? Shan't cost you a dime; Old Swamp is thar, and he'll be a father to you, so will

I, and so will all the boys.

MARY: John!

JOHN: Mary!

MARY: Yes, my friend, we will go with you, and thank heaven for the rough diamond it has thrown in our path.

PIKE: Whoora! for a live woman in the mines. What'll the boys say? they'll peel out o' their skins for joy. A live female woman in the mines! wake snakes and dead niggers! turnpikes and railroads come next and steam engines! whoora for Pike county! wheat bread and chicken fixins now—hoe cakes and slapjacks be damned—whoora! I say. Come to my tent under the oak tree in J street, and turn in. By day-light I'll start three mules and a jackass, a greenhorn and a live woman for Stringtown. Injuns and grizzlies clar the track, or a young airthquake will swaller you. Don't be skeered, gal—don't get mad, John; I mean it all right, but it all comes out tail end foremost. A live woman in the mines! fol lol de lol—lol lol de ral. (*Exeunt, left.*)

SCENE II: *Sacramento, in front of the Round Tent, J Street. Time—morning. Sluice discovered lying asleep in the gutter. Enter Watchman, left.*

WATCHMAN: These eternal broils among rowdies, these infernal cases of drunk slightually, and drunk particularly, with the pleasant pastime of dirking,[14] shooting, grabbing, and stealing are enough to try the patience of any Christian watchman this side of Hangtown.[15] I would resign if it wasn't for the chances, now and then, of plucking a partridge, in the way of hush money. That pays slightually; better, too, than city script or corporation notes. It doesn't do to be too hard on a man who has plenty of money. No, no, he wouldn't look well in the station-house; and then I may as well take a good fee for letting them off, as to let the lawyers and judges get it all for letting them off under color of law—besides, it saves time. Poor devils who have no money, and can't pay, why, they're of no use to anybody, and in the station-house they're removed from temptation, and the county settles their bills. Think I won't resign yet awhile. (*Discovers Sluice.*) Ah! here's a subject of contemplation. (*Watches him.*)

SLUICE: (*Starting from sleep.*) I go it on the red—down—yes I'm down—shove it over here, rake her up, old fel—Dice, one brandy smash—two jarvies and a cocktail, plenty of sugar, boy. (*Rubs his eyes.*) Eh! where am I? O, I thought this was Sacramento. What a dream I had. Come boys, it's day-light, time to go to work; Bill, I'll tend the rocker[16] to-day—you pick and I'll wash. (*Getting awake.*) Why, this ain't the Mines. Where have I got to? I thought I was on my claim. (*Looks about.*) Why, this is Sacramento. I'm in Sacramento or Sacramento is in me, I don't exactly know which.

WATCH: Shouldn't be surprised if it was a leetle of both, my young covey. Oblivious, slightually. (*Aside.*)

SLUICE: (*Gets up.*) Is this me—or somebody else? I had a hat; there's none on my head. (*Feeling for it.*) My coat had a tail to it; there's none on this. I had a pair of boots on; somebody's leg has only one on. Somebody has made a devil of a mistake, somehow. I don't remember going to bed; I don't remember any bed going to me. I—I—I—(*feels around him*). Where's my money? Where's my—my dust—my—my—five—thousand—dollars that I had last night? (*Much alarmed.*)

WATCH: (*Aside.*) Five-thousand dollars! Wonder if the *gentleman* has it about him now. If he hasn't I'll take the *loafer* to the station-house.

SLUICE: (*In alarm.*) It's gone—it's gone—'taint here! My money's gone—I've been robbed! (*Frantically.*) My dust is gone! (*Recollecting.*) O, I know—I re-member—I was drunk—I played—I—I—O, mother! mother! what have I done? O, father! Murder! murder! (*Shouts.*) Help! help! Thieves! Robbers!

WATCH: Hello! what's all this fuss about, youngster! Be quiet, will you?

SLUICE: I've been robbed! I've lost my money! Every dime is gone!

WATCH: Why then, you are a very poor devil.

SLUICE: I had started for home; I had made my pile; I only got into town yester-day; I went into the round tent; they took me in.

WATCH: You was a stranger, I suppose.

SLUICE: They got me drunk—made me play. The gamblers have got it all—I can't go home. O, mother! mother!—O, father! what will you do now? I can never look you in the face again. I want to die—I ain't fit to live! (*Bursts into tears.*)

WATCH: Look here, my lark, I've seen hundreds in the same fix. You are just the goose for the gamblers to pluck; they're always on the watch for greenhorns from the Mines, and have the little jokers always ready. If you hadn't went to the gambling house you wouldn't have been tempted; if you hadn't drank you would not have been drunk; if you had not got drunk you would not have played; if you had not played you would not have lost your money. Do you un-derstand?

SLUICE: (*Agonized.*) Take me to a tree and hang me forty feet high; I ain't fit to live—I want to die.

WATCH: No; I don't think you are worth hanging, so I'll arrest you, and take you to the station-house. A few days in the prison brig or the chain-gang for being uproarous may bring you to your senses. I'll do what I can legally to comfort you.

(*Enter Betsey, left, in men's boots, with a large ox whip in her hand.*)

BETSEY: Mister, whar's the post-office?

WATCH: Corner K and Third streets.

BETSEY: Anan!

WATCH: Corner K and Third streets, madam.

BETSEY: How far away's that from Sacramento?

WATCH: Why, that's Sacramento, madam.

BETSEY: You don't go for to say them places are in Sacramento. It's the post-office I want. Got sich a thing here? a place whar letter is got out of.

WATCH: I believe here's another case of drunk. Where do you hail from, madam?

BETSEY: I don't neither hail, rain, or snow, mister. I want to find the post-office, I do, for I expect thar's a letter from Jess.

WATCH: Well, you must have dropped down from somewhere. The post-office is on the corner of K and Third streets.

BETSEY: Haven't you got a guide book? I had one coming across the Plains, but I threw it away at Hangtown. It was only a Mormon guide, printed at Salt Lake City, and didn't go only to Hangtown. Folks said the trail was plain from thar to Sac City.

WATCH: Ha! ha! you don't need a guide book to go through our streets. Just go through Second street to K, then turn up K to Third, and there is the post-office on the left.[17]

BETSEY: (Addressing Sluice.) Young man, you look as if you'd jist crossed the Plains and had larnt something. Won't you be my guide to the post-office?

SLUICE: Hum! Yes, I crossed the Plains in '49, but I never learned anything till last night in Sacramento. I know more now than I wish I did. (Groans.)

BETSEY: Well, show me the way; I'm a stranger in town.

SLUICE: They're bound to take you in, then. But I'll show you the way to the post-office first and die afterwards.

WATCH: Stay, young man, you're my prisoner.

SLUICE: Your prisoner—what for?

BETSEY: What's he done, mister?

WATCH: He got drunk last night and slept in the street but the worst is, he lost all his money, and that is crime enough to commit any man. Didn't play his cards well.

BETSEY: Ar that a fact? Was yer fool enough to gamble?

SLUICE: Alas! it is too true. I had made a pile, started for home, got into bad company, and like a fool, indeed, lost it all and can't go home. I want to die—I ain't fit to live.

BETSEY: Young man, you ar a fool—you was a fool to gamble, but you ar a bigger fool to cry when the egg is broke. When you was on the Plains, what did you do when your gun missed fire at a buffalo—sit down and cry over it?

SLUICE: No, I picked the priming and tried it again. Any man would do that.

BETSEY: Did yer cry because yer lost the buffalo?

SLUICE: No, I was ready for the next and blazed away.

BETSEY: Right! so don't be a fool, but once in Californy. Pick your priming, put on another cap, go to the Mines, and blaze away for another pile. You're only in a slough—dig out and keep out.

WATCH: She's a true California woman, grit to the back-bone.

SLUICE: She gives my heart ease. Perhaps I can make my pile again; there's hope, anyhow, and I'll try.

BETSEY: Mr. Constable, don't be hard on the man. What may I call your name, mister?

SLUICE: It used to be Bill Sluice when I was at home—'taint much of anything now.

BETSEY: Well, Mr. Constable, don't come it too savage on a broken Sluice. Let me have him; Uncle Jo is sick in my wagon, and I'm tired of driving. He don't play cards any more if my eye is on him. Let him go, I'll take care of him.

WATCH: Ha! ha! ha! Ah! madam, there's no resisting your insinuating manners. I never could resist the glance of the fair sex. Go, young man, and beware of round tents and gambling gentlemen. Can't make anything out of him, anyhow. (Aside, and exit, right.)

BETSEY: Well, Sluice, will you go with me?

SLUICE: Yes, I'll go anywhere—to the devil, if you will, so that I can hide from myself.

BETSEY: Well, take my whip and show me the way to the post-office. Up Second street, down Third street, through B street, across Q street. I wish I had a spellin book—I disremember all the letters.

SLUICE: (*Leading.*) This is the way to the round tent—eh! I mean to the post-office. (*Exeunt.*)

SCENE III: *K Street, corner Third. Enter Sluice and Betsey.*

SLUICE: There's the post-office.

BETSEY: Whar?

SLUICE: There! Don't you see the sign?

BETSEY: What, that little painted board with black letters?

SLUICE: Yes, that's the sign.

BETSEY: Humph! a mighty little sign for sich a big house. 'Taint a quarter as big as the sign on the starn of a Missouri steamboat, nor half so pretty. What does it spell?

SLUICE: Post-office.

BETSEY: Whar's the figger-head?

SLUICE: I don't think they have one any more than I have; if they have they've served it as the gamblers did me—took it in.

BETSEY: Wal, rap at the door. (*He raps gently two or three times, and no response.*) Lord! Sluice, sich raps wouldn't wake a snake under a sage bush. Give me the gad and stand from under. (*Raps furiously.*) Hello! the post-office.

POSTMASTER: (*Puts his head out of the window—his night cap on.*) Who's there, making all that noise?

BETSEY: Ha! ha! ha! I thought I'd raise a figure-head.

POSTMASTER: What do you want at this time in the morning?

BETSEY: Are you the post-office, mister?

POSTMASTER: I am the post*master*, madam. What do you want?

BETSEY: I want my letter—and be quick about it—I'm in a hurry.

POSTMASTER: Go to the devil.

BETSEY: I shan't do no sich thing. Give me my letter, and keep your sauce for them as wants it. I don't.

POSTMASTER: Office opens at eight o'clock—come then. (*Shuts the window.*)

BETSEY: Wal, ef that don't beat a black wolf for impudence. The varmint shows his teeth in your very face. Eight o'clock! Humph! By that time we'd be more'n eight miles out of town. Now, my letter I will have; so thar! I'll have that figger-head out agin, or know the reason why. (*Raps furiously.*) Come out o' yer hole, you old badger, or I'll pen you up so you can't get out.

POSTMASTER: (*Opening the window.*) Didn't I tell you to come at eight o'clock?

BETSEY: And didn't I tell you to get my letter now? You don't sleep another wink till you give me my letter.

POSTMASTER: (*Tartly.*) How do you know you have one?

BETSEY: Wal, I don't, but I ought to have one. Look and see.

POSTMASTER: Where on earth do you come from?

BETSEY: Didn't I come all the way from Pike county, across the Plains? Didn't my Uncle Joe get sick on the Desert, and didn't I drive the team in? Didn't I stand guard agin the Indians? Didn't I—Do you see this pretty plaything? (*Suddenly draws a pistol and presents it.*) Shall I take a lock of yer hair off your figure-head, like I did the scalp lock from a digger on the Humboldt? Say, will you give me my letter—yes or no?

POSTMASTER: I'll do anything to get rid of you. What's your name?

BETSEY: Caroline Elizabeth Martin, commonly know as High Betty Martin, in the Settlements. You'll see it on the letter if you can read hand write. Will you look?

POSTMASTER: Yes, yes—I'll look. (*Disappears.*)

BETSEY: Thar, Sluice, do you see that? Ef you *will* do a thing you will if you only will. You see that some things can be done as well as others, and there's no use to cry for being a fool oncst in a while.

SLUICE: You have taught me a lesson I shan't forget. I'll go to the Mines and be a man again.

POSTMASTER: (*Opens the window and hands out a letter.*) Here, Bedlam. (*Retires.*)

BETSEY: I know'd it! I know'd it! Jess is true as a percussion—a snap and a boo! bang! Thar, Sluice, read it to me. I don't know much about dictionary larnin; we hoed corn and pulled flax, in the Settlements—we did.

SLUICE: (*Opens the letter and reads.*) "Dear Carolina Betsey:—I take my pick in hand—I mean my pen—and hope you ar enjoying the same blessing. My stake is stuck at Stringtown, on Feather River. Beef is four bits a pound, and scarce at that. Hard bread and hard work is plenty sometimes, but difficult to get. I drive three mules and a jackass, and slapjacks and molasses is our common doins; but corn dodgers and hoe cake and possom fat can't be got no how. Take the trail to Stringtown and don't stop at Humbug, for the diggers is poor thar. 'My pen is poor, my ink is pale, / One of my mules has lost his tail.'—Bit off by a grizzly. Respectfully yours, Jessy Jenkins, known here as Pike County Jess."

BETSEY: Wal, I declar! Jess always was a scholard—he licked the schoolmaster oncst—and then he writes so sentimental like, so poetetic—Stringtown, Feather River—three mules and a jackass—thar's whar I'm gwine. Come along, Sluice. Who haw! Gee up, Berry! (*Exeunt.*)

SCENE IV: *Stringtown Hill.—Wild and romantic high mountains around, and in the distance, with deep ravines. A tent is discovered, closed.—Pike is seen lying outside, in his blankets.*

PIKE: (*Rousing up from sleep.*) Cock-a-doodle-doo-oo-oo! (*Crowing.*) The lizards are crawlin out, and it's time for me to crawl out too. The gal and her man seem to sleep—I'll let 'em snooze till I get my mules up.

(*Enter Mary, from the tent.*)

PIKE: Eh, what! rolled out so airly? Did you stand guard all night, gal?

MARY: Good morning, Pike. No, I slept soundly; the ground seemed as soft as a bed of down, and oh! such sweet dreams!

PIKE: All in use, all in use, gal—only get used to it. Feather beds are only a vexation—in fact, they're only modern inventions to make people lazy—and I'll marry no gal who sleeps on one; she'd want me to git up and get breakfast for her. Eh! here's another prairie dog crawling out of his hole—(*Enter John.*) I'll warrant the red ants drove him from his nest.

JOHN: No, I never slept better, and I begin to like mountain life. I turned out to help you pack the mules.

PIKE: No, no, you tried that yesterday, and what work you made of it. Pack turned, your gal rolled down hill, mule rolled after her; pots, pans, and crockery smashed up, and if you hadn't moved your boots, pretty freely you'd have been smashed too.

MARY: For heaven's sake, John, don't pack my mule again, if you have any regard for me. I think something of my own bones yet.

PIKE: The fact ar thar's about as much riggin about a mule to secure a cargo as there is about a clipper.[18] You don't know how to trim your load, and ef you don't trim right and tighten right, your cargo will be turning somersets,[19] as your gal did yesterday, worse nor a circus rider. No greenhorn knows the quirks and flumadiddles of an aparaho.[20]

JOHN: Ha! ha! I hope you don't consider me a greenhorn by this time.

MARY: *I* do, John, of the greenest kind.

PIKE: Thar! the gal git my sentiments exactly. All you are fit for is to hippah mula.[21] Whar did your wife go to comin over Bidwell ridge? humph! took lodgings in a clump of mansinieto[22] bushes. You followed like a ten-pin ball, and Short-Tail came within an ace of making a ten-strike after you, and the rattling of frying-pans and coffee-pots was worse than the gongs of a Chinese theatre.[23]

MARY: It was a Providential escape, however.

PIKE: I don't think Providence had anything to do with it. It was all owing to John's miserable packin. Short-Tail is a varmint that never tempts Providence, nohow; I've driv him a year, and never knew the animal to stampede, lay down, or dodge in the bushes before, and I think it was all because a greenhorn packed him, and a live woman rid him.

JOHN: It is possible, but I won't be a greenhorn long, ha! ha! Well, where are we, Pike?

PIKE: On the pinnacle of Stringtown Hill. That gulch that daylight doesn't shine into is whar the South Fork of Feather flows. To get to it, you've got to roll and tumble about a mile down into the bowels of the airth, and when you get to the bottom, you can hear the tinkers at work on the other side. If it wasn't for the ravines and side gulches, the quickest way to get down would be to roll, but as it is, you'd be squashed into a jelly by going it on the perpendicular over the crags; so we have to go it zigzag, like a water snake, till we fetch up on the first bench for a breathin spell.

MARY: How in the world are we to get to the bottom of such a gulf?

PIKE: Thar's only one way that I knows of.

MARY: How is that?

PIKE: Lend me your petticoat.

MARY: My petticoat? gracious!

JOHN: A petticoat, Pike—you're jesting.

PIKE: A petticoat—I want to borrow a petticoat—I do.

MARY: To get me down the hill?

PIKE: Sartain.

JOHN: Explain.

PIKE: Why, a public officer must always have his vouchers, and I, being commissary and wagon-master, must have mine. I can't get a live woman, three mules, and a jackass into camp at oncst—no human could do it down sich a hill. The boys in the cabin must be short of feed, and they shan't go hungry; so the mules must go with the provisions fust, and you must wait till the next load. Now, if I go into camp and tell the boys I've got a live female woman as part cargo, they'll think I'm drunk or crazy and won't believe a word—but if I show the papers, with a clear bill of health, they'll acknowledge the corn, and tote you in.

MARY: Ha! ha! Well, if I can't reach the diggins without a passport, you shall have it. (*Goes into the tent and brings out a petticoat.*) Here it is, and I hope they'll believe the book.

PIKE: All O.K. Now make yourselves comfortable till I bring up pay dirt. (*Goes out, and is heard driving his mules.*) Get up, Mula! ah, Short-Tail! huppah! Mula—arriva! arrea, Jacky. Huppah! you devils! huppah! (*Exeunt, left.*)

SCENE V: *The Hill, lower down. Jones discovered clinging to a tree.*

JONES: (*Solo.*) Here I am, brought up all standing, with a round turn at that. If this isn't the cussedest hill in all Californy! I don't know which end up I came down. If it hadn't been for this pine, the Lord only knows where I should have went to. I'll hold on to the roots and take an observation. (*Sits down.*) I wonder where this trail leads to—wonder if there is anything to eat at the bottom of the gulch—wonder if I shall live to get there? O, my stomach! um! (*Groans.*) What would I give to see a water cart coming down the hill, loaded with bread, bacon, and brandy cocktails, and smash up against this tree! O, Jones, you won't be Jones much longer. O, my stomach! (*Groans.*)

PIKE: (*Outside.*) Stop that mule! stop that mule! d——n[24] her! don't you see Short-Tail going over the rocks? (*Rushes in.*) Why the d——l didn't you stop that infarnel varmint?

JONES: (*Lugubriously.*) Humph! It was all I could do to stop myself, and if it hadn't been for this tree, my carcass wouldn't have stopped rolling for the next generation. (*Groans.*)

PIKE: It's the first time I ever know'd Short-Tail to stampede; and it's all owin to bein rid by a woman. I believe, in my soul, that woman will make a stampede among all the mules and asses in the diggins.

JONES: Stranger, you haven't got such a thing as a biscuit about ye, have ye? I'm so hungry that I could eat a young digger,[25] and wash it down with about a gallon of brandy, and three of the biggest dams on the Yuba.

PIKE: Why, who ar you—what ar you prospecting here for?

JONES: My name is Jones, and I've stuck my stake here because I can't stick it anywhere else.

PIKE: Jones—I've heard that name before. Any relation of Sam Jones, the fisherman, who fished for clams off Sandy Hook?

JONES: No, I don't belong to that family, though I've been going it hook and line for the last three years.

PIKE: Maybe you're John Jones, stranger?

JONES: Nary time—he was hung, in company with John Brown and John Smith, at Nevada.

PIKE: Wal, who the d——l ar you, anyhow?

JONES: My name's Bill Jones called for short William E. Jones, Esq., type-setter by profession and roller by practice, for I rolled from the top of this hill till I brought up against this tree.

PIKE: O! a printer man, ar ye? Goin to establish a paper in the diggins?

JONES: Well, I've had a press for the last forty-eight hours. My *form* is about *locked up*, and my leader, I think will be an obituary, with an epitaph on the death of the late editor, William E. Jones, Esq. Humph! I'm about knocked into pie—I wish a pie was knocked into me. (*Groans.*)

PIKE: I'm glad to see you, old fellow. Thar's a good opening for a paper at String-town, and I always patronize a paper. What will it be—the Stringtown Ga-zette?

JONES: Yes, and I shall gazette my own death and burial in the maus of the Cay-otes,[26] I reckon. Haven't you got the least slice of pork, a handful of dried beans about you? I havn't ate a mouthful for three days, and I'm as hungry as a printer's devil.

PIKE: What! haven't ate for three days? Why, you are famishing. Hold on till I overhaul[27] "Short-Tail." Why, I'll divide the last biscuit with you, and give you the biggest half. (*Runs out and brings in a pack.*) Here, here, old fellow, here's liquor; here's bacon, here's bread—pitch in, pitch in—thar's beans, thar's cold slapjacks,[28] thar's—thar's—pitch in—no surface diggins, lay hold, and go to the bed rock.

JONES: (*Laughs deliriously.*) Ha! ha! ha! The water cart's come. I say, waiter, a broiled chicken, with butter gravy—don't be particular—cook the whole of her, coop, feathers and all. (*Seizes a bottle.*) Gentlemen, your health—ha! ha! ha! (*Drinks and eats.*) Do you know what I think?

PIKE: Poh! how should I?

JONES: Well, I think that Noah never had a sweeter piece of bacon in the ark than this. Hogs are delicious animals, ain't they?

PIKE: Judging by some speciments I've seen, I think they're rather voracious. All right, all right—a streak of luck for you, Bill Jones. Now tell me how you got in close quarters.

JONES: Why, you see—(*drinks*)—your health—I like good manners next to good fare. I had a claim in Jackass Gulch, but it got so d——d poor, it didn't pay but an ounce a day, and I couldn't stand that, and I determined to find better dig-gins. I heard they were taking out fifty dollars to a man on Humbug Flat, so Jim Simmons, from Whiskey Bar, and Sam Slope, from Shirt Tail Canyon, come along, and we agreed to go prospecting together. We loaded a mule with provi-sions, and struck across the South Fork of Yuba in search of Humbug, and I've found it to a dead certainty.

PIKE: Wal?

JONES: Towards evening of the second day, we halted on a little branch. The boys were gathering wood to build a fire, and I was about unpacking the mule, when an almighty grizzly, with two cubs, rushed out of the chapparel,[29] and made at us with a mouth open seventeen miles wide. It was devil take the hindmost with us; the boys broke for the tall timber; I climbed a tree, while our mule took a stampede as if seven devils was on her trail.

PIKE: Wal, that was funny. Ha! ha! ha! How did you go it on a swinging limb?

JONES: Why, old griz seemed to think my flesh was the sweetest and tried to climb after me, to get a taste of my toe nails, but the tree was too small, she couldn't get up.

PIKE: Ha! ha! Why didn't you come down?

JONES: Why, I thought if she would let me alone, I would her, and more particularly as the boys had run off with the rifles, and my pistol had no cap on. Well, we sat and grinned at each other for about an hour, and I out-grinned her—she got ashamed of herself and concluded to go somewhere else for a supper.

PIKE: What became of the boys?

JONES: D——d if I know. As soon as I thought it would answer, I slid down and hunted about for the mule and shouted for the boys; but they were gone, hook and line, so I wandered about till midnight, when I turned in all alone, without a blanket or a biscuit—but it wasn't long before I found myself in a settlement.

PIKE: What, when you was all alone?

JONES: Yes, for I found that in the dark I had laid down on a nest of red ants, and in ten minutes I wished myself in the mouth of the old bear, just for a change.

PIKE: Why, yes, that was murder by inches, without benefit of a rope.

JONES: When daylight came, I found I wasn't anywhere, with all the world before me. I was teetotally lost, and all I could do, I couldn't find myself; so I kept going on for three days, when I struck this trail, and I knew it would bring me out somewhere, if I could only hold on—and sure enough, it brought me up with a side-winder against this tree, and if you hadn't come along I should have gone to *quad,* and my *composing stick* filled with *dead lines* and a *dash.*[30]

PIKE: Wal, Bill Jones, you're on the right trail, now; a few more rolls will bring you to our cabin right side up.

JONES: I'm fond of rolls, but I like 'em hot and well buttered, best.

PIKE: The boys will be glad to see you. We'll set you up and all take your paper. Plenty of contributors in the diggins, too—in fact, you needn't write any thing yourself. Thar's Old Swamp great on sarmons—can go it like a cart-horse. The Judge is a tall coon on law; Stokes is a ra'al wiggler on polotics and can bray a speech like a jackass, and I'm a riproarer on poetry.

JONES: You a poet?

PIKE: You may lay your life on that! Never read my poem on true love, did you?

JONES: No.

PIKE: I reckon not—the printer man at Sacramento wouldn't print it—didn't 'preciate genius, but you shall print it, and we'll sell it at two bits a copy and divide the profits, old fel. O, it's capital. (*Reciting.*)
  "O, Carolina Betsy's yaller hair
  Has laid my heart and innards bare."

JONES: There, there—take a drink, and let the rest go till we get to the bottom of the hill. There is genuine poetry in your heart, if there is not in your poem, and I'll set *you* up in capitals, if I don't your *rhymes*.

PIKE: Well, help me straighten up Short-Tail, who's lodged in the mansinietos, and we'll straighten the pome when your press gets to grinding.

JONES: Go ahead. For once in my life I'm in luck. (*Exeunt.*)

SCENE VI: *Inside of a miner's cabin; a group of miners variously engaged—some mending clothes, some cooking, some washing clothes at the wash-tub, some lying in bunks; Old Swamp is trying to bake slapjacks in a frying-pan.*

JOE: (*Trying to mend boot with fork.*) I say, Old Swamp, I'm savage as a meat-ax—ain't breakfast most ready. The lizards have been licking their chops the last hour.

OLD SWAMP: (*Trying to turn a cake in the pan.*) Swallow a piece of your boot, Joe, to keep your stomach. This is the last we've got, any how, and unless Pike gets back pretty soon, you'll have a chance to girt up, Indian fashion, unless you're good at catching rats.

JOE: Traps are all broke—powder gone—and rats shy and half starved, Old Swamp. Have to go it on fried boots.

OLD SWAMP: Leetle too much cold water in this batter—the cakes don't get done brown, and don't turn easy.

JOE: Put a little whisky in 'em, Old Swamp—they'll soon turn over on their own hook.

OLD SWAMP: Pshaw! the Judge and Stokes drank up the last drop—not enough left te wet your eye. No matter—the cakes will go further half cooked.

STOKES: (*At the wash tub.*) Judge, I see you are on the bench—what case is on the docket for to-day?

JUDGE: (*Mending a very ragged pair of pants.*) Action for rents—an old suit—parties trying to compromise.

STOKES: What's the prospect, Judge?

JUDGE: (*Holds up the pants.*) Doubtful whether the parties agree. I can see through the *hole*, but the parties may trick anon for a new trial—they're trying to patch it up somehow.

STOKES: How is the evidence?

JUDGE: Strong on one side—and a good deal of re-button testimony will be required to uphold the suit. Old Swamp, I want to examine you.

OLD SWAMP: Want me to swear, Judge?

JUDGE: No, no—you swear wickedly enough every day to answer any court in the mines.

OLD SWAMP: Then you won't take me up for contempt?

JUDGE: Not if you go according to Bacon.

OLD SWAMP: I've been on bacon the last fifteen minutes, and it's the last piece in the cabin; there isn't grease enough in the bone to fry itself—but it will go further half cooked.

JUDGE: Stand aside—such testimony won't pay my fees—you'll starve judge, jury, and all the parties out.

OLD SWAMP: Have to stay proceedings for want of grease to grease the griddle. It's a fact—we can't go on much longer.

STOKES: (*Who is washing a shirt—sleeves rolled up.*) The question of ways and means is before the house.

JOE: "Hark! from the tombs a doleful sound."

STOKES: Mr. Speaker—I call the gentleman to order. A thorough renovation is necessary to our larder, gentlemen; our stores have been consumed; the relentless rats—

JOE: Two-legged rats, Mr. Speaker.

STOKES: I call the gentleman to order. The bill which I am about to offer to the house will have a soaporific effect upon the shirt bosoms of my constituents.

JOE: Hope I shan't have to pay the gentleman's bill, Mr. Speaker; too much liquor in it for a temperance man.

STOKES: I say, Mr. Speaker, my bill will have a soaporific effect.

JUDGE: On the bowels, man—on the bowels. Hang your law and legislation for spare diet; empty stomachs require strong tonics and stimulants.

OLD SWAMP: Not pork enough left to stimulate the stomach of a horned toad— only a mouthful left.

JOE: Enough for a taste all round. Tie a string to it—swallow it and pull it back again—and so let it go around; you'll all have a taste, and a grand operation will be produced.

JUDGE: I object to such practice in my court; some knave of a lawyer will bite the string off, and the bacon will be teetotally incarcerated.

STOKES: Mr. Speaker—the gentleman's plan is ingenious, but will not apply to all cases. Some of my constituents have throats that no string can fathom, if I may judge by the streams of fluid running down.

JOE: Dam them up, then, by tying a string tight outside.

OLD SWAMP: Don't be afraid, boys—if worse comes to worst, we'll mend the traps and go it on rats; I'm great on trappin.

JOE: O, for a friccaseed rat. Here, Old Swamp, fry that—(*throws his boot out*)—don't cook it quite done, it will go further; it has already gone several miles. (*Sings.*)

O, Susannah, don't you cry for me—
I'm eating up my boots in Californi*ee*.

JUDGE: Hark! there's a noise at the door.

JOE: Some poor devil coming to beg a breakfast—I shall have to divide my boot with him. Old Swamp, don't cook it done—'twill go further.

OLD SWAMP: Boys, it's Pike; I know the tramp—it's Pike and the jackass. Plenty to eat now.

(*Enter Pike and Jones.*)

ALL: Huzzah! for Pike—huzza! for Short-Tail, slapjacks and molasses! Pork and beans now, and no mistake.

PIKE: I'm glad to see you, boys. Thar's no place like home arter[31] all, with plenty of hog and hominy—hoe cake and possum fat.

OLD SWAMP: Two days over time, Pike. We concluded the diggers were on your trail, and that you had fell into the stomach of a digger squaw like a roasted caterpillar.

PIKE: Never fell into a woman's bosom as deep as that in all my life. Devil to pay with Short-Tail; got rid by a witch; took the stampede; rolled down hill, and finally, Short-Tail and I got into the editor business, and picked up a printer man, who was mighty near struck off; hadn't ate a mouthful in a month, and the way he pitched into the bacon and brandy was like a greenhorn on his first day's work. Here he is, boys—let him dig for himself now.

JONES: I'm like a licked politician, gentlemen—nothing to say but keep up a devil of a thinking. My long primer was about run out, and if Pike hadn't come along, I shouldn't have had an index by this time.

OLD SWAMP: A miner's latch string is always out—pull, and the door of his heart, as well as his cabin, will open to distress. We'll divide our last biscuit with you.

JUDGE: We will share such as we have with you.

STOKES: I vote aye to that.

JOE: Old Swamp, cook t'other boot now—well done and plenty of gravy.

JONES: No abbreviations of periods to my thanks, gentlemen—I am an exclamation—not a single leaded column in my heart.

PIKE: Thar, Bill Jones, didn't I tell you so? Depend upon it, ef thar's a mean streak in a man so long (*measures the tip of his finger*), it's bound to come out of him in California, and ef he has got a good streak he can't keep it in, no how you can fix it.[32] Boys, do you know what this is? (*Holds up the petticoat.*)

OLD SWAMP: You've been stealing a white shirt, Pike.

STOKES: It's a long petition on parchment, for the relief of widows—grass widows, Mr. Speaker.

JOE: No, no, it's a table-cloth to eat fried boots on. (*Pike gets into it.*)

JUDGE: It's a petticoat, by heavens! O Blackstone, what revolution is at hand?

MINERS: A petticoat! A petticoat! Huzza! huzza!

OLD SWAMP: What female woman have you murdered to get that skin?

PIKE: Do you s'pose I'd kill a woman to get her petticoat? I'd rather destroy a dozen petticoats to get one live woman, you varmints—and you know it, you do. I hope I may never strike a lead[33] if the animal didn't give it to me with her own hands.

STOKES: You've robbed some washerwoman's clothes line in Sacramento.

PIKE: Nary time, old fellow. Haven't been near a clothes line since my mother walloped me with one for drowning kittens in the wash tub. The fact ar, the animal who owns this skin is at the top of the hill, and sends this by Short-Tail, with her compliments, and hopes you'll help her down.

OLD SWAMP: A real live woman comin to the Mines—unpossible!

PIKE: As true as yer born, boys. Short-Tail and I fetched her ourselves—she put the devil into the mule tho'.

JOE: The millenium has come!

PIKE: No, it's only a woman.

JOE: Let's eat breakfast in a hurry and go and tote her into town.

JUDGE: D——n the breakfast, boys—let us go and get a sight of her before the dew carries her off.

STOKES: Slapjacks and molasses would be worse than emetics now. Let's hear from you, old minister—what do you say?

OLD SWAMP: (*Slowly and with emphasis.*) Joe, take down that fiddle and rosin the bow.

JOE: (*Jumps after it.*) It's in tune, and if it ain't it's no matter.

OLD SWAMP: Now, boys, remember you had mothers oncst—don't make fools of yourselves, but make a carcle. (*They circle around Pike.*) Now Joe, give us Hail Columby, Star Spangled, Yankee Doodle, and Rory O'More all at oncst! and, boys, let your legs go prospecting as if the richest kind of a lead was before you. Try your boots, boys—try your boots. (*Plays a lively air; miners dance merrily around Pike in a grotesque manner.*)

PIKE: (*Unable to contain himself, dances inside the ring, crowing.*) Cock-a-doodle-doo-oo-oo!

(*Joe becomes too much excited to play and capers about without music.*)

STOKES: Hello! We've danced the fiddle into the negative. Old Swamp, take it up where Joe left off.

OLD SWAMP: (*Sings.*)

A petticoat flag is the miner's delight—
It awakens sweet thoughts of our mothers at home;
Our sweethearts and wives to dear memory bright:
All the girls we will welcome whenever they come.

Now, boys, get your rifles and pistols—Joe, hand me the whisky bottle. Form line, boys—form line; go it in millintary order. Joe, give us General Washington's most particular grand march. (*Joe plays.*) Shoulder arms! forard march.

MINERS: Huzza! huzza for a "live woman in the mines." (*Exeunt.*)

SCENE VII: *The top of the hill. Miners enter before the tent—give a cheer and fire a salute; Mary screams inside, and John rushes out alarmed.*

JOHN: Good heavens, gentlemen! what is the matter?

MINERS: Old Swamp! Old Swamp!

OLD SWAMP: (*Gets up on a rock.*) Stranger, we were white men oncst; it seems like a very long time ago—but we have a tradition that some of us wore white shirts and short beards, but it is so long, I don't vouch for it. It has been handed down to us, by various letters through the post-office, that we war born into the world, and that our mothers were live female women. It is so long since we have seen a woman, that we don't exactly know what they are, but the doctor here says a woman is a female man of the human *specie*. Pike County Jess showed us a skin of a strange animal and swears it belongs to a female woman of the human specie; he says, too, that you have caught the animal and had her alive on exhibition. Now, stranger, we want to take a look at the thing, and I pledge you my honor we won't stampede her.

JOHN: Ha! ha! ha! gentlemen—well, this is a droll specimen of the mines—yes, I have caught such an animal—rather rabid, but if you will risk the consequences, I'll show her up.

OLD SWAMP: We'll take the chances—trot her out—trot her out.

(*Exit John into the tent. Enter John and Mary.*)

MINERS: Huzza for "a live woman in the mines!" Huzza for our mothers, our wives, and sweethearts at home!

PIKE: Huzza for Carolina Elizabeth Martin!—commonly known as High Betty Martin—that's my gal, it is.

MINERS: Huzza! Huzza!

MARY: Gentlemen, I thank you for your kind reception—may I be able to make you some return?

OLD SWAMP: Hi! gal! won't you sew the buttons on our pants? won't you make light bread and bunkum hoe-cake? won't you make good gruel for a sick miner? won't you make us wear white shirts of a Sunday, and help Pike make poetry and me sarmons?

MARY: Indeed, I'll do all I can for you, I'm sure. O, John, when we were starving in Sacramento, we little thought of finding such warm hearted friends in the mines!

OLD SWAMP: Friends, gal? why we'd all be fathers and mothers and brothers and sisters to you. Boys, a drink all round! here, gal—beauty before age. (*Hands her the bottle; she drinks from it.*[34]) Now, boys, strike the tent. (*Tent is taken down.*) Make a chair for the gal, two o' ye. (*They make a chair by clasping hands.*) Three cheers for the first "live woman in the mines." (*Cheers.*)

JOE: Three cheers for the first white man who brought his wife to the mines.

PIKE: And three cheers for High Betty Martin, who's coming to the mines.

(*The Miners seat Mary between them; others shoulder John; Joe strikes up a march; Pike raises the petticoat for a flag as they march out. Curtain on picture.*)

END OF ACT I

ACT II

SCENE I: *A deep gulf.—Hillsides rocky and steep, and covered with undergrowth. An emigrant wagon a little in the background.*

(Enter Betsey and Sluice.)

BETSEY: Sluice, whar are we?

SLUICE: According to the best of my judgment, we are here.

BETSEY: Lord, Sluice! any fool knows that. But whar's our wharabouts?

SLUICE: In a devilish deep gulch, in my opinion.

BETSEY: How are we to get out of it?

SLUICE: I don't know, unless we wait till the world gets upside-down and fall out.

BETSEY: Ain't thar no cend[35] to it?

SLUICE: Yes, one end has a perpendicular fall over the rocks a hundred feet—the other end hasn't any beginning, so far as I can see.

BETSEY: What on airth did we come down for?

SLUICE: I don't know any other reason than by the force of gravitation, and woman's will. I told you we had better head the gulch, and go around it, but no, down you would come, over rocks and bushes, and now you are like a rat in a trap—can't neither back out nor go further. Now you see where woman's will has brought you to.

BETSEY: I don't care a snap, Bill Sluice. I wasn't going six miles around to make half a mile—I go it on short cuts, I do.

SLUICE: Well, we shall go it on short cuts now, for it won't take long to starve to death here.

BETSEY: Who talks of starving to death? If you are so easily discouraged, you'd better go back to Sacramento and practice in the Round Tent.

SLUICE: I had rather starve to death with you.

BETSEY: Good. If worse comes to worse, we'll pack the cattle, leave the wagon, and work our way to Stringtown.

SLUICE: And leave Uncle Joe sick to be eaten up by the wolves.

BETSEY: No, no, no—that won't do—no, never. You shall go to Stringtown, hunt up Jess, bring him here, and then we'll take our wagon to pieces,³⁶ carry it up the hill wheel at a time, shoulder Uncle Joe, drive the cattle up, put the wagon together, and—whoa! haw! Berry, who's afraid?

SLUICE: A woman's wit, a woman's wit forever! It's a pity you wasn't a man.

BETSEY: Why, Sluice?

SLUICE: You'd make a capital general. You would have fought your way through Mexico as well as General Taylor,³⁷ without men, money or provisions.

BETSEY: I should need better soldiers than you, then.

SLUICE: Can't I shoot—can't I fight—can't I dig?

BETSEY: Yes, and you can lay in the gutter like a loafer.

SLUICE: Um! (Groans.) That's ungenerous.

BETSEY: Pshaw! you draw a close sight, but you can't stand grief—you're like a faithful dog—can fight well, but want somebody to set you on. You'd make a good soldier, but a poor general.

SLUICE: I give it up—there is no use in disputing with a woman. Let her have her own way, and its all sunshine—contradict her, and a thunder storm raises directly. Well, general, what is to be done?

BETSEY: Put a piece of bread and bacon in your pocket, shoulder your rifle, and go out on scout, and see if thar's any place to get our wagon out. I'll stand guard over the cattle and Uncle Joe, and mind, don't you come back without finding a trail—d'ye hear?

SLUICE: (Going.) I'm gone.

BETSEY: Stop!

SLUICE: I'm stopped.

BETSEY: Whar's your rifle?

SLUICE: In the wagon.

BETSEY: Get it. Never stir from your camp in a wild country without your arms. Suppose you meet an Indian, or a grizzly—what show would you have for your own skin?

SLUICE: Right again, general. The fact is, if California is ever invaded by an enemy, with a regiment of Pike County women we can defy the devil. (Gets his rifle, and exits.)

BETSEY: (Sitting down on a rock.) O, dear, what trouble I have in hunting up a man—come two-thousand miles and havn't found him yet; ef it had been any body else but Jess, I'd seen all the men hung first, afore I'd wore out so much shoe-leather in running arter 'em! Ef it hadn't been for him, I'd have been hoein corn and pulling flax on the plantation now, instead of climbing these hills. These pesky men do bother our heads so orfully when they do get in; thar's no getting along without one—and after all thar isn't one in a hundred that's worth the trouble they give us. Then, like a flea, thar's no sartinty of catching one—for just as yer get yer finger on him, like as any way he's hoppin off arter somebody else. Let me catch Jess hoppin arter somebody else. Giminy! wouldn't I give him jessie?—wouldn't I crack him? O, Jess, Jess—you run arter somebody else! O, murder! O, ef he should? O! O! (Weeps.) I'm a poor, lone, lorn woman—Uncle

Joe sick—lost in the mountains—and Jess, my Jess, to serve me so! My courage is gone—my boots worn out—wagon tire getting loose—my best har comb broke—all trying to find a man, and him to use me so. (*Weeps.*) It will break my heart! O! O! O! (*A gun shot is heard.*) Ha! (*Springs up and listens.*) Sluice in trouble? (*Forgets her lamentation instantly; runs to the wagon and seizes a rifle.*) Keep still, Uncle Joe—ef thar's danger, I'm ready for it.

(*Enter Sluice, running.*)

BETSEY: What is it, Sluice—what is it?

SLUICE: O, nothing in particular—no harm done yet—can't say what may come.

BETSEY: Let it come, Sluice; only give us a fair chance for a skrimmage.

SLUICE: I was picking my way through the chapparel, when I discovered fresh digger tracks, and I thought some of the Indians were lurking about to stampede our cattle. Directly I got a glimpse of one of the rascals, and I thought I'd give him leave to quit, so I just put a ball through the top of his hair, and such an almighty yell you never heard, and such a scratching of gravel you never saw, for the black devil ran as if a young earthquake was at his heels—I didn't hurt him though; only gave him a hint to move his boots.

BETSEY: That's right; never take a human life except in self-defense. Ef *they'll* let *us* alone, we will let *them.*[38] Glad it's no worse. Did you find a chance to get the wagon out?

SLUICE: Yes, I found a side ravine, and by taking the point, I think we can get the wagon up—it's a tight squeeze though, for it's a little less than a perpendicular.

BETSEY: We'll go it on the perpendicular then, and go it clar. As for staying here, I shan't do it, so thar. (*To herself.*) And ef I do find Jess in cahoot with any live woman, won't I wake snakes and peel his skin. (*Exit and is heard behind the scenes.*) Whoa—haw Buck! Gee up, Berry!

SCENE II: *Exterior of log cabin. Enter John and Mary. Mary with a broom.*

MARY: Well, Mr. Storekeeper, how do you sell beans to-day?

JOHN: By the pound, generally, Mrs. Express Man.

MARY: Ha! ha! I didn't know but you sold them by the yard—are you sure that you know beans?

JOHN: I profess an acquaintance with them when they are well baked—think I can tell a bean from a broomstick, madam.

MARY: (*Raising her broom, threatening good-naturedly.*) Perhaps I had better test your knowledge.

JOHN: No, no—not now; try me on beans first.

MARY: Well, weigh me out five pounds, then, for dinner.

JOHN: Got the dust to pay for them? No credit here—pay as you go.

MARY: (*Raising her broom.*) I'll raise a dust for you if you don't get the beans—no beans, no dinner!

JOHN: How sharp you are—you shall have the beans.

MARY: And you'll be sharp enough, too, when the beans are cooked.

JOHN: I'll try to get my pay, anyhow.

MARY: No fear of that, for you already have a miner's appetite.

JOHN: Nothing better than our pure mountain air for that.

MARY: O, John, we are so happy, now! Everybody is so kind to us—all are so good natured. Why, I never was happier in my life—and it is so much better here than starving in the city!

JOHN: I never knew I was good for anything till I came here.

MARY: Nor I, either; now I know I am worth beans. Ha! ha!

JOHN: Circumstances make men—aye, and women, too—and if we are only willing to help ourselves, why, in due time—in miner's language—we may strike a lead.

MARY: True—and we have struck the lead—let us follow it. The kind-hearted boys have set us up in business, and scarcely ever seem satisfied unless when they are doing something to help us on.

JOHN: God bless them! Any package for me in your department, madam Express Man?

MARY: Yes, an empty pail and an ax; I want the charges paid.

JOHN: Pail and ax—charges! What are the charges?

MARY: Fill the pail at the spring—cut an armful of wood—and get five pounds of beans.

JOHN: Charges outrageous! I'll forfeit the packages!

MARY: If you do, you'll forfeit your dinner—take your choice—can't cook beans without water and fire.

JOHN: And I can't eat beans without being cooked; I'll take the pail and pay the charges. No getting ahead of a woman, I see.

MARY: And be quick, John dear, for the express will be in soon, and you know what a throng we shall have around us. By the way, I found two letters in the box, this morning, addressed to me.

JOHN: Two letters? Somebody making love to you, I suppose, already.

MARY: Yes, indeed—is that any business of yours? (*Playfully.*)

JOHN: I suppose not, in California, where women do business on their own account, independent of their husbands. Still, I might be just the least bit in the world jealous.

MARY: And with some reason, John—for if they are not love letters, they are loves of letters.

JOHN: I'm all curiosity—besides, I want to know who I've got to shoot.

MARY: No doubt! Well, here they are—read them. (*Handing him the letters.*)

JOHN: They look as if they had been written with a pick or shovel, rather than a pen. (*Reads.*) "For and in consideration of mending pants, sewing on buttons and patching shirts, and trying to make an old man happy by sundry kindnesses—know all men and female women by these here presents: I hereby sell and make over to Mary Wilson, my half interest in claim No. 10—situate, lying and being on Whisky Bar, Feather River diggins, State of Californy, United States of Ameriky—for her whole soul's benefit and behoof, and her husband hasn't anything to do with it." (The deuce he hasn't—setting up for yourself without advertising, are you?) "And I agree to prospect her said claim with pick, shovel and pump, clear to the bed rock, free gratis for nothing, from date."[39] Ambrose Swamp. Shan't shoot old Swamp for that. (*Opens the other.*)

Poetry, eh? this must be a love letter in earnest. (*Reads.*)
"I, Jessie Jenkins by name,
Give Mary Wilson my half claim—
Know'd as number ten
By all the mining men—
Which I, in cahoot
With that ar old brute
Call'd Swamp, on Whisky ba
Hopin she may clar
Ten thousand dollars on sight.
To which I subscribe my hand write
With a pen like a pole—
And may the Lord have mercy on your soul."

Jess Jenkins,
Known as Pike County Jess.—Amen.

Ha! ha! ha! Shan't shoot Pike for that—God bless him! Ah! Mary, Mary, if you havn't fallen in love with the boys, I have; they are doing so much for us, I—I can't—(*Affected. Post horn is heard.*)

MARY: Ah! here is the express rider; hurry, John—hurry. (*He takes the pail and ax and goes out.*)

(*Enter Express Rider with his bags.*)

EXPRESS RIDER: Up to time and a leetle ahead, madam. Run the gauntlet between a pack of cayotes, three grizzlies, and a whole tribe of Digger Indians—killed two horses and jumped a ledge a hundred feet—hung myself by the heels in the bushes—turned forty somersets down a canyon—slept three nights on a snow bank—froze three legs stiff, had 'em amputated and climbed the hill next morning on crutches, and have brought lots of letters for the boys, and newspapers for the old ones. Please take the bags, and give me a glass of brandy and water without any water in it.

MARY: Ha! ha! ha! Merry as an express man yet, I see. Well, come in, come in—we have always something for you. (*Mary goes to the express counter.*)

(*Enter Miners, hastily, as if running from their work. Half a dozen voices at once.*)

MINERS: Any letters for me? Have I got a letter?

MARY: Wheugh! wheugh! One at a time—one at a time—can't look for all at once!

OLD SWAMP: Form a line, boys—form a line; give the gal a chance.

1ST MINER: I'll give five dollars for a letter!

2ND MINER: I'll give ten—only give me a letter!

OLD SWAMP: Form line, boys, or you'll never get a letter. (*They range in line.*) Now, gal, look for me.

MARY: (*Looking over the letters, calls out.*) Ambrose Swamp. (*Hands him a letter.*)

OLD SWAMP: Glory! Here's five dollars. (*Takes the letter and is going off.*)

MARY: It's only a dollar—here's the change.

OLD SWAMP: O, d——n the change—keep it, gal—the letter's from Betsey and the children.

1ST MINER: Jonathan Sims!

MARY: No letter for Jonathan Sims.

1ST MINER: (*Passing on.*) Go to thunder with your express—I won't strike a blow to-day—I'll get drunk.

2ND MINER: Roswell Rattail.

MARY: No letter for Roswell Rattail.

STOKES: William Stokes.

MARY: Letter for William Stokes. (*Hands it.*)

STOKES: Petitioner's prayer has been granted, and bill passed, Mr. Speaker. (*Throwing his purse on the counter.*) Take out an ounce, madam, never mind details. (*Turns off to read his letter, leaving the purse.*)

JUDGE: Edward Smaile.

MARY: Letter for Edward Smaile.

JUDGE: (*Sings and dances.*) Fol lol de riddle lol rol lol lol. (*Throws down money.*) D——n the change. Boys, what'll you drink? I'll treat the whole crowd.

PIKE: Jessie Jenkins, commonly known as Pike County Jess.

MARY: Sorry to say no letter for Pike.

PIKE: No letter! I'll give that gal, High Betty Martin, the sack, by all the weasles that wear a skin, I will. No letter! I'll go and whip Short-Tail out of spite, I will.

JOE: Joseph Nudge.

MARY: No letter for Joseph Nudge.

JOE: No letter? Havn't heard from home in a year. Don't believe I've got any friends in America. D——n the luck—I'll emigrate to the North Pole and fish for grizzlies through the ice.

(*Others are passing in dumb show—some receiving letters, some none—some getting newspapers, and ranging themselves around—some sitting on the floor, some leaning against the wall, reading their letters and papers. Old Swamp is in the foreground, leaning against the wall, reading his letter and wiping his eyes.*)

MARY: Package for Old Swamp.

OLD SWAMP: (*Still absorbed with his letter.*) Anan!

MARY: Pass it over to him. (*Pike takes it and puts it in his hand.*)

PIKE: Here, old fellow. Why—why, Old Swamp, you're cryin—bad news from home?

OLD SWAMP: (*Struggling with emotion.*) N—no; all well, thank God. What's this? (*Holding up the package.*)

PIKE: Don't know—reckon it's a dogeretype;[40] peel the skin off and see.

OLD SWAMP: (*Tears off the paper, and opens it.*) It's my Betsey, and Jennie, and Bill! (*Looks at it a moment—kisses it, much affected.*) My wife! My children! O, if I could fly, wouldn't I be with you. O, the misery of separation! My wife, my children, my home! (*Bursts into tears. Miners gather round respectfully—Mary comes and takes his hand kindly.*)

MARY: My father, there are better days coming—joy shall yet lighten your path, and home and happiness shall be yours again. Courage, my good father. You labor here to make them independent at home, and your love for them and your present self-denial surely will be rewarded. You will yet be happy together.

OLD SWAMP: (*Still affected.*) God bless you, gal. (*Struggling with his feelings.*) I'm an old fool. Somehow, women always get on the soft side of me. (*With fervor.*) I've got the best wife, the best children—thar—thar—read—read it aloud. (*Hands Mary the letter.*)

MARY: (*Reads.*) "My dear husband:—I received your draft for one-thousand dollars safe. I didn't know exactly what to do to get the money, so I took it up to Squire Gibbs. If you had seen him when he looked at the draft—I never saw a politer man—he actually sot a chair for me. 'Did your old man send all this to you? Why, I'll take it, and give you the cash.' I tell you I felt proud of my old man that blessed minute, and I wish I could put my arms about his neck, and if you will come home, I will, and Bill and Jennie will—but you had better not come, for you will be kissed to death. Didn't I feel rich with all that money—I was afraid I should lose it before I got home, but I didn't. I went right off and paid up the mortgage on our place; then I paid the store debt, then the shoemaker, and everybody else, and I had nigh a hundred dollars left, and we didn't owe a dime in the world, and I felt so happy that I sat down and cried—I don't care, I cried like a child. The children thought we were so rich that we needn't take in washing any more, but I told them father might have bad luck, so we must keep at work and save all we could. Bill said he'd bring water, and Jennie said she'd pound the clothes, but I told the darlings they should go to school, for my heart was light enough to do all the work. Bill says he'll never owe nothing to nobody, and he will work for father and mother when they get old and they needn't work at all. We all talk about you every night, and want to see you right bad. Dear husband, let the Californy chunks go, and come home to your chunks here. We send a thousand kisses."

OLD SWAMP: Ain't sich a wife and children worth workin for, boys?

MINERS: Three cheers for Old Swamp and his wife at home!

PIKE: Three cheers for High Betty—no, nary cheer, the gal didn't write me a letter to-day. (*Exeunt.*)

SCENE III: *Front wood glen. Enter Cash and Dice.*

DICE: A pretty mess, we've made of it, Cash. Do you know where we are?

CASH: I know we have got clear of the harpies of the law, and that is all I care for till the thing is blown over a little.

DICE: We've had a lucky escape—but what made you shoot that fellow?

CASH: Shoot him? Who wouldn't have shot him rather than lost the money? Everything was going right till the fellow saw me turn up the wrong card. The fact was, the wax on my fingers had worn smooth, and my thumb slipped, and he saw the trick. He accused me of cheating and grabbed the money. Of course I wouldn't stand that, so I put a bullet through him, grabbed the money, and put out through the back door before the police could arrest me.

DICE: You hadn't much time to spare, for a hornet's nest was raised in less than ten minutes.

CASH: That ten minutes saved me, for I ran to the slough, and, as luck would have it, I found a boat, and in two minutes I was in the chapparel on the other side, made my way to the American,[41] swam that, and was safe in our rendezvous till you came.

DICE: Well, it will blow over in a month, so we can go back again.

CASH: Yes, no trouble about that, for who cares about a miner? They're only fair game for gamblers and lawyers to pluck. The only difference is, we win their money honorably, while the lawyers steal it by law.

DICE: And if there is any fuss, why, we can buy up law, lawyers, judges, witnesses, and jurymen. The only trouble is, it may cost something to prove an alibi, or buy up straw bail.[42]

CASH: Exactly, and if they put us in jail, for form's sake, why, it is not much trouble to break out by getting on the right side of the jailor.

DICE: We'll have a little play-spell now by going on to some of the Bars[43] and prospecting in the pockets of miners at home. They work and we win.

CASH: Right, old fellow. I had rather have a dozen lucky miners at my table than a whole plantation of niggers—I'll make more out of them, and if, now and then, one gets rapped over the head for being too lucky, who cares—whose business is it?

DICE: Good. Well, push ahead—we'll see where this trail leads to. (*Exeunt.*)

SCENE IV: *Stringtown. Pike and Swamp digging on Mary's claim, in the fore-ground—Miners at work in the distance.*

OLD SWAMP: Thar, Pike, we're comin to gravel, and the dirt looks right. (*Examines.*)

PIKE: Mary's claim may turn out a good egg, arter all. Old Swamp, I love that gal.

OLD SWAMP: It's lucky High Betty Martin don't hear you say that—she'd be in your hair worse nor a steel trap into a hairy coon.

PIKE: Geet out, you old varmint. My gal knows I'm true as steel to her. She knows that every gal I love is for her sake, and you know too that I don't want to stampede Mary Wilson.

OLD SWAMP: Humph! I'd trust you about as far as I would a fox with a goose, and your gal wouldn't trust you at all.

PIKE: Pooh! make it up in a minute—Californy gals mighty forgiving. A leetle soft sodder, a trifle of honey, and fair promises, and they'll pull the wool over their own eyes, kiss, and forgive.

OLD SWAMP: But they don't forget, eh? I'd like to know, Pike, how on airth sich an ungainly varmint as you are made out to catch any gal.

PIKE: Ha! ha! ha! Ain't I a beauty—ain't I a roarer, a perfect wild bull on the prairie? Why, the gal don't live on air and hoe-cake that kin stand the glance of my eye. We were at a huskin[44] frolic. When it come to the hoe dig, I pulled High Betty Martin on to the floor for a double shuffle breakdown. O, I'm death on the toe and heel. Well, Bill Sampson steps up, and swore he'd dance with my gal fust, and he gin me a push. He mought as well have tried to upset a steamboat. "Hold on," says I, Bet sees fair play, and I pitched into the varmint, worse nor a gang of niggers into a cotton field. "Go your death, boys," shouted Betty—"I don't care which whips—but, Jess Jenkins, if you don't lick him, I'll lick you." In just two minutes by the watch, Bill Sampson was the worst-licked man in the

Settlement, and he owned up that he thought a young airthquake had hold on him. I popped the question to the gal that very night, and she caved like a young possom—said I was the boy for her beauty. Cock-a-doodle-doo!

OLD SWAMP: What made you fall in love with her?

PIKE: I seed her lift a barrel of whisky plump and square out of the cart on to the ground. I thought the gal what could do that could manage niggers as well as make gingerbread, and I didn't sleep a wink for three nights for thinking of her. (*Enter Jones.*) Here comes the printer man. Well, old fellow, got your press a-going?

JONES: No; hain't dug enough to set up a *form*, nor made money enough to buy the types to set it up with. Have to start for Humbug again.

PIKE: Can't you rig out a printing machine on a sluice box, and make it go on the undershot principle? I'm great on machine poetry—can't you be great on machine printing?

JONES: O yes; no trouble about that; the printing machine would be about equal to your poetry, but then there would be the devil to pay.

PIKE: The devil? what's he got to do with your machine, or my poetry?

JONES: A good deal—every printer has his devil.

PIKE: Well, I know they're as saucy as the devil, but I didn't know they always kept one on hand.

JONES: Always, Pike—and they've got stomachs to fill—you've heard of a man being as hungry as the devil—that means the printer's devil.

PIKE: Yes, I saw you in the same fix onest, and didn't you pitch in?

JONES: Pretty much as I did into a turkey dinner once.

OLD SWAMP: How's that?

JONES: Bought a splendid turkey once, to give the devil, and all the other office imps a grand dinner. Fed him four times a day for six weeks, and when the old sinner got so fat he couldn't stand, I cut his head off, pulled out his feathers, stuffed him with gingerbread and oysters, and hung him outside the house to freeze him tender. Went out the next morning to bring him in to roast, and found he had given me the slip, leaving a card that read "A bird in the hand is worth two in the bush."[45]

PIKE: What! a dead turkey run away? Must have been of the Shanghai[46] breed, and crowed his legs off the nail.

JONES: Some hungry devil stole the turkey and left nothing but the joke for us.

OLD SWAMP: And your guests?

JONES: O, made it up on bacon and eggs, only there wasn't any eggs, and the bacon was boiled codfish.

(*Enter Chinaman, left, much alarmed.*)

CHINAMAN: Me help! Me help! shooty me! bang me shooty! one, tree, five-hundred Indian! O! O! O!

PIKE: Shoot you, bang you, two or three hundred Indians? What the devil do you want with so many Indians?

CHINAMAN: No, no, no! Pop! bang! bullet shooty me!

OLD SWAMP: Indians shoot you?

CHINAMAN: Gold prospect, me hill over. Par one dollar—one dollar, two bit—one dollar half. Indian come! me bang! bang! bullet! pop me! two, three, five hundred!

PIKE: Hey! Indians coming to the Settlement? We must look to it.

OLD SWAMP: That ar a fact. Rally the boys; call all hands; we must drive them back.

PIKE: (*Shouts.*) Indians, boys, Indians! Hurrah for a fight! Fun, boys, fun—drop your tools, and run, boys, run.

(*Miners rush in, with their arms.*)

OLD SWAMP: The diggers are upon us, boys—let's meet them on the hill and surprise them.

PIKE: And lick them before they have a chance to scalp Short-Tail. (*All rush out except Chinaman, with a "Huzzah!"*)

CHINAMAN: Chinaman no fight; Chinaman skin good skin; keep him so. Mellican man big devil—no hurty bullet him.

SCENE V: *Top of the Hill. Enter Betsey, with boots in her hand, and Sluice.*

SLUICE: Here's a trail that leads somewhere, and by the lay of the land, Feather River must be at the bottom of the gulch.

BETSEY: I'm glad on't. I've worn out one pair of good boots in hunting up a man, (*holds up boots*) I wouldn't give another pair for the best man alive, except Jess.

SLUICE: Well, let us go a little higher on the Ridge to ascertain our position. Stringtown cannot be very far off. (*They walk up the stage.*)

(*Enter Pike, Swamp, and party.*)

PIKE: The varmints can't be far off, boys. Stay here—tracks—boots, too. They've killed somebody and stole their clothes—squat, boys, squat! lay low till I take a peep. (*All lay or squat down.*)

OLD SWAMP: Hold, Pike—there's two of 'em. (*Pointing to Sluice and Betsey.*) Squat, boys, squat! (*Betsey and Sluice advance slowly.*)

PIKE: Cock your pieces, boys—don't fire till I give the word. Swamp and I will take them two—as fast as you fire drop down and load. Old Swamp, I'll take that tall squaw—you take the buck. (*Pike and Swamp crouch down behind a tree, as Betsey and Sluice advance.*) Are you ready, Swamp? Say the word. (*Taking aim.*)

OLD SWAMP: Stay, Pike! That's a white woman.

PIKE: No; it's a d——d squaw.

OLD SWAMP: I swear it's a woman.

PIKE: (*Looking close.*) Boys, it's a fact—they are humans from the settlements—get up, and three cheers for another live woman in the mines. (*Miners rise and cheer.*)

BETSEY: (*Drawing a knife and pistol, in alarm, rushes towards Pike, as if to shoot him.*) You varmints! Do you mean to harm a woman?

PIKE: Snakes and alligators! That's Betsey—whoo-ra! whoo-ra!

BETSEY: Jess—Jess—my Jess, it it you? (*They rush into each other's arms.*)

PIKE: Boys, it's my own blessed High Betty Martin herself, it is.

MINERS: (*Shout.*) Hurrah for High Betty Martin and Pike County Jess—Short-Tail and all!

PIKE: Why, Betty, I hope I may be shot if I didn't take you for a Digger squaw; I was going to shoot you.

BETSEY: May I never pull another acre of flax ef I didn't take you for a robber; I was going to knife you.

OLD SWAMP: Ha! ha! One looks like a squaw, and the other like a robber, sure enough, but so long as the heart is in the right place, it's no matter.

PIKE: Well, boys, we'll let the diggers go—the Chinaman was more scared than hurt. (*To Betsey.*) Somebody shot at one of the Johns,[47] and he thought a tribe of Indians was on his trail.

BETSEY: Ha! ha! ha! It was Sluice, thar. He thought he saw an Indian through the bushes, and fired his rifle to scare him off. It's done no harm, and only brought us together sooner.

OLD SWAMP: It's the first time I ever knowed gunpowder to act as a messenger of love.

BETSEY: Well, Sluice—bring up the wagon—I've found the man, and let the boots be hanged. (*Exit all, laughing and cheering.*)

SCENE VI: *Inside of a miner's store—miners lounging around. Cash and Dice seated at a table with a Monte Box.*

DICE: Come, boys, here's a chance for a fortune. Never say die with the money in hand. Come down, boys, come down. (*Miners gather around the table—some throw money on the table.*) Down, boys—any more? all down? (*Draws the cards.*) King—ace—knave in the door. Bank wins. (*Cash scrapes it up.*)

(*Enter Old Swamp as Dice is speaking.*)

OLD SWAMP: Knave in the door? A knave is always in the door of a gambler's bank. Boys, you are fools. Doesn't your money come hard enough, that you must throw it away?

CASH: Come down, gentlemen. Fortune to the brave—don't be backward in coming forward—down—down—all down?

OLD SWAMP: Boys, don't fool away your money. Remember your wives and children at home; save your money for them; don't rob them.

DICE: Bank wins. (*Scrapes it up.*) Come down, boys—no preaching here, old man —plenty of luck and good liquor. Landlord, six juleps, four brandy smashes, at my expense—all down?

OLD SWAMP: The varmints! I've a mind to break their heads, bank and all, the fools.

JONES: (*Who is reading a paper.*) Old Swamp, read this article in the Sacramento paper. (*Hands the paper, pointing to the article.*)

OLD SWAMP: (*Puts on his spectacles and reads.*) It is as true as I am a living man.

JONES: No mistake, they are the very men.

OLD SWAMP: Boys, I want to read you a leetle news—rayther important.

CASH: Come down, come down—don't mind the old fool.

JOE: What is it Old Swamp?

MINERS: Yes, let's hear it.

OLD SWAMP: Boys, keep your eyes skinned while I read—let no one leave the room. (*Reads.*) "Proclamation—One-thousand dollars reward will be paid for the apprehension of a gambler, named Jacob Cash, who committed a brutal murder by shooting a miner named George Doan, on the 17th inst., in Sacramento. Said Cash is about five-feet nine or ten inches in height, sandy hair, grey eyes, dark complexion, with a bold address. The murderer was accompanied in his flight by a confederate named Richard Dice, a man about—"

CASH: The devil! Boys, the game is up for to-day. (*Gathers up the money. To Dice.*) I want to speak with you.

OLD SWAMP: Yes, villains, your game is up. Seize them, boys—they are the rascals. (*Miners make demonstrations of taking them. Cash and Dice rise and draw their pistols.*)

DICE: The first that moves is a dead man. Gentlemen, it is all a mistake—that is not the man—he is as innocent as I am.

OLD SWAMP: Very likely. Birds of a feather flock together.

(*Enter Pike and Betsey.*)

PIKE: What's the row, boys—any chance for me to take a hand?

OLD SWAMP: A murder has been committed in Sacramento—thar stands the murderer. Here's the Governor's proclamation, in black and white, offering a reward of one-thousand dollars for his apprehension.

PIKE: As sure as I'm a Christian, them's the very varmints who tried to stampede Mary Wilson. Boys, I know the dogs—let's pin 'em.

CASH AND DICE: (*Presenting their pistols.*) The first man that stirs gets a bullet in him.

BETSEY: (*Leveling her gun.*) Mister, two can play at that game.

PIKE: High Betty Martin forever; (*Presents his rifle.*) Shall we shoot first, or will you?

(*Enter John and Mary.*)

JOHN: What is this, my friends?—I hope no difficulty among yourselves.

MARY: John, John! there stand the villains who sought to entrap us in Sacramento.

JOHN: The very men. Good heavens! What a strange chance!

DICE: (*To Cash.*) By heavens! The very woman.

PIKE: You've got just one minute to surrender. Ef you don't cave at oncst, we'll make riddles of your carcasses, and send you to the Devil's Monte Bank.

DICE: It's no use—(*To Cash.*)—they're too many. Will you give us the benefit of the law?

PIKE: Law? No—we'll hang you like dogs by miner's law.

OLD SWAMP: No, boys—'bide the law. If the law will do its duty, 'bide the law.

It's time enough to take the law in hand when the authorities become scoundrels—till then, 'bide the law. We'll send them to Sacramento.

PIKE: With one condition, I agree to that. Give them the law of Moses first, so that they will not forget Stringtown—"forty lashes save one."

MINERS: Agreed! Agreed!

DICE: We surrender. Cash, we'll get off easy enough when we get a chance of the law. (*They surrender—and, as they are led out—*)

PIKE: Make them dance to their own music, boys—a fiddle with one string, and a bow in a strong hand. (*A shout is heard without.*)

(*Enter miners, tumultuously—one holding a prospecting pan.*)

MINERS: Mary Wilson! Mary Wilson! Huzza for the "live woman in the Mines!"

JOHN: What is it, boys? I hope you are not going to hang my wife.

STOKES: You be hanged, yourself. Mary Wilson has struck a lead rich—rich as Croesus! Look—look! piles of gold!

MARY: Mine—is it true? O, heavens!

OLD SWAMP: Yes, gal—No. 10 is a ten-strike—it's yours, and no mistake. You are rich, gal, but don't get proud.

MARY: O, I am proud—I am proud of your friendship, I am proud of the miners, my friends, I am proud of everything—everybody in the Mines.

PIKE: We're all proud of you, and—John Wilson, I shall kiss your wife.

BETSEY: (*Good humoredly.*) Jess, if you kiss that man's wife, I'll kiss that woman's husband. (*Throws her arms about John, and kisses him heartily.*)

PIKE: I'm so happy, I could kiss Short-Tail himself, ef it wasn't for stampeding him.

MARY: O, John, are we not well paid for all our trials and misfortunes? How can I ever repay you for your many, many kindnesses? (*To miners.*)

OLD SWAMP: Pshaw! by sewing on our buttons, nursing poor, sick miners, giving kind words to all, and making us think of and love still better our wives and sweethearts at home, as you have done.

PIKE: And by being bridesmaid to my Carolina Betsey, commonly known as High Betty Martin, who is to be spliced to Pike County Jess, by the Judge, this blessed night. (*Advancing to the front of the stage.*) And ef thar's any more female women in these diggins who wants to strike a lead, and go in cahoots with an A No. 1 miner for a husband, she is welcome to Short-Tail to ride on a prospecting tour, to become "A LIVE WOMAN IN THE MINES."

END

FOOTNOTES

[1] *"Old Block"*: pen-name of Alonzo Delano, humorist and playwright.

[2] *Pike County Jess*: his name indicates his origin: Pike County, Missouri; as portrayed by Delano, he's a cousin to the stage-frontiersman, Nimrod Wildfire, in *The Lion of the West*, but he also typifies Pike County men, lacking in polish, but forthright in manner and full of

vitality.

[3]*Modern and Mining*: Delano's "modern" costumes are those of 1857, which now makes them period; mining-garb is depicted in Currier and Ives prints and in the paintings of Christian Nahl and others who captured the Far West on paper and canvas.

[4]*Panama fever*: malaria, Yellow Fever; since many gold-seekers took ship from the East to Panama through the Caribbean, crossing the Isthmus of Panama overland, to take ship again on the Pacific Coast, bound for San Francisco, exposure to the disease was a frequent hazard.

[5]*Thy God my God*: thus spoke Ruth to Naomi, amid the alien corn, in the *Book of Ruth*, 1:16.

[6]*Backed water*: steam-boating term; held back, hesitated.

[7]*Sluice Forks'*: shortly after, Sluice is referred to by Dice as Sluice Box; both are contemptuous. Forks probably is a reference to a fork of a river in the goldfields; a sluice-box was a wooden device, mounted on rockers so it could agitate the gold-bearing sand or dirt—liberally washed over with water, or sluiced—to permit the gold flakes and nuggets to settle in the sluice-box, while the lighter, worthless materials flowed away.

[8]*Round Tent*: a notorious gambling "hell" in Sacramento in the early days of the Gold Rush.

[9]*Diggins*: miners prospected for gold, and when they found it, they staked a "claim," since the land was regarded as previously belonging to no one, even though in some cases goldstrikes were on land owned by Captain John Sutter or Mexican landowners, who had land grants from Spanish or Mexican officials. Seizing another's claim was called "jumping." In the Gold Rush of 1849, the gold sought was in flakes ("colors") and nuggets found in the sand of river and creekbeds or in the earth from which it had to be dug—hence, "diggins"—and washed free of impurities. The process was known as Placer Mining: literally, pleasure mining, from its supposed ease of operation. Later, with the discovery of veins of gold in quartz, "Hard-rock" mining largely replaced the placer process.

[10]*Vamos*: later altered to "vamoose": literally, "let's go," but here used in the sense of "get out."

[11]*Stringtown*: a gold-mining center in Butte County.

[12]*An original*: an eccentric, an original type.

[13]*Carolina Betsey*: she comes from Pike County; is Delano, in choosing this name, thinking of the folk-song "Sweet Betsey from Pike"?

[14]*Dirking*: stabbing.

[15]*Hangtown*: the Gold Rush colloquial name for Placerville; the name also refers to the speedy and popular method of local justice.

[16]*Rocker*: the sluice-box, on rockers.

[17]*On the left*: this is Delano's own footnote: "The post-office was there in 1850."

[18]*Clipper*: clipper-ship.

[19]*Somersets*: somersaults.

[20]*Aparaho*: a Mexican pack-saddle.

[21]*Hippah mula*: Get up, mule!

[22]*Mansinieto*: Manzanita, a Far Western shrub with gnarled branches; literally, "Little Apple."

[23]*Chinese theatre*: Chinese immigrants, flocking to the goldfields and the cities of Sacramento and San Francisco, brought this and othe aspects of their traditional culture with them, so Jess could very well have seen such a performance.

[24]*D--n her*: considering the care British and American dramatists usually took to protect the ears of family audiences in the theatre from strong oaths, Delano was apparently more interested in suggesting some of the actual force and quality of a miner's speech.

[25]*Digger*: a California Indian, living in the Sierra foothills.

[26]*Maus of the Cayotes*: maws of the coyotes, referring to the wolf-like Far Western predator.

[27]*Overhaul*: catch, catch up with.

[28]*Slapjacks*: flapjacks, pancakes.

[29]*Chapparel*: chaparral: scrub-oaks; low, often dense brush, from which horsemen were to protect themselves with "chaps" (shaps).

[30]*Dead lines and a dash*: printer's terms, used here to indicate violent death.

[31]*Arter*: after.

[32]*Fix it*: Delano's own footnote: "The actual expression of a young Pike County man to the author."

[33]*Strike a lead*: hit a vein of gold.

[34]*She drinks from it*: considering the refinement required of melodrama heroines on the Eastern Seaboard, Mary's alacrity in drinking from a communal bottle of what is surely potent "fire-water" suggests a rapid adaptation to Western ways—and possibly a somewhat more realistic portrait of a woman on stage than was the rule. So much for Temperance!

[35]*Cend*: ascend, way of ascent.

[36]*Wagon to pieces*: descending and ascending the steep, rocky mountains and chasms of the Sierras, the emigrants occasionally had to dismantle their wagons and lower (or hoist) them, themselves, and their livestock on ropes secured around trees at the tops of such slopes. Emigrant Gap, in the High Sierras near Lake Tahoe and not far from Grass Valley, of which Delano was a founder, was just such a precipitous challenge to the gold-seekers.

[37]*General Taylor*: Zachary Taylor, a hero of the Mexican War, known popularly as "Old Rough-and-Ready," a name also used, in his honor, to designate a mining center near Grass Valley, memorialized by Bret Harte in *A Millionaire of Rough and Ready*. (The editor of these plays grew up on a ranch outside Rough and Ready.)

[38]*We will let them*: so much for the Indians' birthright to the land before the Forty-Niners arrived!

[39]*Free gratis for nothing, from date*: although this may seem improbable, so lonely were these men without women for the sight of one of the "fair creatures," that similar acts of

generosity were recorded; not to mention the largesse of nuggets and gold-dust that miners are said to have showered on such performers as the almost legendary Lola Montez and little Lotta Crabtree, "The Darling of the Forty-Niners."

[40]*Dogeretype*: Daguerreotype, a pioneer form of photograph, developed by Louis Daguerre, in which a silvered copper-plate, sensitized to light, recorded an image; the process became immensely popular in America, after its 1839 introduction from France.

[41]*American*: the American River; a slough is a swampy inlet.

[42]*Straw bail*: cheap bail intended to be forfeited by flight.

[43]*Bars*: although this suggests fleecing miners in whiskey-bars, it actually refers to mining settlements which took their names from this geological feature, a large sandbar in a river.

[44]*Huskin*: this refers to the popular rural custom of combining communal work—husking corn—with social pleasures; a husking-bee.

[45]*Two in the bush*: as Delano has indicated in his introduction to *A Live Woman in the Mines*, this story was told him by an actual printer—the model for Jones in this play—who assured him the tale was true.

[46]*Shanghai*: this is a reference to the practice of kidnapping men for service on ships bound for the Orient: "Shanghai-ing."

[47]*Johns*: short for the colloquial term for Chinese immigrants: "Chinamen John."

TWO MEN OF SANDY BAR

BY

BRET HARTE

DRAMATIS PERSONA

Sandy, son of Alexander Morton, Sr.
John Oakhurst, his former partner, personating the prodigal son, Sandy
Col. Starbottle, Alexander Morton, Sr.'s legal adviser
Old Morton, Alexander Morton, Sr.
Don Jose, father of Jovita Castro
Capper, a detective
Concho, major-domo of Don Jose's rancho
York, an old friend of Oakhurst
Pritchard, an Australian convict
Soapy & Silky, his pals.
Jackson, confidential clerk of Alexander Morton, Jr. and confederate of Pritchard
Hop Sing, a Chinese laundryman
Servant of Alexander Morton, Sr.—Policeman
Miss Marry Morris, the schoolmistress of Red Gulch, in love with Sandy, and cousin of Alexander Morton, Sr.
Dona Jovita Castro, in love with John Oakhurst and daughter of Don Jose
The Duchess, wife of Pritchard, illegally married to Sandy, and former "dame" of John Oakhurst
Manuela, servant of Castro, and maid to Dona Jovita

ACT I: The Rancho of the Blessed Innocents, and House of Don Jose Castro

ACT II: Red Gulch

ACT III: The Banking-house of Morton & Son, San Francisco

ACT IV: The Villa of Alexander Morton, Sr., San Francisco

COSTUMES

Alexander Morton ("Sandy")—First dress: Mexican vaquero:[1] black velvet trousers, open from knee, over white trousers; laced black velvet jacket, and broad white sombrero; large silver spurs. Second dress: miner's white duck jumper, and white duck trousers; (sailor's) straw hat. Third dress: fashionable morning costume. Fourth dress: full evening dress.
John Oakhurst—First dress: riding dress, black, elegantly fitting. Second and third dress: fashionable. Fourth dress: full evening dress.
Col. Starbottle—First dress: blue double-breasted frock, and white "strapped" trousers; white hat. Second dress: same coat, blue trousers, and black broad-brimmed felt hat; cane, *semper*,[2] ruffles. Third dress: the same. Fourth dress: the same, with pumps.
York—Fashionable morning dress.
Jackson—Business suit.
Concho—First dress: vaquero's dress. Second dress: citizen's dress.

Hop Sing—Dress of Chinese coolie: dark-blue blouse, and dark-blue drawers gathered at ankles; straw conical hat, and wooden sabots.

Don Jose—First dress: serape, black, with gold embroidery. Second dress: fashion-able suit, with broad-brimmed black stiff sombrero.

Old Morton—First, second, third, and fourth dress: black, stiff, with white cravat.

Capper—Ordinary dress of period.

Miss Mary—First dress: tasteful calico morning dress. Second dress and third dress: lady's walking-costume—fashionable. Fourth dress: full dress.

Dona Jovita—First dress: handsome Spanish dress, with manta.[3] Second dress: more elaborate, same quality.

The Duchess—First dress: elaborate but extravagant fashionable costume. Second dress: travelling dress.

Manuela—The *saya y manta*:[4] white waist, and white or black skirt, with flowers.

ACT I

SCENE I: *Courtyard and Corridors of the Rancho.*

MANUELA: (*Arranging supper-table in corridor, solus.*[5]) There! Tortillas, chocolate, olives, and—the whiskey of the Americans! And supper's ready. But why Don Jose chooses tonight, of all nights, with this heretic fog lying over the Mission Hills like a wet serape,[6] to take his supper out here, the saints only know. Perhaps it's some distrust of his madcap daughter, the Dona Jovita; perhaps to watch her—who knows? And now to find Diego. Ah, here he comes. So! The old story. He is getting Dona Jovita's horse ready for another madcap journey. Ah! (*Retires to table.*)

(*Enter cautiously from corridor, Sandy Morton, carrying lady's saddle and blanket; starts on observing Manuela, and hastily hides saddle and blanket in recess.*)

SANDY: (*Aside.*) She's alone. I reckon the old man's at his siesta yet. Ef he'll only hang on to that snooze ten minutes longer, I'll manage to let that gal Jovita slip out to that yer fandango, and no questions asked.
MANUELA: (*Calling Sandy.*) Diego!
SANDY: (*Aside, without heeding her.*) That's a sweet voice for a serenade. Round, full, high-shouldered, and calkilated to fetch a man every time. Only thar ain't, to my sartain knowledge, one o' them chaps within a mile of the rancho. (*Laughs.*)
MANUELA: Diego!
SANDY: (*Aside.*) Oh, go on! That's the style o' them Greasers.[7] They'll stand rooted in their tracks, and yell for a chap without knowin' whether he's in sight or sound.
MANUELA: (*Approaching Sandy impatiently.*) Diego!

SANDY: (*Starting, aside.*) The devil! Why, that's *me* she's after. (*Laughs.*) I clean disremembered that when I kem yer I tole those chaps my name was James— James Smith (*laughs*), and thet they might call me "Jim." And De-a-go's their lingo for Jim. (*Aloud.*) Well, my beauty, De-a-go it is. Now, wot's up?

MANUELA: Eh? no sabe![8]

SANDY: Wot's your little game? (*Embraces her.*)

MANUELA: (*Aside, and recoiling coquettishly.*) Mother of God! He must be drunk again. These Americans have no time for love when they are sober. (*Aloud and coquettishly.*) Let me go, Diego. Don Jose is coming. He has sent for you. He takes his supper tonight on the corridor. Listen, Diego. He must not see you thus. You have been drinking again. I will keep you from him. I will say you are not well.

SANDY: Couldn't you, my darling, keep him from *me*? Couldn't you make him think *he* was sick? Couldn't you say he's exposin' his precious health by sittin' out thar tonight; thet ther's chills and fever in every breath? (*Aside.*) Ef the old Don plants himself in that chair, that gal's chances for goin' out tonight is gone up.

MANUELA: Never. He would suspect at once. Listen, Diego. If Don Jose does not know that his daughter steals away with you to meet some caballero,[9] some lover—you understand, Diego—it is because he does not know, or would not *seem* to know, what every one else in the rancho knows. Have a care, foolish Diego! If Don Jose is old and blind, look you, friend, we are *not*. You understand?

SANDY: (*Aside.*) What the devil does she expect?—money? No! (*Aloud.*) Look yer, Manuela, you ain't goin' to blow on that young gal! (*Putting his arm around her waist.*) Allowin' that she hez a lover, thar ain't nothin' onnateral in thet, bein' a purty sort o' gal. Why, suppose somebody should see you and me together like this, and should jest let on to the old man.

MANUELA: Hush! (*Disengaging herself.*) Hush! He is coming. Let me go, Diego! It is Don Jose!

(*Enter Don Jose, who walks gravely to the table, and seats himself. Manuela retires to table.*)

SANDY: (*Aside.*) I wonder if he saw us. I hope he did: it would shut that Manuela's mouth for a month of Sundays. (*Laughs.*) God forgive me for it! I've done a heap of things for that young gal, Dona Jovita, but this yer gettin' soft on the Greaser maid-servant to help out the missus is a little more than Sandy Morton bargained fur.

DON JOSE: (*To Manuela.*) You can retire. Diego will attend me. (*Looks at Diego attentively. Exit Manuela.*)

SANDY: (*Aside.*) Diego will attend him! Why, blast his yeller skin, does he allow that Sandy Morton hired out as a purty waiter-gal? Because I calkilated to feed his horses, it ain't no reason thet my dooty to animals don't stop there. Pass his hash![10] (*Turns to follow Manuela, but stops.*) Hello, Sandy! wot are ye doin', eh? You ain't going back on Miss Jovita, and jest spile that gal's chances to git out to-night, on'y to teach that God-forsaken old gov'ment mule manners? No! I'll humor the old man, and keep one eye out for the gal. (*Comes to table, and leans familiarly over the back of Don Jose's chair.*)

DON JOSE: (*Aside.*) He seems insulted and annoyed. His manner strengthens my worst suspicions. He has not expected this. (*Aloud.*) Chocolate, Diego.

SANDY: (*Leaning over table carelessly.*) Yes, I reckon it's somewhar thar.

DON JOSE: (*Aside.*) He is unused to menial labor. If I should be right in my suspicions! If he really were Dona Jovita's secret lover! This gallantry with the servants is only a deceit! Bueno! I will watch him. (*Aloud.*) Chocolate, Diego!

SANDY: (*Aside.*) I wonder if the old fool reckons I'll pour it out. Well, seein' he's the oldest—(*Pours chocolate awkwardly, and spills it on the table and Don Jose.*)

DON JOSE: (*Aside.*) He *is* embarassed. I am right. (*Aloud.*) Diego!

SANDY: (*Leaning confidentially over Don Jose's chair.*) Well, old man!

DON JOSE: Three months ago my daughter the Dona Jovita picked you up, a wandering vagabond, in the streets of the Mission. (*Aside.*) He does not seem ashamed. (*Aloud.*) She—she—ahem! The aguardiente, Diego.

SANDY: (*Aside.*) That means the whiskey. It's wonderful how quick a man learns Spanish. (*Passes the bottle, fills Don Jose's glass, and then his own. Don Jose recoils in astonishment.*) I looks toward ye,[11] ole man. (*Tosses off liquor.*)

DON JOSE: (*Aside.*) This familiarity! He *is* a gentleman. Bueno! (*Aloud.*) She was thrown from her horse; her skirt caught in the stirrup; she was dragged; you saved her life. You—

SANDY: (*Interrupting, confidentially drawing a chair to the table, and seating himself.*) Look yer! I'll tell you all about it. It wasn't that gal's fault, ole man. The hoss shied at me, lying drunk in a ditch, you see; the hoss backed, the surcle[12] broke; it warn't in human nature for her to keep her seat, and that gal rides like an angel; but the mustang throwed her. Well, I sorter got in the way o' thet hoss, and it stopped. Hevin' bin the cause o' the hoss shyin', for I reckon I didn't look much like an angel lyin' in that ditch, it was bout the only square thing for me to waltz in and help the gal. Thar, thet's about the way the thing pints. Now, don't you go and hold that agin her!

DON JOSE: Well, well! She was grateful. She has a strange fondness for you Americans, and at her solicitation I gave you—*you*, an unknown vagrant—employment here as groom. You comprehend, Diego. I, Don Jose Castro, proprietor of this rancho, with a hundred idle vaqueros on my hands—I made a place for you.

SANDY: (*Meditatively.*) Umph.

DON JOSE: You said you would reform. How have you kept your word? You were drunk last Wednesday.

SANDY: Thet's so.

DON JOSE: And again last Saturday.

SANDY: (*Slowly.*) Look yer, ole man, don't ye be too hard on me: that was the same old drunk.

DON JOSE: I am in no mood for trifling. Hark ye, friend Diego. You have seen, perhaps—who has not?—that I am a fond, an indulgent father. But even my consideration for my daughter's strange tastes and follies has its limit. Your conduct is a disgrace to the rancho. You must go.

SANDY: (*Meditatively.*) Well, I reckon, perhaps I'd better.

DON JOSE: (*Aside.*) His coolness is suspicious. Can it be that he expects the girl will follow him? Mother of God! perhaps it has already been planned between them. Good! Thank Heaven I can end it here. (*Aloud.*) Diego!

SANDY: Old man.

DON JOSE: For my daughter's sake, you understand—for her sake—I am willing to try you once more. Hark ye! My daughter is young, foolish and romantic. I have reason to believe, from her conduct lately, that she has contracted an intimacy with some Americano, and that in her ignorance, her foolishness, she has allowed that man to believe that he might aspire to her hand. Good! Now listen to me. You shall stay in her service. You shall find out—you are in her confidence—you shall find out this American, this adventurer, this lover if you please, of the Dona Jovita my daughter, and you will tell him this—you will tell him that a union with him is impossible, forbidden; that the hour she attempts it, without my consent, she is *penniless*; that this estate, this rancho, passes into the hands of the Holy Church, where even your laws cannot reach it.

SANDY: (*Leaning familiarly over the table.*) But suppose that he sees that little bluff, and calls ye.

DON JOSE: (*Coldly.*) I do not comprehend you.

SANDY: Suppose he loves that gal, and will take her as she stands, without a cent, or hide or hair of yer old cattle.

DON JOSE: (*Scornfully.*) Suppose—a miracle! Hark ye, Diego! It is now five years since I have known your countrymen, these smart Americanos. I have yet to know when love, sentiment, friendship, was worth any more than a money value in your market.

SANDY: (*Truculently and drunkenly.*) You hev, hev ye? Well, look yar, old man. Suppose I *refuse*. Suppose I'd rather go than act as a spy on that young gal, your darter! Suppose that—hic—allowin' she's my friend, I'd rather starve in the gutters of the Mission than stand between her and the man she fancies. Hey? Suppose I would—damn me! Suppose I'd see you and your derned old rancho in—t'other place—hic—damn me. You hear me, ole man! That's the kind o' man I am—damn me.

DON JOSE: (*Aside, rising contemptuously.*) It is as I suspected. Traitor—Ingrate! Satisfied that his scheme has failed, he is ready to abandon her. And this—*this* is the man for whom she has been ready to sacrifice everything—her home, her father. (*Aloud, coldly.*) Be it so, Diego; you shall go.

SANDY: (*Soberly and seriously, after a pause.*) Well, I reckon I had better. (*Rising.*) I've a few duds, old man, to put up. It won't take me long. (*Goes to exit and pauses.*)

DON JOSE: (*Aside.*) Ah! he hesitates! He is changing his mind. (*Sandy returns slowly to table, pours out glass of liquor, nods to Don Jose and drinks.*)

SANDY: I looks towards ye, ole man. Adios! (*Exit Sandy.*)

DON JOSE: His coolness is perfect. If these Americans are cayotes[13] in their advances, they are lions in retreat! Bueno! I begin to respect him. But it will be just as well to set Concho to track him to the Mission, and I will see that he leaves the rancho alone. (*Exit Jose.*)

(*Enter hurriedly Jovita Castro in riding habit, with whip.*)

JOVITA: So! Chiquita not yet saddled, and that spy Concho haunting the plains for the last half-hour. What an air of mystery! Something awful, something deliciously dreadful has happened! Either my amiable drunkard has forgotten to dispatch Concho on his usual fool's errand, or he is himself lying helpless in some ditch. Was there ever a girl so persecuted? With a father wrapped in mystery, a lover nameless and shrouded in the obscurity of some Olympian height, and her only confidant and messenger a Bacchus instead of a Mercury! Heigh ho! And in another hour Don Juan—he told me I might call him John—will be waiting for me outside the convent wall! What if Diego fails me? To go there alone would be madness! Who else would be as charmingly unconscious and inattentive as this American vagabond! (*Crosses.*) Ah, my saddle and blanket hidden! He *has* been interrupted. Someone has been watching. This freak of my father's means something. And tonight, of all nights, the night that Oakhurst was to disclose himself and tell me all! What is to be done? Hark! (*Diego, without, singing:* "*Oh, here's your aguardiente, drink it down!*") It is Diego; and Mother of God! drunk again!

(*Enter Sandy, carrying pack, intoxicated; staggers to center, and, observing Jovita, takes off his hat respectfully.*)

JOVITA: (*Shaking him by the shoulders passionately.*) Diego! How dare you! And at such a time!

SANDY: (*With drunken solemnity.*) Miss Jovita, did ye ever know me to be drunk afore at such a time?

JOVITA: No.

SANDY: Zachy so. It's abnormal. And it means—the game's up.

JOVITA: I do not understand. For the love of God, Diego, be plain!

SANDY: (*Solemnly and drunkenly.*) When I say your game's up, I mean the old man knows it all. You're blowed upon.[14] Hearken, miss! (*Seriously and soberly.*) Your father knows all that I know, but, as it wasn't my business to interfere with, I hev sorter helped along. He knows that you meet a stranger, an American, in these rides with me.

JOVITA: (*Passionately.*) Ingrate! You have not dared to tell him! (*Seizing him by the collar and threatening him with the horsewhip.*)

SANDY: (*Rising with half-drunken, half-sober solemnity.*) One minit, miss! one minit! Don't ye! don't ye do that! Ef ye forget (and I don't blame ye for it), ef ye forget that I'm a man, don't ye, don't ye forget that you're a woman! Sit ye down, sit ye down, so! Now, ef ye'll kindly remember, miss, I never saw this yer man, yer lover. Ef ye'll recollect, miss whenever you met him, I allers hung back and waited round in the mission, or in the fields beyond for ye, and allowed ye to hev your own way, it bein' no business o' mine. Thar isn't a man on the ranch who, ef he'd had a mind to watch ye, wouldn't hev known more about yer lover than I do.

JOVITA: (*Aside.*) He speaks truly. He always kept in the background. Even Don Juan never knew that I had an attendant until I told him. (*Aloud.*) I made a mistake, Diego. I was hasty. What am I to do? He is waiting for me even now.

SANDY: (*With drunken gravity.*) Well, ef ye can't go to him, I reckon it's the square thing for him to come to ye.

JOVITA: Recollect yourself, Diego. Be a man!

SANDY: Thash jus wot I say. Let him be a man, and come to ye here. Let him ride up to this ranch like a man, and call out to yer father that he'll take ye jist as ye are, without the land. And if the old man allows, rather than hev ye marry that stranger, he'll give this yer place to the church, why, let him do it, and be damned.

JOVITA: (*Recoiling, aside.*) So! That is their plan. Don Jose has worked on the fears or the cupidity of this drunken ingrate.

SANDY: (*With drunken submission.*) Ye was speaking to me, miss. Ef ye'll take my advice—a drunken man's advice, miss—ye'll say to that lover of yours, ef he's afeard to come for ye here, to take ye as ye stand, he ain't no man for ye. And ontil he does, ye'll do as the ole man says. Fur ef I do say it, miss—and thar ain't no love lost between us—he's a good father to ye. It ain't every day that a gal kin afford to swap a father like that, as she *does know*, fur the husband that she *don't*! He's a proud old fool, miss, but to ye, to ye, he's clar grit all through.

JOVITA: (*Passionately, aside.*) Tricked, fooled, like a child! and through the means of this treacherous, drunken fool. (*Stamping her foot.*) Ah! we shall see! You are wise, you are wise, Don Jose, but your daughter is not a novice, nor a helpless creature of the Holy Church. (*Passionately.*) I'll—I'll become a Protestant tomorrow!

SANDY: (*Unheeding her passion, and becoming more earnest and self-possessed.*) Ef ye hed a father, miss, ez instead o' harkinin' to your slightest wish, and surroundin' ye with luxury, hed made your infancy a struggle for life among strangers, and your childhood a disgrace and a temptation; ef he had left ye with no company but want, with no companions but guilt, with no mother but suffering; ef he had made your home, this home, so unhappy, so terrible, so awful, that the crowded streets and gutters of a great city was something to fly to for relief; ef he had made his presence, his very name—your name, miss, allowin' it was your father—ef he had made that presence so hateful, that name so infamous, that exile, that flyin' to furrin' parts, that wanderin' among strange folks ez didn't know ye, was the only way to make life endurable; and ef he'd given ye—I mean this good old man Don Jose, miss—ef he'd given ye as part of yer heritage a taint, a weakness in yer very blood, a fondness for a poison, a poison that soothed ye like a vampire bat and sucked yer lifeblood (*seizing her arm*) ez it soothed ye; ef this curse that hung over ye dragged ye down day by day, till hating him, loathing him, ye saw yerself day by day becoming more and more like him, till ye knew that his fate was yours, and yours his—why then, Miss Jovita (*rising with an hysterical drunken laugh*), why then, I'd run away with ye myself—I would, damn me!

JOVITA: (*Who has been withdrawing from him scornfully.*) Well acted, Diego. Don Jose should have seen his pupil. Trust me, my father will reward you. (*Aside.*) And yet there were tears in his drunken eyes. Bah! it is the liquor: he is no longer sane. And, either hypocrite or imbecile, he is to be trusted no longer. But where and why is he going? (*Aloud.*) You are leaving us, Diego.

SANDY: (*Quietly.*) Well, the old man and me don't get on together.

JOVITA: (*Scornfully.*) Bueno! I see. Then you abandon me?

SANDY: (*Quickly.*) To the old man, miss—not the young one. (*Walks to the table and begins to pour out liquor.*)

JOVITA: (*Angrily.*) You would not dare to talk to me thus, if John Oakhurst—ah!

(*Checking herself.*)

SANDY: (*Drops glass on table, hurries to center and seizes Dona Jovita.*) Eh! Wot! Wot name did you say? (*Looks at her amazed and bewildered.*)

JOVITA: (*Terrified, aside.*) Mother of God! What have I done? Broken my sacred pledge to keep his name secret. No! No! Diego did not hear me! Surely this wretched drunkard does not know him. (*Aloud.*) Nothing. I said nothing: I mentioned no name.

SANDY: (*Still amazed, frightened, and bewildered, passing his hand over his forehead slowly.*) Ye mentioned no name? Surely. I am wild, crazed. Tell me, miss—ye didn't—I know ye didn't, but I thought it sounded like it—ye didn't mention the name of—of—of—John Oakhurst?

JOVITA: (*Hurriedly.*) No, of course not! You terrify me, Diego. You are wild.

SANDY: (*Dropping her hand with a sigh of relief.*) No, no! In course ye didn't. I was wild, miss, wild; this drink has confused me yer. (*Pointing to his head.*) There are times when I hear that name, miss—times when I see his face. (*Sadly.*) But it's when I've took too much—too much. I'll drink no more—no more!—tonight—tonight! (*Drops his head slowly in his hands.*)

JOVITA: (*Looking at Diego—aside.*) Really, I'm feeling very uncomfortable. I'd like to ask a question of this maniac. But nonsense! Don Juan gave me to understand Oakhurst wasn't his real name; that is, he intimated there was something dreadful and mysterious about it that mustn't be told—something that would frighten people. *Holy Virgin!* it has! Why, this reckless vagabond here is pale and agitated. Don Juan shall explain this mystery tonight. But then, how shall I see him? Ah, I have it. The night of the last fiesta, when I could not leave the rancho, he begged me to show a light from the flat roof of the upper corridor, that he might know I was thinking of him—dear felllow! He will linger tonight at the Mission; he will see the light; he will know that I have not forgotten. He will approach the rancho; I shall manage to slip away at midnight to the ruined Mission. I shall—ah, it is my father! Holy Virgin, befriend me now with self-possession. (*Stands quietly, looking toward Sandy, who still remains buried in thought, as—*)

(*Enter Don Jose; regards his daughter and Diego with a sarcastic smile.*)

DON JOSE: (*Aside.*) Bueno! It is as I expected—an explanation, an explosion, a lover's quarrel, an end to romance. From his looks I should say she has been teaching the adventurer a lesson. Good! I could embrace her! (*Crosses to Sandy—aloud.*) You still here!

SANDY: (*Rising with a start.*) Yes! I—a—I was only taking leave of Miss Jovita that hez been kind to me. She's a good gal, ole man, and won't be any the worse when I'm gone—Good-bye, Miss Jovita (*extending his hand*), I wish ye luck.

JOVITA: (*Coldly.*) Adios, friend Diego. (*Aside, hurriedly.*) You will not expose my secret?

SANDY: (*Aside.*) It ain't in me, miss. (*To Don Jose, going.*) Adios, ole man. (*Shouldering his pack.*)

DON JOSE: Adios, friend Diego. (*Formally.*) May good luck attend you! (*Aside.*)

You understand, on your word as—as—as—*a gentleman!*—you have no further communication with this rancho, or aught that it contains.

SANDY: (*Gravely.*) I hear ye, ole man. Adios. (*Goes to gateway, but pauses at table, and begins to fill a glass of aguardiente.*)

DON JOSE: (*Aside, looking at his daughter.*) I could embrace her now. She is truly a Castro. (*Aloud to Jovita.*) Hark ye, little one! I have news that will please you, and—who knows?—perhaps break up the monotony of the dull life of the rancho. Tonight come to me two famous caballeros, Americanos, you understand: they will be here soon, even now. Retire, and make ready to receive them. (*Exit Jovita.*)

DON JOSE: (*Aside, looking at Sandy.*) He lingers. I shall not be satisfied until Concho has seen him safely beyond the Mission wall.

(*Enter Concho.*)

CONCHO: Two caballeros have dismounted in the corral and seek the honor of Don Jose's presence.

DON JOSE: Bueno! (*Aside.*) Follow that fellow beyond the Mission. (*Aloud.*) Admit the strangers. Did they give their names?

CONCHO: They did, Don Jose—Colonel Culpepper Starbottle and the Don Alexandro Morton.

SANDY: (*Dropping glass of aguardiente, and staggering stupidly to the center, confronting Don Jose and Concho, sitll holding bottle.*) Eh! Wot? Wot name did you say? (*Looks stupidly and amazedly at Concho and Don Jose, and then slowly passes his hand over his forehead. Then slowly and apologetically.*) I axes your pardon, Don Jose, and yours, sir (*to Concho*), but I thought ye called me. No!—that ez—I mean—I mean—I'm a little off color here (*pointing to his head*). I don't follow suit—I—eh—eh! Oh!—ye'll pardon me, sir, but thar's names—perhaps yer darter will remember that I was took a bit ago on a name—thar's names sorter hangin' round me yer (*pointing to his head*), that I thinks I hear—but bein' drunk—I hopes ye'll excoos me. Adios. (*Staggers to gateway, Concho following.*)

CONCHO: (*Aside.*) There is something more in this than Don Jose would have known. I'll watch Diego, and keep an eye on Miss Jovita too.

(*Exit, following Sandy, who, in exit, jostles against Colonel Starbottle entering, who stops and leans exhaustedly at the wall to get his breath; following him closely, and oblivious of Sandy Morton, Alexander Morton, Sr. Enter Col. Starbottle and Alexander Morton, Sr.*)

SCENE 2: *The Same.*

COL. STARBOTTLE: (*Entering, to Don Jose.*) Overlooking the insult of —er—er[15] —inebriated individual, whose menial position in this—er—er—houshold precludes a demand for personal satisfaction, sir, I believe I have the honor of addressing Don Jose Castro. Very good, sir. Permit me, sir, to introduce myself as Colonel Culpepper Starbottle—damn me! the legal adviser of Mr. Alexander Morton, Sr., and I may add, sir, the friend of that gentleman, and as such, sir—er—er—personally—personally responsible.

ALEXANDER MORTON: (*Puritanically and lugubriously.*) As a God-fearing and forgiving Christian, Mr. Castro, I trust you will overlook the habitual profanity of the erring but well-meaning man, who, by the necessities of my situation, accompanies me. I am the person—a helpless sinner—mentioned in the letters which I believe have preceded me. As a professing member of the Cumberland Presbyterian Church, I have ventured, in the interest of works rather than faith, to overlook the plain doctrines of the church in claiming sympathy of a superstitious papist.

STARBOTTLE: (*Interrupting, aside to Alexander Morton.*) Ahem! ahem! (*Aloud to Don Jose.*) My friend's manner, sir, reminds me of—er—er—Ram Bootgum Sing, first secretary of Turkish legation at Washington in '45; most remarkable man—damn me—most remarkable—and warm personal friend. Challenged Tod Robinson for putting him next to Hebrew banker at dinner, with remark—damn me—that they were both believers in the profit! he, he! Amusing, perhaps; irreverent, certainly. Fought with scimitars. Second pass, Ram divided Tod in two pieces—fact, sir—just here (*pointing*)—in—er—er—region of moral emotions. Upper half called to me—said to me warningly—last words—never forget it—"Star,"—always called me Star—"respect man's religious convictions." Legs dead; emotion confined to upper part of body—pathetic picture. Ged, sir, something to be remembered!

DON JOSE: (*With grave Spanish courtesy.*) You are welcome, gentlemen, to the rancho of the Blessed Fisherman. Your letters, with honorable report, are here. Believe me, senores, in your modesty you have forgotten to mention your strongest claim to the hospitality of my house—the royal right of strangers.

MORTON: Angels before this have been entertained as strangers, says the Good Book, and that, I take it, is your authority for this ceremoniousness which else were but lip-service and papist airs. But I am here in the performance of a duty, Mr. Castro—the duty of a Christian father. I am seeking a prodigal son. I am seeking him in his winehusks and among his harl—

STARBOTTLE: (*Interrupting.*) A single moment. (*To Don Jose.*) Permit me to—er—explain. As my friend Mr. Morton states, we are, in fact, at present engaged in—er—er—quest—er—pilgrimage that possibly to some, unless deterred by considerations of responsibility—personal responsibility, sir—Ged, sir, might be looked upon as visionary, enthusiastic, sentimental, fanatical. We are seeking a son, or, as my friend tersely and scripturally expresses it—er—er—prodigal son. I say scripturally, sir, and tersely, but not, you understand it, literally, nor I may add, sir, legally. Ged, sir, as a precedent, I admit we are wrong. To the best of my knowledge, sir, the—er—Prodigal Son sought his own father. To be frank, sir—and Ged, sir, if Culpepper Starbottle has a fault, it is frankness, sir . . . As Nelse Buckthorne said to me in Nashville, in '47, "You would infer, Colonel Starbottle, that I equivocate." I replied, "I do, sir, and permit me to add that equivocation has all the guilt of a lie, with cowardice superadded." The next morning at nine o'clock, Ged, sir, he gasped to me—he was lying on the ground, hole through his left lung just here (*illustrating with Don Jose's coat*)—he gasped, "If you have a merit, Star, above others, it is frankness!" his last words, sir—damn me . . . To be frank, sir, years ago, in the wild exuberance of youth, the son of this gentleman left his—er—er—er—boyhood's home, owing to an innocent but natural misunderstanding with the legal protector of his youth—

MORTON: (*Interrupting gravely and demurely.*) Driven from home by my own sinful and unregenerate hand—

STARBOTTLE: (*Quickly.*) One moment, a simple moment. We will not weary you with—er—er—history, or the vagaries of youth. He—er—came to California in '49. A year ago, touched by—er—er—parental emotion and solicitude, my friend resolved to seek him here. Believing that the—er—er—lawlessness of—er—er—untrammeled youth and boyish inexperience might have led him into some trifling indiscretion, we have sought him successively in hospitals, alms-houses, reformatories, State's prisons, lunatic and inebriate asylums, and—er—er—even on the monumental inscriptions of the—er—er—country churchyards. We have thus far, I grieve to say, although acquiring much and valuable information of a varied character and interest, as far as the direct matter of our search—we have been, I think I may say, unsuccessful. Our search has been attended with the—er—disbursement of some capital under my—er—er—direction, which, though large, represents quite inadequately the—er—er—earnestness of our endeavors.

(*Enter Manuela.*)

MANUELA: (*To Don Jose.*) The Dona Jovita is waiting to receive you.

DON JOSE: (*To Morton.*) You shall tell me further of your interesting pilgrimage hereafter. At present my daughter awaits us to place this humble roof at your disposal. I am a widower, Don Alexandro, like yourself. When I say that, like you, I have an only child, and that I love her, you will understand how earnest is my sympathy. This way, gentlemen. (*Leading to door in corridor, and awaiting them.*)

STARBOTTLE: (*Aside.*) Umph! an interview with lovely woman means—er—intoxication, but—er—er—no liquor. It's evident that the Don doesn't drink. Eh! (*Catches sight of table in corridor, and bottle.*) Oh, he does, but some absurd Spanish formality prevents his doing the polite thing before dinner. (*Aloud, to Don Jose.*) One moment sir, one moment. If you will—er—er—pardon the—er—seeming discourtesy, for which I am, I admit—er—personally responsible, I will for a few moments enjoy the—er—er—delicious air of the courtyard, and the beauties of Nature as displayed in the—er—sunset. I will—er—rejoin you and the—er—er—ladies a moment later.

DON JOSE: The house is your own, senor: do as you will. This way, Don Alexandro. (*Exit Don Jose and Morton, Sr.*)

STARBOTTLE: "Do as you will." Well, I don't understand Spanish ceremony, but that's certainly good English. (*Going to table.*) Eh! (*Smelling decanter.*) Robinson County whiskey! Umph! I have observed that the spirit of American institutions, sir, are already penetrating the—er—er—superstitions of—er—foreign and effete civilizations. (*Pours out glass of whiskey and drinks; pours again, and observes Manuela watching him respectfully.*) What the devil is that girl looking at? Eh! (*Puts down glass.*)

MANUELA: (*Aside.*) He is fierce and warlike. Mother of God! But he is not so awful as that gray-haired caballero, who looks like a fasting St. Anthony. And he loves aguardiente: he will pity Diego the more. (*Aloud.*) Ahem! Senor. (*Courtesies coquettishly.*)

STARBOTTLE: (*Aside.*) Oh, I see. Ged! not a bad-looking girl—a trifle dark, but Southern, and—er—tropical. Ged, Star, Star, this won't do, sir; no, sir. The filial affections of Aeneas are not to be sacrificed through the blandishments of—er—Dodo—I mean a Dido.

MANUELA: Ah senor, you are kind, you are good! You are an Americano, one of a great nation. You will feel sympathy for a poor young man—a mere muchaco[16]—one of your own race, who was a vaquero here, senor. He has been sent away from us here disgraced, alone, hungry, perhaps penniless. (*Wipes her eyes.*)

STARBOTTLE: The devil! Another prodigal. (*Aloud.*) My dear, the case you have just stated would appear to be the—er—er—normal condition of the—er—youth of America. But why was he discharged? (*Pouring out liquor.*)

MANUELA: (*Demurely glancing at the colonel.*) He was drunk, senor.

STARBOTTLE: (*Potently.*) Drunkenness, my child, which is—er—weakness in the—er—er—gentleman, in the subordinate is a crime. What—er—excites the social impulse and exhilarates the fancy of the—er—master of the house, in the performance of his duty, renders the servant unfit for his. Legally it is a breach of contract. I should give it as my opinion—for which I am personally responsible—that your friend Diego could not recover. Ged! (*Aside.*) I wonder if this scapegoat could be our black sheep.

MANUELA: But that was not all, senor. It was an excuse only. He was sent away for helping our young lady to a cavalier. He was discharged because he would not be a traitor to her. He was sent away because he was too good, too honorable—too—(*Bursts out crying.*)

STARBOTTLE: (*Aside.*) Oh, the devil! *this* is no Sandy Morton. (*Coming forward gravely.*) I have never yet analyzed the—er—er—character of the young gentleman I have the honor to assist in restoring to his family and society, but judging—er—calmly—er—dispassionately, my knowledge of his own father—from what the old gentleman must have been in his unregenerate state, and knowing what he is now in his present reformed Christian condition, I should say clamly and deliberately that the son must be the most infernal and accomplished villain unhung. Ged, I have a thought, an inspiration. (*To Manuela, tapping her under the chin.*) I see, my dear; a lover, ha, ha! Ah, you rogue! Well, well, we will talk of this again. I will—er—er—interest myself in this Diego. (*Exit Manuela.*)

STARBOTTLE: (*Solus.*) How would it do to get up a prodigal? Umph! Something must be done soon: the old man grows languid in his search. My position as a sinecure is—er—in peril. A prodigal ready-made! But could I get a scoundrel bad enough to satisfy the old man? Ged, that's serious. Let me see: he admits that he is unable to recognize his own son in face, features, manner or speech.

Good! If I could pick up some rascal whose—er—irregularities didn't quite fill the bill, and could say—Ged!—that he was reforming. Reforming! Ged, Star! That very defect would show the hereditary taint, demn me! I must think of this seriously. Ged, Star! the idea is—an inspiration of humanity and virtue. Who knows? it might be the saving of the vagabond—a crown of glory to the old man's age. Inspiration, did I say? Ged, Star, it's a *duty*—a sacred, solemn duty, for which you are responsible—personally responsible.

(*Lights down half. Enter from corridor Morton, Don Jose, Dona Jovita, and Manuela.*)

JOVITA: (*Stepping forward with exaggerated Spanish courtesy.*) A thousand graces await your Excellency, Commander Don—Don—
STARBOTTLE: (*Bowing to the ground with equal delight and exaggerated courtesy.*) Er—Coolpepero!
JOVITA: Don Culpepero! If we throw ourselves unasked at your excellency's feet (*courtesy*), if we appear unsought before the light of your excellency's eyes (*courtesy*), if we err in maidenly decorum in thus seeking unbidden your excellency's presence (*courtesy*), believe us, it is the fear of some greater, some graver indecorum in our conduct that has withdrawn your excellency's person from us since you have graced our roof with your company. We know, Senor Commander, how superior are the charms of the American ladies. It is in no spirit of rivalry with them, but to show—Mother of God!—that we are not absolutely ugly, that we intrude upon your excellency's solitude. (*Aside.*) I shall need the old fool, and shall use him.
STARBOTTLE: (*Who has been bowing and saluting with equal extravagance, during this speech—aside.*) Ged! she is beautiful! (*Aloud.*) Permit me—er—Dona Jovita, to correct—Ged, I must say it, correct erroneous statements. The man who should—er—utter in my presence remarks, disparaging those—er—charms it is my privilege to behold, I should hold responsible—Ged! personally responsible. You—er—remind me of—er—incident, trifling perhaps, but pleasing, Charleston in '52—a reception at John C. Calhoun's. A lady, one of the demnedest beautiful women you ever saw, said to me, "Star!"—she always called me Star—"you avoided me, you have, Star! I fear you are no longer my friend."—"Your friend, madam," I said. "No, I've avoided you because I am your lover." Ged, Miss Jovita, a fact—demn me. Sensation. Husband heard garbled report. He was old friend, but jealous, rash, indiscreet. Fell at first fire—umph—January 5th. Lady—beautiful woman—never forgave: went into convent. Sad affair. And all a mistake—demn me—all a mistake, though perhaps extravagant gallantry and compliment. I lingered here, oblivious perhaps of—er—beauty, in the enjoyment of Nature.
JOVITA: Is there enough for your excellency to share with me, since it must be my rival? See, the fog is clearing away: we shall have moonlight. (*Don Jose and Morton seat themselves at table.*) Shall we not let these venerable caballeros enjoy their confidences and experiences together? (*Aside.*) Don Jose watches me like a fox, does not intend to lose sight of me. How shall I show the light three

times from the courtyard roof? I have it! (*Takes Starbottle's arm.*) It is too pleasant to withdraw. There is a view from the courtyard wall your excellency shall
see. Will you accompany me? The ascent is easy.

STARBOTTLE: (*Bowing.*) I will ascend, although, permit me to say, Dona Jovita,
it would be—er—impossible for me to be nearer—er—heaven, than—er—at
present.

JOVITA: Flatterer! Come, you shall tell me about this sad lady who died. Ah,
Don Culpepero, let me hope all your experiences will not be so fatal to us! (*Exit
Dona Jovita and Starbottle.*)

MORTON: (*Aside.*) A forward daughter of Baal, and, if I mistake not, even now
concocting mischief for this foolish, indulgent, stiff-necked father. (*Aloud.*)
Your only daughter, I presume.

DON JOSE: My darling, Don Alexandro. Motherless from her infancy. A little wild
and inclined to gaiety, but I hope not seeking for more than these walls afford. I
have checked her but seldom, Don Alexandro, and then I did not let her see my
hand on the rein that held her back. I do not ask her confidence always: I only
want to know that when the time comes it can be given to me without fear.

MORTON: Umph!

DON JOSE: (*Leaning forward confidentially.*) To show that you have not intrusted
your confidence regarding your wayward son—whom may the saints return to
you!—to unsympathetic or inexperienced ears, I will impart a secret. A few
weeks ago I detected an innocent intimacy between this foolish girl and a vagabond vaquero in my employ. You understand, it was on her part romantic, visionary; on his, calculating, shrewd, self-interested, for he expected to become
my heir. I did not lock her up. I did not tax her with it. I humored it. Today I
satisfied the lover that his investment was not profitable, that a marriage without my consent entailed the loss of the property and then left them together.
They parted in tears, think you, Don Alexandro? No, but mutually hating each
other. The romance was over. An American would have opposed the girl, have
driven her to secrecy, to an elopement, perhaps. Eh?

MORTON: (*Scornfully.*) And you believe that they have abandoned their plans?

DON JOSE: I am sure—hush! she is here!

(*Enter on roof of corridor, Starbottle and Jovita.*)

STARBOTTLE: Really, a superb landscape! An admirable view of the—er—fog—
rolling over the Mission Hills, the plains below, and the—er—er—single figure
of—er—motionless horseman—

JOVITA: (*Quickly.*) Some belated vaquero. Do you smoke, Senor Commander?

STARBOTTLE: At times.

JOVITA: With me. I will light a cigarette for you: it is the custom. (*Starbottle
draws match from his pocket, and is about to light, but is stopped by Dona
Jovita.*) Pardon, your excellency, but we cannot endure your American mat-
ches. There is a taper in the passage. (*Starbottle brings taper; Dona Jovita turns
to light cigarette but manages to blow out candle.*) I must try your gallantry
again. That is once I have failed. (*Significantly. Starbottle relights candle,
business, same results.*) I am stupid and nervous tonight. I have failed *twice*.

(With emphasis. Starbottle repeats business with candle. Dona Jovita lights cigarette, hands it to the colonel.) Thrice, and I have succeeded. (*Blows out candle.*)
STARBOTTLE: A thousand thanks! There is a—er—er—light on the plain.
JOVITA: (*Hastily.*) It is the vaqueros returning. My father gives a festa to peons in honor of your arrival. There will be a dance. You have been patient, Senor Commander: you shall have my hand for a waltz.

(*Enter vaqueros, their wives and daughters. A dance, during which the "sembi canca[17]" is danced by Col. Starbottle and Dona Jovita. Business, during which the bell of Mission Church, faintly illuminated beyond the wall, strikes twelve. Dancers withdraw hurriedly, leaving alone Manuela, Dona Jovita, Starbottle, Don Jose, and Concho. Concho formally hands keys to Don Jose.*)

DON JOSE: (*Delivering keys to Morton with stately impressiveness.*) Take them, Don Alexandro Morton, and with them all that they unlock for bliss or bale. Take them, noble guest, and with them the homage of this family—tonight, Don Alexandro, your humble servants. Good night, gentlemen. May a thousand angels attend you, O Don Alexandro, and Don Culpepero!
JOVITA: Good night, Don Alexandro. May your dreams tonight see all your wishes fulfilled! Good night, O Senor Commander. May she you dream of be as happy as you!
MANUELA AND CONCHO: (*Together.*) Good night, O senores and illustrious gentlemen! May the Blessed Fisherman watch over you! (*Both parties retreat into opposite corridors, bowing.*)

SCENE 3: *The same. Stage darkened. Fog passing beyond wall outside, and occasionally obscuring moonlit landscape beyond. Enter Jovita softly, from corridor. Her face is partly hidden by Spanish mantilla.*

JOVITA: All quiet at last; and, thanks to much aguardiente, my warlike admirer snores peacefully above. Yet I could swear I heard the old Puritan's door creak as I descended. Pshaw! What matters! (*Goes to gateway, and tries gate.*) Locked! Carramba! I see it now. Under the pretext of reviving the old ceremony, Don Jose has locked the gates, and placed me in the custody of his guest. Stay! There is a door leading to the corral from the passage by Concho's room. Bueno! Don Jose shall see! (*Exit.*)

(*Enter cautiously Old Morton.*)

MORTON: I was not mistaken! It was the skirt of that Jezebel daughter that whisked past my door a moment ago, and her figure that flitted down that corridor. So! The lover driven out of the house at four p.m., and at twelve o'clock at night the young lady trying the gate secretly. This may be Spanish resignation and filial submission, but it looks very like Yankee disobedience and forwardness. Perhaps it's well that the keys are in my pocket. This fond confiding papist may find the heretic American father of some service. (*Conceals himself behind pillar of corridor.*)

(*After a pause the head of John Oakhurst appears over the wall of corridor: he climbs up to roof of corridor, and descends very quietly and deliberately to stage.*)

OAKHURST: (*Dusting his clothing with his handkerchief.*) I never knew before why these Spaniards covered their adobe walls with whitewash. (*Leans against pillar in shadow.*)

(*Re-enter Jovita, hastily.*)

JOVITA: All is lost; the corral door is locked; the key is outside, and Concho is gone —gone where? Madre di Dios! to discover, perhaps to kill him.
OAKHURST: (*Approaching her.*) No.
JOVITA: Juan! (*Embracing him.*) But how did you get here? This is madness!
OAKHURST: As you did not come to the Mission, I came to the rancho. I found the gate locked—by the way, is not that a novelty here?—I climbed the wall. But you, Miss Castro, you are trembling! Your little hands are cold!
JOVITA: (*Glancing around.*) Nothing, nothing! But you are running a terrible risk. At any moment we may be discovered.
OAKHURST: I understand you: it would be bad for the discoverer. Never fear, I will be patient.
JOVITA: But I feared that you might meet Concho.
OAKHURST: Concho—Concho—(*meditatively*). Let me see—tall, dark, long in the arm, weighs about one hundred and eighty, and active.
JOVITA: Yes; tell me! You have met him?
OAKHURST: Possibly, possibly. Was he a friend of yours?
JOVITA: No!
OAKHURST: That's better. Are his pursuits here sedentary or active?
JOVITA: He is my father's major-domo.
OAKHURST: I see: a sinecure. (*Aside.*) Well, if he has to lay up for a week or two, the rancho won't suffer.
JOVITA: Well?
OAKHURST: Well!
JOVITA: (*Passionately.*) There, having scaled the wall, at the risk of being discovered—this is all you have to say! (*Turning away.*)
OAKHURST: (*Quietly.*) Perhaps, Jovita. (*Taking her hand with grave earnestness.*) To a clandestine intimacy like ours there is but one end. It is not merely elopement, not merely marriage, it is exposure! Sooner or later you and I must face the eyes we now shun. What matters if tonight or later?
JOVITA: (*Quickly.*) I am ready. It was you who—
OAKHURST: It was I who first demanded secrecy, but it was I who told you when we last met that I would tell you why tonight.
JOVITA: I am ready; but hear me, Juan, nothing can change my faith in you.
OAKHURST: (*Sadly.*) You know not what you say. Listen, my child. I am a gambler. Not the man who lavishes his fortune at the gaming-table for excitement's

sake; not the fanatic who stakes his own earnings—perhaps the confided earnings of others—on a single coup. No, he is the man who loses—whom the world deplores, pities, and forgives. I am the man who wins—whom the world hates and despises.

JOVITA: I do not understand you, Juan.

OAKHURST: So much the better, perhaps. But you must hear me. I make a profession—an occupation more exacting, more wearying, more laborious, than that of your meanest herdsmen—of that which others make a dissipation of the senses. And yet, Jovita, there is not the meanest vaquero in this ranch who, playing against me, winning or losing, is not held to be my superior. I have no friends—only confederates. Even the woman who dares to pity me must do it in secret.

JOVITA: But you will abandon this dreadful trade. As the son of the rich Don Jose, no one dare scorn you. My father will relent. I am his heiress.

OAKHURST: No more, Jovita, no more. If I were the man who could purchase the world's respect though a woman's weakness for him, I should not be here tonight. I am not here to sue your father's daughter with hopes of forgiveness, promises of reformation. Reformation, in a man like me, means cowardice or self-interest. (*Old Morton, becoming excited, leans slowly out from the shadow of the pillar, listening intently.*) I am here to take, by force if necessary, a gambler's wife—the woman who will share my fortunes, my disgrace, my losses, who is willing to leave her old life of indulgence, of luxury, of respectability, for mine. You are frightened, little dove: compose yourself. (*Soothing her tenderly and sadly.*) You are frightened at the cruel hawk who has chosen you for a mate.

MORTON: (*Aside.*) God in heaven! This is like *him!* like me!—before the blessed Lord lifted me into regeneration. If it should be! (*Leans forward anxiously from pillar.*)

OAKHURST: (*Aside.*) Still silent! Poor dove, I can hear her foolish heart flutter against mine. Another moment decides our fate. Another moment: John Oakhurst and freedom, or Red Gulch and—she is moving. (*To Jovita.*) I am harsh, little one, and cold. Perhaps I have had much to make me so. (*With feeling.*) But when I first met you; when, lifting my eyes to the church porch, I saw your beautiful face; when, in sheer recklessness and bravado, I raised my hat to you; when you—you, Jovita—lifted your brave eyes to mine, and there, there in the sanctuary, returned my salute—the salutation of the gambler, the outcast, the reprobate—then, then I swore that you should be mine, if I tore you from the sanctuary. Speak now, Jovita: if it was coquetry, speak now; I forgive you: if it was sheer wantonness, speak now; I shall spare you: but if—

JOVITA: (*Throwing herself in his arms.*) Love, Juan! I am yours, now and forever. (*Pause.*) But you have not told me all. I will go with you tonight—now. I leave behind me all—my home, my father, my—(*pause*) my name. You have forgotten, Juan, you have not told me what I change *that* for: you have not told me *yours.*

(*Old Morton, in eager excitement, leans beyond shadow of pillar.*)

OAKHURST: (*Embracing her tenderly, with a smile.*) If I have not told you who I am, it was because, darling, it was more important that you should know what I am. Now that you know that—why—(*embarrassedly*) I have nothing more to tell. I did not wish you to repeat the name of Oakhurst—because—(*aside*) how the devil shall I tell her that Oakhurst was my real name, after all, and that I only feared she might divulge it?—(*aloud*) because—because—(*determinedly*) I doubted your ability to keep a secret. My real name is—(*looks up and sees Morton leaning beyond pillar*) is a secret. (*Pause, in which Oakhurst slowly recovers his coolness.*) It will be given to the good priest who tonight joins our fate forever, Jovita—forever, in spite of calumny, opposition, or spies! the padre whom we shall reach, if enough life remains in your pulse and mine to clasp these hands together. (*After a pause.*) Are you content?

JOVITA: I am.

OAKHURST: Then there is not a moment to lose. Retire, and prepare yourself for a journey. I will wait here.

JOVITA: I am ready now.

OAKHURST: (*Looking toward pillar.*) Pardon, my darling: there was a bracelet—a mere trifle—I once gave you. It is not on your wrist. I am a trifle superstitious, perhaps: it was my first gift. Bring it with you. I will wait. Go! (*Exit Jovita.*)

(*Oakhurst watches her exit, lounges indifferently toward gate; when opposite pillar suddenly seizes Morton by the throat, and drags him noiselessly to center.*)

OAKHURST: (*Hurriedly.*) One outcry—one single word—and it is your last. I care not who *you* may be!—who I am—you have heard enough to know, at least, that you are in the grip of a desperate man. (*Keys fall from Morton's hand. Oakhurst seizes them.*) Silence! on your life.

MORTON: (*Struggling.*) You would not dare! I command you—

OAKHURST: (*Dragging him to gateway.*) Out you must go.

MORTON: Stop, I command you! *I* never turned *my* father out of doors!

OAKHURST: (*Gazing at Morton.*) It is an *old* man! I release you. Do as you will, only remember that that girl is mine forever, that there is no power on earth will keep me from her.

MORTON: On conditions.

OAKHURST: Who are you that make conditions? You are not—her father?

MORTON: No, but I am *yours!* Alexander Morton, I charge you to hear me.

OAKHURST: (*Starting in astonishment; aside.*) Sandy Morton, my lost partner's father! This is fate.

MORTON: You are astonished: but I thought so. Ay, you will hear me now! I am your father, Alexander Morton, who drove you, a helpless boy, into disgrace and misery. I know your shameless life: for twenty years it was mine, and worse, until, by the grace of God, I reformed, as you shall. I have stopped you in a disgraceful act. Your mother—God forgive me!—left *her* house for *my* arms, as wickedly, as wantonly, as shamelessly—

OAKHURST: Stop, old man! Stop! Another word, (*seizing him*) and I may forget your years.

MORTON: But not your blood. No, Alexander Morton, I have come thousands of miles for one sacred purpose—to save you; and I shall, with God's will, do it now. Be it so, one one condition. You shall have this girl; but lawfully, openly, with the sanction of Heaven and your parents.

OAKHURST: (*Aside.*) I see a ray of hope. This is Sandy's father; the cold, insensate brute, who drove him into exile, the one bitter memory of his life. Sandy disappeared, irreclaimable, or living alone, hating irrevocably the author of his misery: why should not I—

MORTON: (*Continuing.*) On one condition. Hear me, Alexander Morton. If within one year, you, abandoning your evil practices, your wayward life, seek to reform beneath my roof, I will make this proud Spanish Don glad to accept you as the more than equal of his daughter.

OAKHURST: (*Aside.*) It would be an easy deception. Sandy has given me the details of his early life. At least, before the imposition was discovered I shall be—(*Aloud.*) I—I—(*Aside.*) Perdition! *she* is coming! There is a light moving in the upper chamber. Don Jose is awakened. (*Aloud.*) I—I—accept.

MORTON: It is well. Take these keys, open yonder gate, and fly! (*As Oakhurst hesitates.*) Obey me. I will meet your sweetheart, and explain all. You will come here at daylight in the morning, and claim admittance, not as a vagabond, a housebreaker, but as my son. You hesitate. Alexander Morton, I, your father, command you. Go!

(*Oakhurst goes to the gate, opens it, as the sound of Diego's voice, singing in the fog, comes faintly in.*)

Oh, yer's your Sandy Morton,
    Drink him down!
Oh, yer's your Sandy Morton,
    Drink him down!
Oh, yer's your Sandy Morton,
For he's drunk, and goin' a-courtin',
Oh, yer's your Sandy Morton,
    Drink him down!

(*Oakhurst recoils against gate, Morton hesitates as window in corridor opens, and Don Jose calls from upper corridor.*)

DON JOSE: Concho! (*Pause.*) 'Tis that vagabond Diego, lost his way in the fog. Strange that Concho should have overlooked him. I will descend.

MORTON: (*To Oakhurst.*) Do you hear?

(*Exit Oakhurst through gateway. Morton closes gate, and returns to center. Enter Jovita hurriedly.*)

JOVITA: I have it here. Quick! There is a light in Don Jose's chamber; my father is coming down. (*Sees Morton and screams.*)

MORTON: (*Seizing her.*) Hush! for your own sake; for *his*; control yourself. He is gone, but he will return. (*To Jovita, still struggling.*) Hush, I beg, Miss Jovita. I beg, I command you, my daughter. Hush!

JOVITA: (*Whispering.*) His voice has changed. What does this mean? (*Aloud.*) Where has he gone? And why are *you* here?

MORTON: (*Slowly and seriously.*) He has left me here to answer the unanswered question you asked him. (*Enter Don Jose and Col. Starbottle.*) I am here to tell you that I am his father, and that he is Alexander Morton.

(*Tableaux. Curtain.*)

END OF ACT I

ACT II

SCENE I: *Red Gulch. Canon of river, and distant view of Sierras, snow-ravined. Schoolhouse of logs in right middle distance. Ledge of rocks in center. On steps of schoolhouse, two large bunches of flowers. Enter Starbottle, slowly climbing rocks, panting and exhausted. Seats himself on rock, foreground, and wipes his face with his pocket-handkerchief.*

STARBOTTLE: This is evidently the er—locality. Here are the—er—groves of Academus—the heights of er—Ida! I should say that the unwillingness which the—er—divine Shakespeare points out in the—er—"whining schoolboy" is intensified in—er—climbing this height, and the—er—alacrity of his departure must be in exact ratio to his gravitation. Good idea. Ged! say it to school-ma'am. Wonder what she's like? Humph! the usual thin, weazened, hatchet-faced Yankee spinster, with an indecent familiarity with Webster's Dictionary! And this is the woman, Star, you're expected to discover and bring back to affluence and plenty. This is the new fanaticism of Mr. Alexander Morton, Sr. Ged! not satisfied with dragging his prodigal son out of merited obscurity, this miserable old lunatic commissions *me* to hunt up another of his abused relatives; some forty-fifth cousin, whose mother he had frozen, beaten, or starved to death! And all this to please his prodigal! Ged! if that prodigal hadn't presented himself that morning, I'd have picked up—er—some—er—reduced gentleman—Ged, that knew how to spend the old man's money to better advantage. (*Musing.*) If this school mistress were barely good-looking, Star—and she's sure to have fifty thousand from the old man—Ged, you might get even with Alexander Sr., for betrothing his prodigal to Dona Jovita, in spite of the—er—evident preference that the girl showed for you. Capital idea! If she's not positively hideous, I'll do it! Ged! I'll reconnoitre first! (*Musing.*) I could stand one eye; yes—er—single eye wouldn't be positively objectionable in the—er—present experiments of science toward the—er—the substitution of glass.[18] Red hair, Star, is—er—Venetian—the beauty of Giorgione. (*Goes up to schoolhouse window, and looks in.*) Too early! Seven empty benches; seven desks splashed with ink. The—er—rostrum of the awful Minerva empty, but—er—adorned with flowers, nosegays—demn me! And here, here on the—er—very threshold (*looking down*), floral tributes. The—er—conceit of these New England schoolma'ams, and their—er—evident Jesuitical influence over the young, is fraught, sir, fraught with—er—darkly political significance. Eh, Ged! there's a caricature on the blackboard. (*Laughing.*) Ha, ha! Absurd chalk outline of ridiculous fat person. Evidently the schoolma'am's admirer. Ged! immensely funny! Ah! boys will be boys. Like you, Star, just like you—always up to tricks like that. A sentence scrawled below the figure seems to be—er—explanation. Hem! (*Takes out eyeglass.*) Let's see. (*Reading.*) "This is old"—old—er—old—demme, sir—"Starbottle!" This is infamous. I haven't been forty-eight hours in the place, and to my certain knowledge haven't spoken to a child. Ged, sir, it's the—er—posting of a libel! The woman, the—er—female, who permits this kind of thing, should be made responsible—er—personally responsible. Eh, hush! What have we here? (*Retires to ledge of rocks.*)

(*Enter Miss Mary, reading letter.*)

MISS MARY: Strange! Is it all a dream? No! here are the familiar rocks, the distant snow-peaks, the schoolhouse, the spring below. An hour ago I was the poor schoolmistress of Red Gulch, with no ambition nor hope beyond this mountain wall, and now—oh, it must be a dream! But here is the letter. Certainly this is no delusion: it is too plain, formal, business-like. (*Reads.*)

My Dear Cousin—I address the only surviving child of my cousin Mary and her husband John Morris, both deceased. It is my duty as a Christian relative to provide you with a home—to share with you that wealth and those blessings that Providence has vouchsafed me. I am aware that my conduct to your father and mother, while in my sinful and unregenerate state, is no warrantee for my present promises, but my legal adviser, Colonel Starbottle, who is empowered to treat with you, will assure you of the sincerity of my intention, and my legal ability to perform it. He will conduct you to my house; you will share its roof with me and my prodigal son Alexander, now by the grace of God restored, and mindful of the error of his ways. I enclose a draft for one-thousand dollars; if you require more, draw upon me for the same.

Your cousin,
Alexander Morton, Sr.

My mother's cousin—so! Cousin Alexander! a rich man, and reunited to the son he drove into shameful exile. Well! we will see this confidential lawyer, and until then—until then—why, we are the schoolmistress of Red Gulch and responsible for its youthful prodigals! (*Going to the schoolhouse door. Stopping to examine flowers.*) Poor, poor Sandy! Another offering, and, as he fondly believes, unknown and anonymous! As if he were not visible in every petal and leaf! The mariposa blossom of the plain. The snow-flower I longed for, from those cool snow-drifts beyond the ridge. And I really believe he was sober when he arranged them. Poor fellow! I begin to think that the dissipated portion of this community are the most interesting. Ah! some one behind the rock—Sandy, I'll wager. No! a stranger!

STARBOTTLE: (*Aside, and advancing.*) If I could make her think I left those flowers! (*Aloud.*) When I state that—er—I am perhaps—er—stranger—

MISS MARY: (*Interrupting him coldly.*) You explain, sir, your appearance on a spot which the rude courtesy of even this rough miner's camp has preserved from intrusion.

STARBOTTLE: (*Slightly abashed, but recovering himself.*) Yes—Ged!—that is, I—er—saw you admiring—er—tribute—er—humble tribute of flowers. I am myself passionately devoted to flowers. Ged! I've spent hours—in—er—bending over the—er—graceful sunflower, in—er—plucking the timid violet from the overhanging but reluctant bough, in collecting the—er—*fauna*—I mean the—er—*flora*—of this—er—district.

MISS MARY: (*Who has been regarding him intently.*) Permit me to leave you in uninterrupted admiration of them. (*Handing him flowers.*) You will have ample time in your journey down the gulch to indulge your *curiosity!*

(*Hands Starbottle flowers, enters schoolhouse, and quietly closes door on Starbottle, as Sandy Morton enters cautiously and sheepishly. Sandy stops in astonishment on observing Starbottle and remains by wing.*)

STARBOTTLE: (*Smelling flowers, and not noticing Miss Mary's absence.*) Beautiful—er—exquisite. (*Looking up at closed door.*) Ged! Most extraordinary disappearance! (*Looks around and discovers Sandy; examines him for a moment through his eyeglass, and then, after a pause, inflates his chest, turns his back on Sandy, and advances to schoolhouse door. Sandy comes quickly, and, as Starbottle raises his cane to rap on door, seizes his arm. Both men, regarding each other fixedly, holding each other, retreat slowly and cautiously to center. Then Starbottle disengages his arm.*)

SANDY: (*Embarrassedly but determinedly.*) Look yer, stranger. By the rules of this camp, this place is sacred to the schoolma'am and her children.

STARBOTTLE: (*With lofty severity.*) It is! Then—er—permit to me to ask, sir, what *you* are doing here.

SANDY: (*Embarrassed, dropping his head in confusion.*) I was—passing. There is no school today.

STARBOTTLE: Then, sir, Ged! permit me to—er—*demand—demand*, sir—an apology. You have laid, sir, your hand upon my person—demn me! Not the first time, sir, either; for, if I am not mistaken, you are the—er—inebriated menial, sir, who two months ago jostled me, sir—demn me—as I entered the rancho of my friend Don Jose Castro.

SANDY: (*Starting, aside.*) Don Jose! (*Aloud.*) Hush, hush! She will hear you. No—that is—(*Stops, confused and embarrassed. Aside.*) She will hear of my disgrace. He will tell her the whole story.

STARBOTTLE: I shall await your apology one hour. At the end of that time, if it is not forthcoming, I shall—er—er—waive your menial antecedents, and expect the—er—satisfaction of a gentleman. Good morning, sir. (*Turns to schoolhouse.*)

SANDY: No, no; you shall not go!

STARBOTTLE: Who will prevent me?

SANDY: (*Grappling him.*) I will. (*Appealingly.*) Look yer, stranger, don't provoke me, I, a desperate man, desperate and crazed with drink—don't ye, don't ye do it! For God's sake, take your hands off me! Ye don't know what ye do. Ah! (*Wildly, holding Starbottle firmly, and forcing him backward to precipice beyond ledge of rocks.*) Hear me. Three years ago, in a moment like this, I dragged a man—my friend—to this precipice. I—I—no! no!—don't anger me now! (*Sandy's grip on Starbottle relaxes slightly and his head droops.*)

STARBOTTLE: (*Coldly.*) Permit me to remark, sir, that any reminiscence of your—er—friend—or any other man is—er—at this moment, irrelevant and impertinent. Permit me to point out the—er—fact, sir, that your hand is pressing heavily, demned heavily, on my shoulder.

SANDY: (*Fiercely.*) You shall not go!

STARBOTTLE: (*Fiercely.*) Shall not?

(*Struggle. Starbottle draws derringer from his breastpocket, and Sandy seizes his arm. In this positon, both parties struggle to ledge of rocks, and Col. Starbottle is forced partly over.*)

MISS MARY: (*Opening schoolhouse door.*) I thought I heard voices. (*Looking toward ledge of rocks, where Col. Starbottle and Sandy are partly hidden by trees. Both men relax grasp of each other at Miss Mary's voice.*)

STARBOTTLE: (*Aloud and with voice slightly raised, to Sandy.*) By—er—leaning over this way a moment, a single moment, you will—er—perceive the trail I speak of. It follows the canyon to the right. It will bring you to—er—the settlement in an hour. (*To Miss Mary, as if observing her for the first time.*) I believe I am—er—right, but, being—er—more familiar with the locality, you can direct the gentleman better.

(*Sandy slowly sinks on his knees beside rock, with his face averted from schoolhouse, as Col. Starbottle disengages himself and advances jauntily and gallantly to schoolhouse.*)

STARBOTTLE: In—er—er—showing the stranger the—er—way, I perhaps interrupted our interview. The—er—observances of—er—civility and humanity must not be foregone, even for—er—the ladies. I—er—believe I address Miss Mary Morris. When I—er—state that my name is Colonel Starbottle, charged on mission of—er—delicate nature, I believe I—er—explain *my* intrusion.

(*Miss Mary bows, and motions to schoolhouse door; Col. Starbottle, bowing deeply, enters, but Miss Mary remains standing by door, looking toward trees that hide Sandy.*)

MISS MARY: (*Aside.*) I am sure it was Sandy's voice! But why does he conceal himself?

SANDY: (*Aside, rising slowly to his feet, with his back to schoolhouse door.*) Even this conceited bully overcomes me and shames me with his readiness and tact. He was quick to spare her—a stranger—the spectacle of two angry men. I—I—must needs wrangle before her very door! Well, well! better out of her sight forever, than an object of pity or terror. (*Exit slowly and with downcast eyes.*)

MISS MARY: (*Watching the trail.*) It *was* Sandy! And this concealment means something more than bashfulness. Perhaps the stranger can explain. (*Enters schoolhouse, and closes door.*)

SCENE 2: *The same. Enter Concho, lame, cautiously. Pauses, and then beckons to Hop Sing, who follows.*

CONCHO: (*Impatiently.*) Well! you saw him?

HOP SING: Me see him.

CONCHO: And you recognized him?

HOP SING: No shabe likoquize.[19]

CONCHO: (*Furiously.*) You knew him, eh? Carramba! You *knew* him.

HOP SING: (*Slowly and sententiously.*) Me shabe man you callee Diego. Me shabbee Led Gulchee call Sandy. Me shabbee man Poker Flat callee Alexandlee Molton. Allee same, John![20] Allee same!

CONCHO: (*Rubbing his hands.*) Bueno! Good John! good John! And you knew he was called Alexander Morton? And go on—good John—go on!

HOP SING: Me plentee washee shirtee—Melican man Poker Flat. Me plentee washee shirt Alexandlee Molton. Always litee, litee on shirt allee time. (*Pointing to tail of his blouse, and imitating writing with finger.*) Alexandlee Molton. Melican man tellee me—shirt say Alexandlee Molton—shabbee?[21]

CONCHO: Bueno! Excellent John. Good John. His linen marked Alexander Morton. The proofs are gathering! (*Crosses.*)—the letter I found in his pack, addressed to Alexander Morton, Poker Flat, which first put me on his track; the story of his wife's infidelity, and her flight with his partner to Red Gulch, the quarrel and fight that separated them, his flight to San Jose, his wanderings to the mission of San Carmel, to the rancho of the Holy Fisherman. The record is complete!

HOP SING: Alexandlee Molton—

CONCHO: (*Hurriedly, returning to Hop Sing.*) Yes! good John; yes, good John—go on. Alexander Morton—

HOP SING: Alexandlee Molton. Me washee shirt, Alexandlee Molton; he no pay washee. Me washee flowty dozen hep—four bittie dozen—twenty dollar hep. Alexandlee Molton no payee. He say, "Go to hellee!" You pay me (*extending his hand.*)

CONCHO: Car—! (*Checking himself.*) *Poco tiempo,*[22] John! In good time, John. Forty dollar—yes. Fifty dollar! Tomorrow, John!

HOP SING: Me no likee "tomollow!" Me no likee "nex time, John!" Allee time Melican man say, "Chalkee up, John," "No smallee change, John,"—umph. Plenty foolee me!

CONCHO: You shall have your money, John, but go now—you comprehend. Carramba! go! (*Pushes Hop Sing to wing.*)

HOP SING: (*Expostulating.*) Flowty dozen, hep, John! twenty dollar, John. Sabe. Flowty—twenty—(*gesticulating with fingers.*)

(*Exit Hop Sing, pushed off by Concho.*)

CONCHO: The pagan dolt! But he is important. Ah! If he were wiser, I should not rid myself of him so quickly! And now for the schoolmistress—the sweetheart of Sandy. If these men have not lied, he is in love with her, and, if he is, he has told her his secret before now, and she will be swift to urge him to his rights. If he has not told her—umph! (*Laughing.*) It will not be a *day*—an *hour*—before she will find out if her lover is Alexander Morton, the rich man's son, or "Sandy," the unknown vagabond. Eh, friend Sandy! It was a woman that locked up your secret; it shall be a woman, Madre di Dios![23] who shall unlock it. Ha! (*Goes to door of schoolhouse as door opens, and appears Col. Starbottle.*)

CONCHO: (*Aside.*) A thousand devils! the lawyer of the old man Morton. (*Aloud.*) Pardon, pardon! I am a stranger. I have lost my way on the mountain. I am seeking a trail. Senor, pardon!

STARBOTTLE: (*Aside.*) Another man seeking the road! Ged, I believe he's lying too. (*Aloud.*) It is before you, sir, *down*—down the mountain!

CONCHO: A thousand thanks, senor. (*Aside.*) Perdition catch him! (*Aloud.*) Thanks, senor. (*Exit.*)

STARBOTTLE: Ged, I've seen that face before. Ged, it's Castro's major-domo. Demn me, but I believe all his domestics have fallen in love with the pretty schoolma'am.

(*Enter Miss Mary from schoolhouse.*)

MISS MARY: (*Slowly refolding letter.*) You are aware, then, of the contents of this note, and you are the friend of Alexander Morton, Sr.?

STARBOTTLE: Permit me a moment, a single moment, to—er—er—explain. I am Mr. Morton's legal adviser. There is—er—sense of—er—responsibility—er—personal responbility, about the term "friend," that at the—er—er—present moment I am not—er—prepared to assume. The substance of the letter is before you. I am here to—er—express its spirit. I am here (*with great gallantry*) to express the—er—yearnings of cousinly affection. I am aware—er—that *our* conduct—if I may use the—er—the plural of advocacy—I am aware that—er—*our* conduct has not in the past years been of—er—er—exemplary character. I am aware that the—er—death of our lamented cousin, your sainted mother, was—er—hastened—I may—er—say precip—itated—by our—er—indiscretion. But we are here to—er—confess judgment—with—er—er—costs.

MISS MARY: (*Interrupting.*) In other words, your client my cousin, having ruined my father, having turned his own widowed relation out of doors, and sent me, her daughter, among strangers to earn her bread; having seen my mother sink and die in her struggle to keep her family from want—this man now seeks to condone his offenses—pardon me, sir, if I use your own legal phraseology—by offering me a home; by giving me part of his ill-gotten wealth, the association of his own hypocritical self, and the company of his shameless, profligate son—

STARBOTTLE: (*Interrupting.*) A moment, Miss Morris—a single moment! The epithets you have used, the—er—vigorous characterization of our—er—conduct, is—er—within the—er—strict rules of legal advocacy, correct. We are—er—rascals! we are—er—scoundrels! we are—er—well, I am not-—er—prepared to say that we are not—er—demn me—hypocrites! But the young man you speak of—our son, whose past life (speaking as Colonel Starbottle) no one more sincerely deprecates than myself—that young man has reformed; has been for the past few months a miracle of sobriety, decorum, and industry; has taken, thanks to the example of—er—friends, a position of integrity in his father's business, of filial obedience in his father's household; is, in short, a paragon and, demn me, I doubt if he's his father's son.

MISS MARY: Enough, sir! You are waiting for my answer. There is no reason why it should not be as precise, as brief, and as formal as your message. Go to my cousin; say that you saw the person he claims as his relation; say that you found her, a poor schoolmistress, in a rude mining-camp, dependent for her bread on the scant earnings of already impoverished men, dependent for her honor on the rude chivalry of outcasts and vagabonds; and say that then and there she repudiated your kinship and respectfully declined your invitation.

STARBOTTLE: (*Aside.*) Ged! Star! this is the—er—female of your species! This is the woman—the—er—one woman—for whom you are responsible, sir!—personally responsible!

MISS MARY: (*Coldly.*) You have my answer, sir.

STARBOTTLE: Permit me—er—single moment—a single moment! Between the—er—present moment, and that of my departure—there is an—er—interval of twelve hours. May I, at the close of that interval—again present myself—without prejudice, for your final answer?

MISS MARY: (*Indifferently.*) As you will, sir. I shall be here.

STARBOTTLE: Permit me. (*Takes her hand gallantly.*) Your conduct and manner, Miss Morris, remind me—er—singularly—of—er—beautiful creature—one of the—er—first families. (*Observing Miss Mary regarding him amusedly, becomes embarrassed.*) That is—er—I mean—er—er—good morning, Miss Morris! (*Passes by the schoolhouse door, retreating and bowing, and picks up flowers from doorstep.*) Good morning!

MISS MARY: Excuse me, Colonel Starbottle (*with winning politeness*), but I fear I must rob you of those flowers. I recognize them now as the offering of one of my pupils. I fear I must revoke my gift (*taking flowers from astonished colonel's hand*), all except a single one for your buttonhole. Have you any choice, or shall I (*archly*) choose for you? Then it shall be this. (*Begins to place flowers in buttonhole, Col. Starbottle exhibiting extravagant gratitude in dumb show. Business prolonged through Miss Mary's speech.*) If I am not wrong, colonel, the gentleman to whom you so kindly pointed out the road this morning was not a stranger to you. Ah! I am right. There,—one moment,—a sprig of green, a single leaf, would set off the pink nicely. Here he is known only as "Sandy;" you know the absurd habits of this camp. Of course he has another name. There! (*Releasing the colonel.*) It is much prettier now.

STARBOTTLE: Ged, madam! The rarest exotic—the Victoria Regina—is not as—er—graceful—er—tribute!

MISS MARY: And yet you refuse to satisfy my curiosity?

STARBOTTLE: (*With great embarrassment, which at last resolves itself into increased dignity of manner.*) What you ask is—er—er—impossible! You are right: the—er—gentleman you allude to is known to me under—er—er—another name. But honor—Miss Morris, honor!—seals the lips of Colonel Starbottle. (*Aside.*) If she should know he was a menial! No. The position of the man you have challenged, Star, must be equal to your own. (*Aloud.*) Anything, Miss Morris, but—er—that!

MISS MARY: (*Smiling.*) Be it so. Adios, Colonel Starbottle.

STARBOTTLE: (*Gallantly.*) Au revoir, Miss Morris. (*Exit, impressively.*)

MISS MARY: So! Sandy conceals another name, which he withholds from Red Gulch. Well! Pshaw! What is that to me? The camp is made up of refugees, —men who perhaps have good reason to hide a name that may be infamous, the name that would publish a crime. Nonsense! Crime and Sandy! No, shame and guilt do not hide themselves in those honest but occasionally somewhat bloodshot eyes. Besides, goodness knows! the poor fellow's weakness is palpable enough. No, that is not the reason. It is no guilt that keeps his name hidden, —at least, not his. (*Seating herself, and arranging flowers in her lap.*) Poor Sandy! he must have climbed the eastern summit to get this. See, the rosy sunrise still lingers in its very petals; the dew is fresh upon it. Dear little mountain baby! I really believe that fellow got up before daylight, to climb that giddy height and secure its virgin freshness. And to think, in a moment of spite, I'd have given it to that bombastic warrior! (*Pause.*) That was a fine offer you refused just now, Miss Mary. Think of it: a home of luxury, a position of assured respect and homage; the life I once led, with all its difficulties smoothed away, its uncertainty dispelled,—think of it! My poor mother's dream fulfilled,—I, her daughter, the mistress of affluence, the queen of social power! What a temptation! Ah, Miss Mary, *was* it a temptation? Was there nothing in your free life here that stiffened your courage, that steeled the adamant of your refusal? Or was it only the memory of your mother's wrongs? Luxury and wealth! Could you command a dwelling more charming than this? Position and respect! Is not the awful admiration of these lawless men more fascinating than the perilous flattery of gentlemen like Colonel Starbottle? Is not the devotion of these outcasts more complimentary than the lip-service of perfumed gallantry? (*Pause.*) It's very odd he doesn't come. I wonder if that conceited old fool said anything to him. (*Rises, and then seats herself smiling.*) He *has* come. He is dodging in and out of the manzanita[24] bushes below the spring. I suppose he imagines my visitor still here. The bashful fool! If anybody should see him, it would be enough to make a petty scandal! I'll give him a talking-to. (*Pause.*) I wonder if the ridiculous fool has gone to sleep in those bushes. (*Rises.*) Well, let him; it will help him to recover his senses from last night's dissipation; and you, Miss Mary, it is high time you were preparing the lessons for tomorrow. (*Goes to schoolhouse, enters door, and slams it behind her; after a moment reappears with empty bucket.*) Of course there's no water, and I am dying of thirst. (*Goes slowly to left and pauses embarrassedly and bashfully, presently laughs,—then suddenly frowns and assumes an appearance of indignation.*) Miss Mary Morris, have you become such an egregious fool that you dare not satisfy the ordinary cravings of human nature, just because an idle, dissipated, bashful blockhead— nonsense! (*Exit, brandishing pail.*)

SCENE 3: *The Same.*

(*A pause. Sandy's voice, without.*) This way, miss: the trail is easier.
(*Miss Mary's voice, without.*) Never mind me, look after the bucket.

(*Enter Sandy, carrying bucket with water, followed by Miss Mary. Sandy sets bucket down.*)

MISS MARY: There, you've spilt half of it. If it had been whiskey, you'd have been more careful.
SANDY: (*Submissively.*) Yes, miss.
MISS MARY: (*Aside.*) "Yes, miss!" The man will drive me crazy with his saccharine imbecility. (*Aloud.*) I believe you would assent to anything, even if I said you were—an impostor!
SANDY: (*Amazedly.*) An impostor, Miss Mary?
MISS MARY: Well, I don't know what other term you use in Red Gulch to express a man who conceals his real name under another.
SANDY: (*Embarrassed, but facing Miss Mary.*) Has anybody been tellin' ye I was an imposter, miss? Has that derned old fool that I saw ye with—
MISS MARY: "That old fool," as you call him, was too honorable a gentleman to disclose your secret, and too loyal a friend to traduce you by an epithet. Fear nothing, Mr. "Sandy"; if you have limited your confidence to *one* friend, it has not been misplaced. But, dear me, don't think I wish to penetrate your secret. No. The little I learned was accidental. Besides, his business was with me; perhaps, as his friend, you already know it.
SANDY: (*Meekly.*) Perhaps, miss, he was too honorable a gentleman to disclose *your* secret. His business was with me.
MISS MARY: (*Aside.*) He has taken a leaf out of my book! He is not so stupid after all. (*Aloud.*) *I* have no secret. Colonel Starbottle came here to make me an offer.
SANDY: (*Recoiling.*) An offer!
MISS MARY: Of a home and independence. (*Aside.*) Poor fellow! how pale he looks! (*Aloud.*) Well, you see, I am more trustful than you. I will tell you *my* secret, and you shall aid me with your counsel. (*They sit on ledge of rocks.*) Listen! My mother had a cousin once,—a cousin cruel, cowardly, selfish, and dissolute. She loved him, as women are apt to love such men,—loved him so that she beguiled her own husband to trust his fortunes in the hands of this wretched profligate. The husband was ruined, disgraced. The wife sought her cousin for help for her necessities. He met her with insult and proposed that she should fly with him.
SANDY: One moment, miss: it wasn't his pardner,—his pardner's wife,—eh?

MISS MARY: (*Impatiently.*) It was the helpless wife of his own blood, I tell you. The husband died broken-hearted. The wife, my mother, struggled in poverty, under the shadow of a proud name, to give me an education, and died while I was still a girl. Today this cousin—this more than murderer of my parents—old, rich, self-satisfied, *reformed*, invites me, by virtue of that kinship he violated and despised, to his home, his wealth, his—his family rooftree! The man you saw was his agent.

SANDY: And you—

MISS MARY: Refused.

SANDY: (*Passing his hand over his forehead.*) You did wrong, Miss Mary.

MISS MARY: Wrong, sir? (*Rising.*)

SANDY: (*Humbly, but firmly.*) Sit ye down, Miss Mary. It aint for ye to throw your bright young life away yer in this place. It ain't for such as ye to soil your fair young hands by raking in the ashes to stir up the dead embers of a family wrong. It ain't for ye—ye'll pardon me, Miss Mary, for sayin' it—it ain't for ye to allow when it's *too late* fur a man to reform, or to go back of his reformation. Don't ye do it, miss, fur God's sake,—don't ye do it! Harkin, Miss Mary. If ye'll take my advice—a fool's advice, maybe—ye'll go. And when I tell ye that that advice, if ye take it, will take the sunshine out of these hills, the color off them trees, the freshness outer them flowers, the heart's blood outer me,—ye'll know that I ain't thinkin' o' myself, but of ye. And I wouldn't say this much to ye, Miss Mary, but you're goin' away. There's a flower, miss, you're wearin' in your bosom,—a flower I picked at daybreak this morning, five miles away in the snow. The wind was blowing chill around it, so that my hands that dug for it were stiff and cold, but the roots were warm. Miss Mary, as they are now in your bosom. Ye'll keep that flower, Miss Mary, in remembrance of my love for ye, that kept warm and blossomed through the snow. And, don't start, Miss Mary,—for ye'll leave behind ye, as I did, the snow and rocks through which it bloomed. I axes your parding, miss: I'm hurtin' yer feelin's, sure.

MISS MARY: (*Rising with agitation.*) Nothing,—nothing, but climbing these stupid rocks has made me giddy; that's all. Your arm. (*To Sandy impatiently.*) Can't you give me your arm? (*Sandy supports Miss Mary awkwardly toward shoolhouse. At door Miss Mary pauses.*) But if this reformation is so easy, so acceptable, why have you not profited by it? Why have you not reformed? Why have I found you here, a disgraced, dissipated, anonymous outcast, whom an honest girl dare not know? Why do you presume to preach to me? Have you a father?

SANDY: Hush, Miss Mary, hush! I had a father. Harkin. All that you have suffered from a kinship even so far removed, I have known from the hands of one who should have protected me. *My* father was—but no matter. You, Miss Mary, came out of your trials like gold from the washing. I was only the dirt and gravel to be thrown away. It is too late, Miss Mary, too late. My father has never sought me, would turn me from his doors had I sought him. Perhaps he is only right.

MISS MARY: But why should he be so different from others? Listen. This very cousin whose offer I refused had a son,—wild, wayward, by all report the most degraded of men. It was part of my cousin's reformation to save this son, and, if it were possible, snatch him from that terrible fate which seemed to be his only inheritance—

SANDY: (*Eagerly.*) Yes, miss.

MISS MARY: To restore him to a regenerated home. With this idea he followed his prodigal to California. I, you understand, was only an afterthought, consequent upon his success. He came to California upon this pilgrimage two years ago. He had no recollection, so they tell me, by which he could recognize this erring son and at first his search was wild, profitless, and almost hopeless. But by degrees, and with a persistency that seemed to increase with his hopelessness, he was rewarded by finding some clue to him at—at—at—

SANDY: (*Excitedly.*) At Poker Flat?

MISS MARY: Ah, perhaps you know the story—at Poker Flat. He traced him to the Mission of San Carmel.

SANDY: Yes, miss: go on.

MISS MARY: He was more successful than he deserved, perhaps. He found him. I see you know the story.

SANDY: Found him! Found him! Miss, did you say found him?

MISS MARY: Yes, found him. And today Alexander Morton, the reclaimed prodigal is part of the household I am invited to join. So you see, Mr. Sandy, there is still hope. What has happened to him is only a promise to you. Eh! Mr. Sandy—what is the matter? Are you ill? Your exertion this morning, perhaps. Speak to me! Gracious heavens, he is going mad! No! No! Yes—it cannot be—it is—he *had* broken his promise: he is drunk again.

SANDY: (*Rising, excited and confused.*) Excuse me, miss, I am a little onsartain here (*pointing to his head.*) I can't—I disremember—what you said jus' now; ye mentioned the name o' that prodigal that was found.

MISS MARY: Certainly: compose yourself,—my cousin's son, Alexander Morton. Listen, Sandy; you promised *me*, you know; you said for *my* sake you would not touch a drop. (*Enter cautiously toward schoolhouse the Duchess, stops on observing Sandy, and hides behind rock.*)

SANDY: (*Still bewildered and incoherent.*) I reckon. Harkin, miss, is that thar thing (*Pointing towards rock where Duchess is concealed.*)—is that a tree, or—or—a woman? Is it sorter movin' this way?

MISS MARY: (*Laying her hand on Sandy's.*) Recover your senses, for Heaven's sake, Sandy,—for *my* sake! It is only a tree.

SANDY: (*Rising.*) Then, miss, I've broke my word with ye: I'm drunk. P'r'aps I'd better be a-goin' (*Looking round confusedly.*) till I'm sober. (*Going toward L.*)

MISS MARY: (*Seizing his hand.*) But you'll see me again, Sandy, you'll come here—before—before I go?

SANDY: Yes, miss,—before ye go. (*Staggers stupidly toward L. Aside.*) Found him! Found Alexander Morton! It's a third time, Sandy, the third time: it means—it means—you're mad! (*Laughs wildly, and exits.*)

MISS MARY: (*Springing to her feet.*) There is a mystery behind all this, Mary Morris, that you—you—must discover. That man was *not* drunk; he *had not* broken his promise to me. What does it all mean? I have it. I will accept the offer of this Alexander Morton. I will tell him the story of this helpless man, this poor, poor, reckless Sandy. With the story of his own son before his eyes, he cannot but interest himself in his fate. He is rich; he will aid me in my search for Sandy's father, for Sandy's secret. At the worst, I can only follow the advice of this wretched man—an advice so generous, so kind, so self-sacrificing. Ah—

SCENE 4. *The same. Enter the Duchess, showily and extravagantly dressed. Her manner at first is a mixture of alternate shyness and bravado.*

THE DUCHESS: I heerd tell that you was goin' down to 'Frisco[25] tomorrow, for your vacation and I couldn't let ye go till I came to thank ye for your kindness to my boy—little Tommy.

MISS MARY: (*Aside, rising abstractedly, and recalling herself with an effort.*) I see —a poor outcast, the mother of my anonymous pupil. (*Aloud.*) Tommy! a good boy—a dear, good little boy.

DUCHESS: Thankee, miss, thankee. If[26] I am his mother, thar ain't a sweeter, dearer, better boy lives than him. And if I ain't much as says it, thar ain't a sweeter, dearer, angeler teacher than he's got. It ain't for you to be complimented by me, miss; it ain't for such as me to be comin' here in broad day to do it, neither, but I come to ask a favor,—not for me, miss, but for the darling boy.

MISS MARY: (*Aside—abstractedly.*) This poor, degraded creature will kill me with her wearying gratitude. Sandy will not return, of course, while she is here. (*Aloud.*) Go on. If I can help you or yours, be assured I will.

DUCHESS: Thankee, miss. You see, thar's no one the boy has any claim on but me, and I ain't the proper person to bring him up. I did allow to send him to 'Frisco, last year, but when I heerd talk that a schoolma'am was comin' up, and you did, and he sorter tuk to ye natril[27] from the first, I guess I did well to keep him yer. For, oh, miss, he loves ye so much, and if you could hear him talk in his purty way, ye wouldn't refuse him anything.

MISS MARY: (*With fatigued politeness and increasing impatience.*) I see. I see; pray go on.

DUCHESS: (*With quiet persistency.*) It's natril he should take to ye miss; for his father, when I first knowed him, miss, was a gentleman like yourself, and the boy must forget me sooner or later—and I ain't goin' to cry about *that*.

MISS MARY: (*Impatiently.*) Pray tell me how I can serve you.

DUCHESS: Yes, miss; you see, I came to ask you to take my Tommy—God bless him for the sweetest, bestest boy that lives!—to take him with you. I've money plenty, and it's all ours and his. Put him in some good school whar ye kin go and see and sorter help him to—forget—his mother. Do with him what you like. The worst you can do will be kindness to what he would learn with me. You will; I know you will, won't you? You will make him as pure and as good as yourself, and when he has grown up and is a gentleman, you will tell him his father's name—the name that hasn't passed my lips for years—the name of Alexander Morton.

MISS MARY: (*Aside.*) Alexander Morton! The prodigal! Ah, I see—the ungathered husks of his idle harvest.

DUCHESS: You hesitate, Miss Mary. (*Seizing her.*) Do not take your hand away. You are smiling. God bless you! I know you will take my boy. Speak to me, Miss

Mary.

MISS MARY: (*Aloud.*) I will take your child. More than that, I will take him to his father.

DUCHESS: No, no! for God's sake, no, Miss Mary! He has never seen him from his birth; he does not know him. He will disown him. He will curse him—will curse me!

MISS MARY: Why should he? Surely his crime is worse than yours.

DUCHESS: Hear me, Miss Mary. (*Aside.*) How can I tell her? (*Aloud.*) One moment miss. I was once—ye may not believe it, miss—as good, as pure, as you. I had a husband, the father of this child. He was kind, good, easy, forgiving—too good for me, miss, too simple and unsuspecting. He was what the world calls a fool, miss: he loved me too well—the kind o' crime, miss,—beggin your pardon, and all precepts to the contrary—the one thing that women like me never forgives. He had a pardner, miss, that governed him as *he* never governed me; that held him with the stronger will, and maybe *me* too. I was young, miss—no older than yourself then, and I ran away with him; left all and ran away with my husband's pardner. My husband—nat'rally—took to drink. I axes your pardin', miss, but ye'll see now, allowin' your larnin', that Alexander Morton ain't the man as will take my child.

MISS MARY: Nonsense. You are wrong. He has reformed; he has been restored to his home—your child's home, your home if you will claim it. Do not fear: I will make that right.

(*Enter Sandy slowly and sheepishly; stops on observing the Duchess and stands amazed and motionless.*)

MISS MARY: (*Observing Sandy—aside.*) He *has* returned. Poor fellow! How shall I get rid of this woman? (*Aloud.*) Enough. If you are sincere, I will take your child, and, God help me! bring him to his home and yours. Are you satisfied?

DUCHESS: Thank ye! Thank ye, miss, but—but thar's a mistake somewhar. In course—it's natural—ye don't know the father of that child, my boy Tommy, under the name o' Alexander Morton. Yur's thinking, like as not, of another man. The man I mean lives yer, in this camp; they calls him Sandy, miss,—*Sandy!*

MISS MARY: (*After a pause, coming forward, passionately.*) Hush! I have given you my answer, be it Alexander Morton or Sandy. Go now: bring me the child this evening at my house. I will meet you there. (*Leads the Duchess to wing. The Duchess endeavors to fall at her feet.*)

DUCHESS: God bless you miss!

MISS MARY: (*Hurriedly embracing her.*) No more, no more—but go! (*Exit Duchess. Miss Mary returns hurriedly to center, confronting Sandy.*)

MISS MARY: (*To Sandy, hurriedly and excitedly.*) You have heard what that woman said. I do not ask you under what *alias* you are known here; I only ask a single question[28]—Is *she* your wife? Are you the father of her child?

SANDY: (*Sinking upon his knees before her, and covering his face with his hands.*) I am!

MISS MARY: Enough! (*Taking flower from her bosom.*) Here, I give you back the flower you gave me this morning. It has faded and died here upon my breast. But I shall replace it with your foundling—the child of that woman, born like that flower in the snow! And I go now, Sandy, and leave behind me, as you said this morning, the snow and rocks in which it bloomed. Good-by! Farewell, farewell—forever! (*Goes toward schoolhouse as—*)

(*Enter Col. Starbottle.*)

MISS MARY: You are here in season, sir. You must have come for an answer to your question. You must first give me one to mine. Who is this man (*Pointing to Sandy.*), the man you met upon the rocks this morning?

STARBOTTLE: Ahem! I am—er—now fully prepared and responsible, I may say, miss—er—personally responsible, to answer that question. When you asked it this morning, the ordinary courtesy of the—er—code of honor threw a—er—cloak around the—er—antecedents of the—er—man whom I—er—elected by a demand from personal satisfaction, to the equality of myself, an—er—gentleman! That—er—cloak is now removed. I have waited six hours for an apology or a—er—reply to my demand. I am now free to confess that the—er—person you allude to was first known by me, three months ago, as an inebriated menial,—a groom in the houshold of my friend Don Jose Castro,—by the—er—simple name of "Diego."

MISS MARY: (*Slowly.*) I am satisfied. I accept my cousin's invitation. (*Exit slowly, supported by Col. Starbottle.*)

(*As Starbottle and Miss Mary exeunt, Concho and Hop Sing enter cautiously. Sandy slowly rises to his feet, passes his hand across his forehead, looks around toward exit of Starbottle and Miss Mary.*)

SANDY: (*Slowly, but with more calmness of demeanor.*) Gone, gone—forever! No: I am not mad, nor crazed with drink. My hands no longer tremble. There is no confusion here. (*Feeling his forehead.*) I heard them all. It was no dream. I heard her every word. Alexander Morton, yes, they spoke of Alexander Morton. She is going to him, to my father. She is going—she, Mary, my cousin—she is going to my father. He has been seeking me—has found—ah! (*Groans.*) No, no, Sandy! Be patient, be calm; you are not crazy—no, no, good Sandy, good old boy! Be patient, be patient; it is coming, it is coming. Yes, I see; some one has leaped into my place; some one has leaped into the old man's arms. Some one will creep into *her* heart! No! by God. No! I am Alexander Morton. Yes, yes! But how, how shall I prove it?—how? Who (*Concho steps cautiously forward towards Sandy unobserved.*) will believe the vagabond, the outcast—my God!—the crazy drunkard?

CONCHO: (*Advancing and laying his hand on Sandy.*) I will!

SANDY: (*Staggering back amazedly.*) You!

CONCHO: Yes—I, I,—Concho! You know me, Diego, you know me—Concho, the major-domo of the Blessed Innocents. Ha! You know me now. Yes, I have come to save you. I have come to make you strong. So—I have come to help you strip the Judas that has stepped into your place—the sham prodigal that has had the fatted calf and the ring—ah! ah!

SANDY: You? You do not know me!

CONCHO: Ah! you think, you think, eh? Listen: since you left, I have tracked *him—the impostor*, this Judas, this coyote—step by step, until his tracks crossed yours, and then I sought you out. I know all. I found a letter you had dropped; that brought me to Poker Flat. Ah, you start! I have seen those who knew you as Alexander Morton. You see! Ah, I am wise.

SANDY: (*Aside.*) It is true. (*Aloud.*) But (*Suspiciously.*) Why have you done this? You, Concho?—you were not my friend.

CONCHO: No, but *he* is my enemy. Ah, you start! Look at me, Alexander Morton, Sandy, Diego! You knew a man, strong, active, like yourself. Eh! Look at me now! Look at me, a cripple! Eh! lame and crushed here (*Pointing to his leg.*), broken and crushed here (*Pointing to his heart.*), by him,—the impostor! Listen, Diego. The night I was sent to track you from the rancho, he—this man—struck me from the wall, dashed me to the earth, and made *my body*, broken and bruised, a stepping-stone to leap the wall into your place, Diego—into your father's heart—into my master's home. They found me dead, they thought—no, not dead, Diego! It was sad, they said—unfortunate. They nursed me; they talked of money—eh, Diego!—money! They would have pensioned me to hush scandal—eh! I was a dog, a foreigner, a Greaser! Eh! That is why I am here. No! I love you not, Diego; you are of his race; but I hate—Mother of God!—I *hate* him!

SANDY: (*Rising to his feet, aside.*) Good! I begin to feel my courage return; my nerves are stronger. Courage, Sandy! (*Aloud.*) Be it so, Concho; there is my hand! We will help each other,—you to my birthright; I to your revenge! Hark ye! (*Sandy's manner becomes more calm and serious.*) This impostor is *no* craven, *no* coyote. Whoever he is, he must be strong. He has most plausible evidences. We must have rigid proofs. I will go with you to Poker Flat. There is one man, if he be living, knows me better than any man who lives. He has done me wrong—a great wrong, Concho—but I will forgive him. I will do more— I will ask his forgiveness. He will be a witness no man dare gainsay—my partner—God help him and forgive him as I do!—John Oakhurst.

CONCHO: Oakhurst your parnter!

SANDY: (*Angrily.*) Yes. Look ye, Concho, he has wronged me in a private way: that is *my* business, not *yours*, but he was *my* partner; no one shall abuse him before me.

CONCHO: Be it so. Then sink here! Rot here! Go back to your husks, O prodigal! Wallow in the ditches of this camp, and see your birthright sold for a dram of aguadiente! Lie here, dog and coyote that you are, with your mistress under the protection of your destroyer! For I tell you—I, Concho, the cripple—that the man who struck me down, the man who stepped into your birthright, the man who tomorrow welcomes your sweetheart in his arms, who holds the custody of your child, is your partner—John Oakhurst!

SANDY: (*Who has been sinking under Concho's words, rising convulsively to his feet.*) God be merciful to me a sinner! (*Faints.*)

CONCHO: (*Standing over his prostrate body exultingly.*) I am right. You are wise, Concho, you are wise! You have found Alexander Morton.

HOP SING: (*Advancing slowly to Sandy's side, and extending open palm.*) Me washee shirt flo you, flowty dozen hab. You no payee me. Me wantee twenty dollar hep. Sabe!

(*Curtain.*)

END OF ACT II

ACT III

SCENE 1: *The bank parlor of Morton & Son, San Francisco. Room richly furnished; two square library desks, left and right. At right, safe in wall; at left, same with practicable doors. Folding-door in flat, leading to counting-room. Door in left to private room of Alexander Morton, Sr.; door in right to private room of Morton, Jr. Alexander Morton, Sr., discovered at desk, right, opening and reading letters.*

MORTON, SR.: (*Laying down letter.*) Well, well, the usual story; letters from all sorts of people, who have done or intend to do all sorts of things for my reclaimed prodigal. (*Reads.*) "Dear Sir: Five years ago I loaned some money to a stranger who answers the description of your recovered son. He will remember Jim Parker—Limping Jim, of Poker Flat. Being at present short of funds, please send twenty dollars, amount loaned, by return mail. If not convenient, five dollars will do as installment." Pshaw! (*Throws letter aside, and takes up another.*) "Dear Sir: I invite your attention to inclosed circular for a proposed Home for Dissipated and Anonymous Gold-Miners. Your well-known reputation for liberality, and your late valuable experience in the reformation of your son, will naturally enlist your broadest sympathies. We inclose a draft for five-thousand dollars, for your signature." We shall see! Another: "Dear Sir: The Society for the Formation of Bible Classes in the Upper Stanislaus[29] acknowledge your recent munificent gift of five-hundred dollars to the cause. Last Sabbath Brother Hawkins, of Poker Flat, related with touching effect the story of your prodigal to an assemblage of over two hundred miners. Owing to unusual expenses, we regret to be compelled to draw upon you for five-hundred dollars more." So! (*Putting down letter.*) If we were given to pride and vainglory, we might well be puffed up with the fame of our works and the contagion of our example: yet I fear that, with the worldly-minded, this praise of charity to others is only the prayerful expectation of some personal application to the praiser. (*Rings handbell.*)

(*Enter Jackson*)

(*To Jackson*) File these letters (*Handing letters.*) with the others. There is no answer. Has young Mr. Alexander come in yet?

JACKSON: He only left here an hour ago. It was steamerday yesterday: he was up all night, sir.

OLD MORTON: (*Aside.*) True. And the night before he traveled all night, riding two hours ahead of one of our defaulting agents, and saved the bank a hundred-thousand dollars. Certainly his devotion to business is unremitting. (*Aloud.*) Any news from Colonel Starbottle?

JACKSON: He left this note, sir, early this morning.

OLD MORTON: (*Takes it, and reads.*) "I think I may say on my own personal responsibility, that the mission is successful. Miss Morris will arrive tonight with a female attendant and child." (*To Jackson.*) That is all, sir. Stop! Has any one been smoking here?

JACKSON: Not to my knowledge, sir.

OLD MORTON: There was a flavor of stale tobacco smoke in the room this morning when I entered, and ashes on the carpet. I *know* that young Mr. Alexander has abandoned the pernicious habit. See that it does not occur again.

JACKSON: Yes, sir. (*Aside.*) I must warn Mr. Alexander that his friends must be more careful, and yet those ashes were good for a deposit of fifty-thousand.

OLD MORTON: Is any one waiting?

JACKSON: Yes, sir,—Don Jose Castro and Mr. Capper.

OLD MORTON: Show in the Don; the policeman can wait.

JACKSON: Yes, sir. (*Exit.*)

OLD MORTON: (*Taking up Starbottle's note.*) "Miss Morris will arrive tonight." And yet he saw her only yesterday. This is not like her mother: no. She would never have forgiven and forgotten so quickly. Perhaps she knew not my sin and her mother's wrongs; perhaps she has—has—*Christian* forgiveness (*Sarcastically.*); perhaps, like my prodigal, she will be immaculately perfect. Well, well, at least her presence will make my home less lonely. "An attendant and child." A child! Ah, if *he*, my boy, my Alexander, were still a child, I might warm this cold, cold heart in his sunshine! Strange that I cannot reconstruct from this dutiful, submissive, obedient, industrious Alexander—this redeemed outcast, this son who shares my life, my fortunes, my heart—the foolish, willful, thoughtless, idle boy that once defied me. I remember (*musing, with a smile*) how the little rascal, ha, ha! once struck me,—*struck me!*—when I corrected him: ha, ha! (*Rubbing his hands with amusement, and then suddenly becoming grave and lugubrious.*) No, no. These are the whisperings of the flesh. Why should I find fault with him for being all that a righteous conversion demands,—all that I asked and prayed for? No, Alexander Morton: it is you, *you*, who are not yet regenerate. It is *you* who are ungrateful to Him who blessed you, to Him whose guiding hand led you to—

(*Enter Jackson.*)

JACKSON: Don Jose Castro.

(Enter Don Jose.)

DON JOSE: A thousand pardons, senor, for interrupting you in the hours of business; but it is—it is of business I would speak. *(Looking around.)*

OLD MORTON: *(To Jackson.)* You can retire. *(Exit Jackson.)* Be seated, Mr. Castro; I am at your service.

DON JOSE: It is of your—your son—

OLD MORTON: Our firm is Morton & Son; in business we are one, Mr. Castro.

DON JOSE: Bueno! Then to you as to him I will speak. Here is a letter I received yesterday. It has significance, importance perhaps. But whatever it is, it is something for you, not me, to know. If I am wronged much, Don Alexandro, *you*, you are wronged still more. Shall I read it? Good. *(Reads.)* "The man to whom you have affianced your daughter is not the son of Alexander Morton. Have a care. If I do not prove him an impostor at the end of six days, believe me one, and not your true friend and servant, Concho." In six days, Don Alexandro, the year of probation is over, and I have promised my daughter's hand to your son. *(Hands letter to Morton.)*

OLD MORTON: *(Ringing bell.)* Is that all, Mr. Castro?

DON JOSE: All, Mr. Castro? Carramba! is it not enough?

(Enter Jackson.)

OLD MORTON: *(To Jackson.)* You have kept a record of this business during the last eighteen months. Look at this letter. *(Handing letter.)* Is the handwriting familiar?

JACKSON: *(Taking letter.)* Can't say, sir. The form is the old one.

OLD MORTON: How many such letters have you received?

JACKSON: Four-hundred-and-forty-one, sir. This is the four-hundred-and-forty-second application for your son's position, sir.

DON JOSE: Pardon. This is not an application; it is only information or caution.

OLD MORTON: *(To Jackson.)* How many letters of information or caution have we received?

JACKSON: This makes seven-hundred-and-eighty-one, sir.

OLD MORTON: How, sir! *(Quickly.)* There were but seven-hundred-and-seventy-nine last night.

JACKSON: Beg pardon, sir! The gentleman who carried Mr. Alexander's valise from the boat was the seven-hundred-and-eightieth.

OLD MORTON: Explain yourself, sir.

JACKSON: He imparted to me, while receiving his stipend, the fact that he did not believe young Mr. Alexander was your son. An hour later, sir, he also imparted to me confidentially that he believed you were his father, and requested the loan of five dollars, to be repaid by you, to enable him to purchase a clean shirt and appear before you in respectable conditions. He waited for you an hour and expressed some indignation that he had not an equal show with others, to throw himself into your arms.

DON JOSE: *(Rising, aside, and uplifting his hands.)* Carramba! These Americans are of the Devil! *(Aloud.)* Enough, Don Alexandro! Then you think this letter is only worth—

OLD MORTON: One moment. I can perhaps tell you exactly its market value. (*To Jackson.*) Go on, sir.

JACKSON: At half-past ten, sir, then being slightly under the influence of liquor, he accepted the price of a deck passage to Stockton.

OLD MORTON: How much was that?

JACKSON: Fifty cent.

OLD MORTON: Exactly so! There you have, sir (*To Don Jose.*), the market value of the information you have received. I would advise you, as a business matter, not to pay more. As a business matter, you can at any time draw upon us for the amount. (*To Jackson.*) Admit Mr. Capper. (*Exit Jackson.*)

DON JOSE: (*Rising with dignity.*) This is an insult, Don Alexandro.

OLD MORTON: You are wrong, Mr. Castro; it is *business*; sought, I believe, by yourself. Now that it is transacted, I beg you to dine with me tomorrow to meet my niece. No offense, sir, no offense. Come, come! Business, you know, business.

DON JOSE: (*Relaxing.*) Be it so! I will come. (*Aside.*) These Americanos, these Americanos, are of the Devil! (*Aloud.*) Adios. (*Going.*) I hear, by report, that you have met with the misfortune of a serious loss by robbery?

OLD MORTON: (*Aside.*) So our mishap is known everywhere! (*Aloud.*) No serious misfortune, Mr. Castro, even if we do not recover the money. Adios.

(*Exit Don Jose.*)

OLD MORTON: The stiff-necked Papist! That he should dare, for the sake of his black-browed, froward daughter, to question the faith on which I have pinned my future! Well, with God's blessing, I gave him some wholesome discipline. If it were not for my covenant with Alexander—and nobly he has fulfilled his part—I should forbid his alliance with the blood of this spying Jesuit.

(*Enter Mr. Jackson, leading in Capper.*)

JACKSON: Policeman, sir.

CAPPER: (*Turning sharply.*) Who's that man?

OLD MORTON: Jackson, clerk.

CAPPER: Umph! Been here long?

OLD MORTON: A year. He was appointed by my son.

CAPPER: Know anything of his previous life?

OLD MORTON: (*Stiffly.*) I have already told you he is an appointee of my son's.

CAPPER: Yes! (*Aside.*) "Like master, like man." (*Aloud.*) Well, to business. We have worked up the robbery. We have reached two conclusions—one, that the work was not done by professionals; the other, consequent upon this, that you can't recover the money.

OLD MORTON: Excuse me, sir, but I do not see the last conclusion.

CAPPER: Then listen. The professional thief has only one or two ways of disposing of his plunder, and these ways are always well known to us. Good! Your stolen coin has not been disposed of in the regular way, through the usual hands which we could at any time seize. Of this we are satisfied.

OLD MORTON: How do you know it?

CAPPER: In this way. The only clue we have to the identification of the missing money were two boxes of Mexican doubloons.

OLD MORTON: (*Aside.*) Mr. Castro's special deposit! He may have reason for his interest. (*Aloud.*) Go on.

CAPPER: It is a coin rare in circulation in the interior. The night after the robbery the dealer of a monte-table in Sacramento paid out five-thousand dollars in doubloons. He declared it was taken in at the table and could not identify the players. Of course, *of course!* So far, you see, you are helpless. We have only established one fact, that the robber is—is—(*Significantly.*) a gambler.

OLD MORTON: (*Quietly.*) The regular trade of the thief seems to me to be of little importance, if you cannot identify him or recover my money. But go on, sir, go on; or is this all?

CAPPER: (*Aside.*) The old fool is blind. That is natural. (*Aloud.*) It is not all. The crime will doubtless be repeated. The man who has access to your vaults, who has taken only thrity-thousand dollars, when he could have secured half a million—this man, who has already gambled that thirty-thousand away—will not stop there. He will in a day or two, perhaps today, try to retrieve his losses out of *your* capital. *I* am here to prevent it.

OLD MORTON: (*Becoming interested.*) How?

CAPPER: Give me, for forty-eight hours, free access to this building. Let me conceal myself somewhere, anywhere, within these walls. Let it be without the knowledge of your clerks, even of *your son!*

OLD MORTON: (*Proudly.*) Mr. Alexander Morton is absent today. There is no other reason why he should not be here to consent to the acts of his partner and father.

CAPPER: (*Quickly.*) Very good. It is only to insure absolute secrecy.

OLD MORTON: (*Aside.*) Another robbery might excite a suspicion, worse for our credit than our actual loss. There is a significant earnestness about this man that awakens my fears. If Alexander were only here. (*Aloud.*) I accept. (*Capper has been trying doors.*)

CAPPER: What room is this?

OLD MORTON: My son's; I would prefer—

CAPPER: And this?

OLD MORTON: Mine, sir; if you choose—

CAPPER: (*Locking door and putting key in his pocket.*) This will do. Oblige me by making the necessary arrangements in your counting-room.

OLD MORTON: (*Hesitating and aside.*) He is right; perhaps it is only prudence, and I am saving Alexander additional care and annoyance. (*Exit*)

(*Enter Mr. Shadow cautiously.*)

SHADOW: (*In a lisping whisper to Capper.*) I've got the litht of the clerkth complete.

CAPPER: (*Triumphantly.*) Put it in your pocket, Shadow. We don't care for the lackeys now; we are after the master.

SHADOW: Eh! the mathter?

CAPPER: Yes: the master—the young master, the reclaimed son, the reformed prodigal! ha, ha!—the young man who compensates himself for all this austere devotion to business and principle by dipping into the old man's vaults when he wants a *pasear*:[30] eh, Shadow? That's the man we're after. Look here! *I* never took any stock in that young man's reformation. Ye don't teach old sports like him new tricks. They're a bad lot, father and son,—eh, Shadow?—and he's a chip of the old block. I spotted him before this robbery, before we were ever called in here professionally. I've had my eye on Alexander Morton, alias John Oakhurst, and, when I found the old man's doubloons raked over a monte-table at Sacramento, I knew where to look for the thief. Eh, Shadow?

SHADOW: (*Aside.*) He ith enormouth, thith Mithter Capper.

(*Enter Old Morton.*)

OLD MORTON: I have arranged everything. You will not be disturbed or suspected here in my private office. Eh! (*Looking at Shadow.*) Who slipped in here?

CAPPER: Only my Shadow, Mr. Morton, but I can rid myself even of that. (*Crosses to Shadow.*) Take this card to the office and wait for further orders. Vanish, Shadow! (*Exit Shadow.*)

(*Enter Jackson.*)

JACKSON: Mr. Alexander has come in, sir. (*Old Morton and Capper start.*)

OLD MORTON: Where is he?

JACKSON: In his private room, sir.

MORTON: Enough; you can go. (*Exit Jackson.*)

CAPPER: (*Crossing to Morton.*) Remember, you have given your pledge of secrecy. Beware! Your honor, your property, the credit and reputation of your bank are at stake.

OLD MORTON: (*After a pause of hesitation, with dignity.*) I gave you my word, sir, while my son was not present. I shall save myself from breaking my word with you, or concealing anything from him, by withdrawing myself. For the next twenty-four hours, this room (*Pointing to private room.*) is yours.

(*Each regards the other. Exit Old Morton as Capper exits in private room. After a pause, door of other room opens, and Harry York appears, slightly intoxicated, followed by John Oakhurst.*)

HARRY YORK: (*Looking around.*) By Jove! Morton, but you've got things in style here. And this yer's the gov'nor's desk, and here old Praise God Barebones sits opposite ye. Look yer, old boy (*Throwing himself in chair.*), I kin allow how it comes easy for ye to run this bank, for it's about as exciting, these times, as faro was to ye in '49, when I first knew ye as Jack Oakhurst, but how the devil you can sit opposite that stiff embodiment of all the Ten Commandments, day by day, damn it! That's wot *gets* me! Why, the first day I came here on business, the old man froze me so that I couldn't thaw a deposit out of my pocket. It chills me to think of it.

OAKHURST: (Hastily.) I suppose I am accustomed to him. But come, Harry: let me warm you. (Opens door of safe, and discovers cupboard, decanter, and glasses.)

YORK: (Laughing.) By Jove! under the old man's very nose. Jack, this is like you. (Takes a drink.) Well, old boy, this is like old times. But you don't drink?

OAKHURST: No, nor smoke. The fact is, Harry, I've taken a year's pledge. I've six days still to run: after that (Gloomily.), why (With a reckless laugh.), I shall be Jack Oakhurst again.

YORK: Lord! to think of your turning out to be anybody's son, Jack!—lest of all, his! (Pointing to chair.)

OAKHURST: (Laughing recklessly.) Not more strange than that I should find Harry York, the spendthrift of Poker Flat, the rich and respected Mr. York, produce-merchant of San Francisco.

YORK: Yes, but, my boy, you see I didn't strike it—in a rich father. I gave up gambling, married and settled down, saved my money, invested a little here and there, and—worked for it, Jack, damn me—worked for it like a damned horse!

OAKHURST: (Aside.) True, this is not work.

YORK: But that ain't my business with ye now, old boy: it's this. You've had some trials and troubles in the bank lately—a defalcation of agents one day, a robbery next. It's luck, my boy, luck! But ye know people will talk. You don't mind my sayin' that there's rumors round. The old man's mighty unpopular because he's a saint, and folks don't entirely fancy you because you used to be the reverse. Well, Jack, it amounts to 'bout this: I've withdrawn my account from Parkinson's, in Sacramento, and I've got a pretty heavy balance on hand—nigh on two-hundred-thousand—in bonds and certificates here, and if it will help you over the rough places, old boy, as a deposit, yer it is. (Drawing pocket-book.)

OAKHURST: (Greatly affected, but endeavoring to conceal it.) Thank you, Harry old fellow—but—

YORK: (Quickly.) I know: I'll take the risk, a business risk. You'll stand by me all you can, old boy; you'll make it pay all you can, and if you lose it—why—all right!

OAKHURST: (Embarrassed.) As a deposit with Morton & Son, drawing two per cent monthly interest—

YORK: Damn Morton & Son! I'll back it with Jack Oakhurst, the man I know.

OAKHURST: (Advancing slowly.) I'll take it, Harry.

YORK: (Extending his hand.) It's a square game, Jack!

OAKHURST: (Seizing his hand with repressed emotion.) It's a square game, Harry York, if I live.

YORK: Then I'll travel. Goodnight, old boy. I'll send my clerk around in the morning to put things right. Goodnight. (Going.)

OAKHURST: (Grasping York's hand.) One moment—no—nothing! Goodnight. (Exit York.)

(Oakhurst follows him to door, and then returns to desk, throwing himself in chair, and burying his face in his hands.)

OAKHURST: (*With a deep feeling.*) It needed but this to fill the measure of my degradation. I have borne the suspicions of the old man's enemies, the half-pitying, half-contemptuous sympathy of his friends, even his own cold, heartless, fanatical fulfillment of his sense of duty, but *this*—this confidence from one who had most reason to scorn me, this trust from one who knew me as I *was*—this is the hardest burden. And he, too, in time will know me to be an impostor. He too—a reformed man, but he has honorably retraced his steps and won the position I hold by a trick, an imposture. And what is all my labor beside his honest sincerity? I have fought against the chances that might discover my deception, against the enemies who would overthrow me, against the fate that put me here, and I have been successful—yes, a successful impostor! I have even fought against the human instinct that told this fierce, foolish old man that *I* was an alien to his house, to his blood; I have even felt him scan my face eagerly for some reflection of his long-lost boy, for some realization of his dream, and I have seen him turn away, cold, heartsick, and despairing. What matters that I have been to him devoted, untiring, submissive, ay, a better son to him than his own weak flesh and blood would have been? He would tomorrow cast me forth to welcome the outcast, Sandy Morton. Well, what matters? (*Recklessly.*) Nothing. In six days it will be over; in six days the year of my probation will have passed; in six days I will disclose to him the deceit I have practiced and will face the world again as Jack Oakhurst the gambler, who staked and lost *all* on a single cast. And Jovita! Well, well!—the game is made: it is too late to draw out now. (*Rings bell. Enter Jackson.*) Who has been here?

JACKSON: Only Don Jose, and Mr. Capper the detective.

OAKHURST: The detective? What for?

JACKSON: To work up the robbery, sir.

OAKHURST: True! Capper, Capper, yes! A man of wild and ridiculous theories, but well meaning, brave, and honest. (*Aside.*) This is the old man's idea. He does not know that I was on the trail of the thieves an hour before the police were notified. (*Aloud.*) Well, sir?

JACKSON: He told your father he thought the recovery of the money hopeless, but he came to caution us against a second attempt.

OAKHURST: (*Aside, starting.*) True! I had not thought of that. (*Excitedly.*) The success of their first attempt will incite them to another; the money they have stolen is gone by this time. (*Aloud.*) Jackson, I will stay here tonight and tomorrow night, and relieve your regular watchman. You will, of course, say nothing of my intention.

JACKSON: Yes, sir. (*Lingering.*)

OAKHURST: (*After a pause.*) That is all, Mr. Jackson.

JACKSON: Beg your pardon, Mr. Morton, but Colonel Starbottle, with two ladies, was here half an hour ago, and said they would come again when you were alone.

OAKHURST: Very well; admit them.

JACKSON: Beg pardon, sir, but they seemed to avoid seeing your father until they had seen you. It looked mysterious, and I thought I would tell you first.

OAKHURST: (*Laughing.*) Admit them, Mr. Jackson. (*Exit Jackson.*) This poor fellow's devotion is increasing. He, too, believes that his old associate in dissipation, John Oakhurst, *is* the son of Alexander Morton. He, too, will have to share in the disgrace of the impostor. Ladies! umph! (*Looking down at his clothes.*) I'm afraid the reform of Alexander Morton hasn't improved the usual neatness of John Oakhurst. I haven't slept, nor changed my clothes, for three days. (*Goes to door of Morton, Sr.'s room.*) Locked, and the key on the inside! That's strange. Nonsense! the old man has locked his door and gone out through the private entrance. Well, I'll find means of making my toilet here. (*Exit into private room.*)

(*Enter Jackson, leading in Col. Starbottle, Miss Mary, the Duchess, and child of three years.*[31])

JACKSON: Mr. Alexander Morton, Jr., is in his private room. He will be here in a moment. (*Exit Jackson.*)

STARBOTTLE: One moment, a single moment, Miss Mary. Permit me to—er—if I may so express myself, to—er—group the party, to—er—place the—er—present company into position I have—er—observed as part of my—er—legal experience, that in cases of moral illustration a great, I may say—er—tremendous, effect on the—er—jury, I mean the—er—guilty party, has been produced by the attitude of the—er—victim and martyr. You, madam, as the—er—injured wife (*Placing her.*), as Moral Retribution, leaning toward and slightly appealing to me, the image of—er—er—Inflexible Justice! (*Inflates his chest, puts his hand in his bosom, and strikes an attitude.*)

(*Door of young Morton's room opens and discloses Mr. Oakhurst gazing at the group. He starts slightly on observing the Duchess, but instantly recovers himself, and faces the company coldly. The Duchess starts on observing Oakhurst and struggles in confusion towards the door, dragging with her the child and Miss Mary, who endeavors to reassure her. Col. Starbottle looks in astonishment from one to the other and advances to front.*)

STARBOTTLE: (*Aside.*) The—er—tableau, although striking in moral forces, is apparently—er—deficient in moral stamina.

MISS MARY: (*Angrily to the Duchess.*) I'm ashamed of you! (*To Oakhurst, advancing.*) I don't ask pardon for my intrusion. If you are Alexander Morton, you are my kinsman, and you will know that I cannot introduce myself better than as the protector of an injured woman. Come here! (*To the Duchess, dragging her towards Oakhurst.*) (*To Oakhurst.*) Look upon this woman: she claims to be—

STARBOTTLE: (*Stepping between Miss Mary and the Duchess.*) A moment, Miss Mary, a single moment! Permit me to—er—explain. The whole thing, the—er—situation reminds me, demn me, of most amusing incident at Sacramento in '52. Large party at Hank Suedecois'; know Hank? Confirmed old bach of sixty. Dinner for forty. Everything in style, first families, Ged,—Judge Beeswinger, Mat Boompointer, and Maje Blodgett of Alabam'; know old Maje Blodgett? Well, Maje was there. Ged, sir, delay—everybody waiting. I went to Hank. "Hank," I says, "What's matter? Why delay?"—"Star," he says,—always called me Star,—"Star,—it's cook!"—"Demn cook," I says, "discharge cook—only a black mulatto anyway!" "Can't, Star," he says, "impossible!"—"Can't?" says I.

"No," says he. "Listen, Star," he says, "family secret! Honor—Can't discharge cook, because cook—demn it—'s *my wife!*" Fact sir, fact—showed marriage certificate—married privately seven years! Fact, sir—

DUCHESS: (*To Miss Mary.*) Some other time, miss. Let us go now. There's a mistake, miss, I can't explain. Some other time, miss! See, miss, how cold and stern he looks! Another time, miss! (*Struggling.*) For God's sake, miss, let me go!

MISS MARY: No! This mystery must be cleared up now, before I enter *his* house—before I accept the charge of this—

STARBOTTLE: (*Interrupting and crossing before Miss Mary.*) A moment—a single moment, miss. (*To Oakhurst.*) Mr. Morton, you will pardon the exuberance, and perhaps, under the circumstances, somewhat natural impulsiveness, of the—er—sex, for which I am perhaps responsible; I may say—er—personally, sir—personally responsible—

OAKHURST: (*Coldly.*) Go on, sir.

STARBOTTLE: The lady on my right is—er—the niece of your father,—your cousin. The lady on my left, engaged in soothing the—er—bashful timidity of infancy, is—er—that is—er—claims to be, the mother of the child of Alexander Morton.

OAKHURST: (*Calmly.*) She is right.

MISS MARY: (*Rushing forward.*) Then you are—

OAKHURST: (*Gently restraining her.*) You have another question to ask; let me ask it. (*Crossing to the Duchess.*) You have heard my answer. Madam, are you the legal wife of Alexander Morton?

DUCHESS: (*Sinking upon her knees, and dropping her face in her hands.*) No!

OAKHURST: Enough: I will take the child. Pardon me, Miss Morris, but you have heard enought to know that your mission is accomplished, but that what else passes between this woman and myself becomes no stranger to hear. (*Motions toward room.*)

MISS MARY: (*Aside.*) It is *his* son. I am satisfied. (*Going.*) Come, colonel. (*Exeunt into room Starbottle and Miss Mary.*)

DUCHESS: (*Crossing to Oakhurst and falling at his feet.*) Forgive me, Jack, forgive me! It was no fault of mine. I did not know that you were here. I did not know that you had taken his name!

OAKHURST: Hush—on your life!

DUCHESS: Hear me, Jack! I was anxious only for a home for my child. I came to *her*—the schoolmistress of Red Gulch—for aid. I told her the name of my boy's father. She—she brought me here. Oh, forgive me, Jack! I have offended you!

OAKHURST: How can I believe you? You have deceived *him*—you have deceived me. Listen! When I said, a moment ago, you were not the wife of Alexander Morton, it was because I knew that your first husband—the Australian convict Pritchard—was still living; that you had deceived Sandy Morton as you had deceived me. That was why I left you. Tell me, have you deceived me also about him, as you did about the other? Is *he* living, and with you, or dead, as you declared?

DUCHESS: (*Aside.*) He will kill me if I tell him. (*Aloud.*) No, no. He is gone—is dead these three years.

OAKHURST: You swear!

DUCHESS: (*Hesitates, gasps, and looks around for her child; then seizing it and drawing it toward her.*) I—swear.

OAKHURST: Enough. Seek not to know why *I* am here and under his name. Enough for you that it has saved your child's future and secured him his heritage past all revocation. Yet remember! a word from you within the next few days destroys it all. After that, I care not what you say.

DUCHESS: Jack! One word, Jack, before I go. I never thought to bring my shame to you!—to *him*!

OAKHURST: It was no trick, then, no contivance that brought her here. No; it was fate. And at least I shall save this child.

(*Re-enter Starbottle, Miss Mary, and Duchess.*)

STARBOTTLE: (*Impressively.*) Permit me, Mr. Alexander Morton, as the friend of my—er—principal, to declare that we have received—honorable—honorable— satisfaction. Allow me, sir, to grasp the hand, the—er—cherished hand of a gentleman who, demn me! has fulfilled all his duties to—er—society and gentlemen. And allow me to add, sir, should any invidious criticism of the present—er—settlement be uttered in my presence, I shall hold that critic responsible, sir—er—personally responsible!

MISS MARY: (*Sweeping truculently and aggressively up to John Oakhurst.*) And permit *me* to add, sir, that if you can see your way clearly out of this wretched muddle, it's more than I can. This arangement may be according to the California code of morality, but it doesn't accord with my Eastern ideas of right and wrong. If this foolish, wretched creature chooses to abandon all claim upon you, chooses to run away from you—why, I suppose, as a *gentleman*, according to your laws of honor, you are absolved. Goodnight, Mr. Alexander Morton. (*Goes to door, and exit, pushing out Starbottle, the Duchess, and child. Mr. Oakhurst sinks into chair at desk, burying his face in his hand. Re-enter slowly and embarrassedly, Miss Mary; looks toward Oakhurst and comes slowly down stage.*)

MISS MARY: (*Aside.*) I was too hard on him. I was not so hard on Sandy, when I thought that he—he—was the father of her child. And he's my own flesh and blood, too, and—he's crying. (*Aloud.*) Mr. Morton.

OAKHURST: (*Slowly lifting his head.*) Yes, Miss Mary.

MISS MARY: I spoke hastily just then. I—I—thought—you see—I—(*Angrily and passionately.*) I mean this. I'm a stranger. I don't understand your Californian ways, and I don't want to. But I believe you've done what you thought was right, according to a *man's* idea of right; and—there's my hand. Take it, take it; for it's a novelty, Mr. Morton: it's the hand of an honest girl!

OAKHURST: (*Hesitates, then rises, sinks on one knee, and raises Miss Mary's fingers to his lips.*) God bless you, miss! God bless you!

MISS MARY: (*Retreating to center door.*) Goodnight, goodnight (*Slowly.*)—cousin —Alexander. (*Exit. Dark stage.*)

OAKHURST: (*Rising swiftly.*) No, no; it is false! Ah! She's gone. Another moment, and I would have told her all. Pshaw! courage, man! It is only six days more, and you are free, and this year's shame and agony forever ended.

(*Enter Jackson.*)

JACKSON: As you ordered, sir, the night watchman has been relieved and has just gone.

OAKHURST: Very good, sir; and you?

JACKSON: I relieved the porter, sir, and I shall bunk on two chairs in the counting-room. You'll find me handy, if you want me, sir. Goodnight, sir. (*Exit.*)

OAKHURST: I fear these rascals will not dare to make their second attempt tonight. A quiet scrimmage with them—enough to keep me awake or from thinking—would be a good fortune. No, no! no such luck for you tonight, John Oakhurst! You are playing a losing game. . . . Yet the robbery was a bold one. At eleven o'clock, while the bank was yet lighted, and Mr. Jackson and another clerk were at work here, three well-dressed men pick the lock of the counting-house door, enter, and turn the key on the clerks in this parlor, and carry away a box of doubloons, not yet placed in the vaults by the porter, and all this done so cautiously that the clerks within knew nothing of it, until notified of the open street door by the private watchman, and so boldly that the watchman, seeing them here, believed them clerks of the bank, and let them go unmolested. No: this was the coincidence of good luck, not of bold premeditation. There will be no second sttempt. (*Yawns.*) If they don't come soon, I shall fall asleep. Four nights without rest will tell on a man, unless he has some excitement to back him. (*Nods.*) Hallo! What was that? Oh! Jackson in the counting-room getting to bed. I'll look at that front-door myself. (*Takes revolver from desk and goes to door, tries lock, comes down stage with revolver, examines it, and lays it down.*) (*Slowly and quietly.*) The door is locked on the outside: that may have been an accident. The caps are taken from my pistol: that was not! Well, here is the vault, and here is John Oakhurst: to reach the one, they must pass the other. (*Takes off his coat, seizes poker from grate, and approaches safe.*) Ha! some one is moving in the old man's room. (*Approaches door of room as . . .*)

(*Enter noiselessly and cautiously from room Pritchard, Silky, and Soapy. Pritchard and his confederates approach Oakhurst from behind, carrying lariat, or slip-noose.*)

OAKHURST: (*Listening at door.*) Good. At least I know from what quarter to expect the attack. Ah!

PRITCHARD: (*Throws slip-noose over Oakhurst from behind; Oakhurst puts his hand in his breast as the slip-noose is drawn across his bosom, pinioning one arm over his breast, and the other at his side. Silky and Soapy, directed by Pritchard, drag Oakhurst to chair facing front, and pinion his legs. Pritchard regarding him.*)

OAKHURST: (*Very coolly.*) You have left me my voice, I suppose, because it is useless.

PRITCHARD: That's so, pard. 'Twon't be no help to ye.

OAKHURST: Then you have killed Jackson.

PRITCHARD: Lord love ye, no! That ain't like us, pard! Jackson's tendin' door for us, and kinder lookin' out gin'rally for the boys. Thar's nothin' mean about Jackson.

SOAPY: No! Jackson's a squar man. Eh, Silky?

SILKY: Ez white a man[32] ez they is, pard!

OAKHURST: (*Aside.*) The traitor! (*Aloud.*) Well!

PRITCHARD: Well, you want ter know our business. Call upon a business man in business hours. Our little game is this, Mr. Jack Morton Alexander Oakhurst. When we was here the other night, we was wantin' a key to that theer lock (*pointing to vault*), and we sorter dropped in in passin' to get it.

OAKHURST: And suppose I refuse to give it up?

PRITCHARD: We were kalkilatin' on yer bein' even that impolite, wasn't we, boys?

SILKY AND SOAPY: We was that.

PRITCHARD: And so we got Mr. Jackson to take an impression of it in wax. Oh, he's a squar man—is Mr. Jackson!

SILKY: Jackson is a white man, Soapy!

SOAPY: They don't make no better men nor Jackson, Silky.

PRITCHARD: And we've got a duplicate key here. But we don't want any differences, pard: we only want a squar game. It seemed to us—some of your old pards as knew ye, Jack—that ye had a rather soft thing here, reformin' and we thought ye was kinder throwin' off the boys, not givin' 'em any hand in the game. But thar ain't anythin' mean about us. Eh, boys?

SOAPY: We is allers ready to chip in ekal[33] in the game. Eh, Silky?

SILKY: That's me, Soapy.

PRITCHARD: Ye see, the boys is free and open handed, Jack. And so the proposition we wanter make to ye, Jack, is this. It's reg'lar on the squar. We reckon, takin' Mr. Jackson's word—and thar ain't no man's word ez is better nor Jackson's—that there's nigh on to two-millions in that vault, not to speak of a little speshil de-posit o' York's, ez we learn from that accommodatin' friend, Mr. Jackson. We propose to share it with ye, on ekal terms—us five—countin' Jackson, a squar man. In course, we takes the risk o' packin' it away tonight comfortable. Ez your friends, Jack, we allow tis yer little arrangement to be a deuced sight easier for you than playin' Sandy Morton on a riglar salary, with the chance o' the real Sandy poppin' in upon ye any night.

OAKHURST: It's a lie. Sandy is dead.

PRITCHARD: In course, in course! That is your little game! But we kalkilated, Jack, even on that, on yer bein' rambunktious and contrary, and so we went ter Red Gulch, and found Sandy. Ye know I take a kind o' interest in Sandy; he's the second husband of my wife, the woman you run away with, pard. But thar's nothin' mean about me! eh, boys?

SILKY: No! he's the forgivingest kind of a man, is Pritchard.

SOAPY: That's so, Silky.

PRITCHARD: And thinkin' ye might be dubious, we filled Sandy about full o' rye whiskey, and brought him along, and one of our pards is preambulatin' the streets with him, ready to bring him on call.

OAKHURST: It's a lie, Pritchard—a cowardly lie!

PRITCHARD: Is it? Hush!

SANDY: (*Without singing.*)—

    Oh, yer's yer Sandy Morton,
      Drink him down!
    Oh, yer's yer Sandy Morton,
      Drink him down!
    Oh, yer's yer Sandy Morton,
      All alive and just a-snortin'!
    Oh, yer's yer Sandy Morton,
      Drink him down!

PRITCHARD: We don't propose to run him in yer, 'cept we're took, or yer unaccommodatin' to the boys.

OAKHURST: And if I refuse?

PRITCHARD: Why, we'll take what we can get, and we'll leave Sandy Morton with you yer, to sorter alleviate the old man's feelin's over the loss of his money. There's nothin' mean about us; no! eh, boys? (*Going toward safe.*)

OAKHURST: Hear me a moment, Henry Pritchard. (*Pritchard stops abreast of Oakhurst.*) Four years ago you were assaulted in the Arcade Saloon in Sacramento. You would have been killed, but your assailant suddenly fell dead by a pistol-shot fired from some unknown hand. I stood twenty feet from you with folded arms, but that shot was fired by me—me, Henry Pritchard—through my clothes, from a derringer hidden in my waistcoat! Understand me, I do not ask your gratitude now. But that pistol is in my right hand and now covers you. Make a single motion—of a muscle—and it is your last.

PRITCHARD: (*Motionless, but excitedly.*) You dare not fire! No, dare not! A shot here will bring my pal and Sandy Morton to confront you. You will have killed me to save exposure, have added murder to imposture! You have no witness to this attempt!

CAPPER: (*Opening door of room at the same moment that two policemen appear at door center, and two at other room.*) You are wrong: he has five (*Crossing to Silky and Soapy and laying his hands on their shoulders.*), and, if I mistake not, he has two more in these gentlemen, whom I know, and who will be quite as willing to furnish the necessary State's evidence of the robbery as of the fact that they never knew any other Alexander Morton than the gentleman who sits in that chair.

SOAPY: That's so, Silky.

SILKY: That's so, Soapy.

CAPPER: (*To policemen.*) Take them away.

(*Exit policemen with Pritchard, Soapy, and Silky.*)

(*Capper unbinds Oakhurst.*)

OAKHURST: Then I have to thank you, Mr. C.

CAPPER: Yes! "A man of ridiculous theories, but well meaning, brave, and honest." No, sir; don't apologize: you were right, Mr. Oakhurst. It is I who owe *you* an apology. I came here, believing *you* were the robber, having no faith in you or your reformation, expecting,—yes, sir,—hoping, to detect you in the act. Hear me! From the hour you first entered the bank, I have shadowed your every movement; I have been the silent witness of all that has passed in this room. You have played a desperate game, Mr. Oakhurst, but I'll see you through it. If you are true to your resolve, for the next six days, I will hold these wretches silent. I will protect your imposture with the strong arm of the law. I don't like *your* theories, sir, but I believe you to be well-meaning, and I know you to be brave and honest.

OAKHURST: (*Grasping his hand.*) I shall not forget this. But Sandy—

CAPPER: I will put my men on his track and have him brought quietly here. I can give you no aid beyond that. As an honorable man, I need not tell you your duty. Settle it with *him* as best you can.

OAKHURST: You are right; I *will* see him! (*Aside.*) Unless he has changed, he will listen to me; he will obey me.

CAPPER: Hush! (*Blows out candle.*) Stand here!

(*Capper and Oakhurst retreat to wing, as enter Morton, Sr., from his room.*)

MORTON: The private door open, the room dark, and Capper gone. I don't like this. The more I think of the mystery of that man's manner this morning, the more it seems to hide some terrible secret I must fathom! There are watches here. (*Strikes a light, as Capper draws Oakhurst, struggling, back into shadow.*) What's this? (*Picking up key.*) The key of the vault. A chair overturned. (*Touches bell.*) No answer! Jackson gone! My God! A terrible suspicion haunts me! No. Hush! (*Retreats to private room as other door opens and—*)

(*Enter Sandy.*)

SANDY: (*Drunkenly.*) Shoo! Shoo! boys, whar are ye, boys, eh? Pritchard, Silky, Soapy! Whar are ye, boys?

MORTON: (*Aside.*) A crime has been committed, and here is one of the gang. God has delivered him into my hands. (*Draws revolver and fires, as Oakhurst breaks from Capper, and strikes Morton's pistol. Capper at same moment seizes Sandy and drags him in room. Morton and Oakhurst struggle to center.*)

MORTON: (*Relaxing hold of Oakhurst.*) Alexander! Good God! Why are you here? Why have you stepped between me and retribution? You hesitate. God in heaven! Speak, Alexander, my son, speak for God's sake! Tell me—tell me that this detective's suspicions are not true. Tell me that you are not—not—no, I cannot say it. Speak, Alexander Morton, I command you! Who is this man you have saved? Is it—is it—your accomplice?

OAKHURST: (*Sinking at his feet.*) Don't ask me! You know not what you ask. I implore you—

CAPPER: (*Appearing quietly from room and locking door behind him.*) Your son has acted under *my* orders. The man he has saved, as he has saved you, was a *decoy*—one of my policemen.

(*Tableau: Capper, Morton, Oakhurst. Curtain.*)

END OF ACT III

ACT IV

SCENE 1: *Mr. Morton's villa, Russian Hill. Night. Oakhurst's bedroom. Sofa in alcove center, door in flat, left. Sandy Morton discovered, unconscious, lying on sofa; Oakhurst standing at his head, two policemen at his feet. Candles on table, left.*

OAKHURST: That will do. You are sure he was unconscious as you brought him in?

1ST POLICEMAN: Sure, sir? He hasn't known anything since we picked him up on the sidewalk outside the bank.

OAKHURST: Good! You have fulfilled your orders well, and your chief shall know it. Go now. Be as cautious in going out as you were on entering. Here is the private staircase. (*Opens door.*) (*Exit policemen.*)

OAKHURST: (*Listening.*) Gone! and without disturbing any one. So far, luck has befriended me. He will sleep tonight beneath his father's roof. His father! umph! would the old man recognize him here? Would he take to his heart this drunken outcast, picked from the gutters of the street and brought here by the strong arm of the law? Hush! (*A knock without.*) Ah, it is the colonel; he is prompt to the hour. (*Opens door cautiously, and admits Col. Starbottle.*)

STARBOTTLE: (*Looking around, and overlooking Sandy.*) I presume the other— er—principal is not yet on the ground?

OAKHURST: (*Motioning to sofa.*) He is!

STARBOTTLE: (*Starting as he looks toward sofa.*) Ged, you don't mean to say it's all *over*, without witnesses, without my—er—presence?

OAKHURST: Pardon me, Colonel Starbottle, but if you look again, you will perceive that the gentleman is only a drunk.

STARBOTTLE: Eh? Ged, not uncommon, sir, not uncommon! I remember singular incident at—er—Louisville in '47. Old Judge Tollim—know old Judge Tolly?— Ged! he came to ground drunk, sir; couldn't stand! Demn me, sir, had to put him into position with kitchen poker down his back, and two sections of lightning-rod in his—er—trousers, demn me! Firm, sir, firm, you understand, here (*Striking his breast.*), but—here (*Striking his legs.*)—er—er—wobbly! No, sir! Intoxication of principal not a bar, sir, to personal satisfaction! (*Goes toward sofa with eyeglass.*) Good Ged! why it's Diego! (*Returning stiffly, to Oakhurst.*) Excuse me, sir, but this is a case in which I cannot act. Cannot, sir—impossible! absurd! pre—post—er—ous! I recognize in the—er—inebriated menial on yonder sofa, a person, sir, who, having already declined my personal challenge, is—er—excluded from the consideration of gentlemen. The person who lies there, sir, is Diego—a menial of Don Jose Castro,—alias "Sandy," the vagabond of Red Gulch.

OAKHURST: You have omitted one title, his true one. He is Alexander Morton, son of the master of this house.

STARBOTTLE: (*Starting in bewilderment.*) Alexander Morton! (*Aside.*) Ged! my first suspicions were correct. Star, you have lost the opportunity of making your fortune as a scoundrel, but you have, at a pecuniary sacrifice, preserved your honor.

OAKHURST: Yes. Hear me, Colonel Starbottle. I have summoned you here tonight, as I have already intimated, on an affair of honor. I have sought you as my father's legal counsel, as a disinterested witness, as a gentleman of honor. The man who lies before you was once my friend and partner. I have wronged him doubly. As his partner, I ran away with the woman he believed, and still believes, to be his wife; as his friend, I have for a twelvemonth kept him from the enjoyment of his home, his patrimony, by a shameful deception. I have summoned you tonight to witness my confession; as a lawyer, to arrange those details necessary to restore to him his property; as a man of honor, to receive from me whatever retribution he demands. You will be a witness to our interview. Whatever befalls me here, you will explain to Mr. Morton—to Jovita—that I accepted it as a man and did not avoid here or elsewhere the penalty of my crime. (*Folding his arms.*)

STARBOTTLE: Umph! The case is, as you say, a delicate one, but not—not—peculiar. No, sir, Ged! sir, I remember Tom Marshall—know Tom Marshall of Kentucky?—said to me, "Star!"—always calls me Star—"how in blank, sir, can you remember the *real* names of your clients?"—"Why," says I, "Tom"—always called him Tom—"yesterday I was called to make a will—most distinguished family of Virginia—as lawyer and gentleman, you understand; can't mention name. Waited for signature—most distinguished name; Ged, sir, man signed Bloggins,—Peter Bloggins. Fact, demme! 'Mistake,' I said,—'excitement; exaltation of fever. *Non compos*. Compose yourself, Bob.'—'Star,' he said,—always called me Star—'for forty-seven years I have been an impostor!' —his very words, sir. 'I am not—' you understand, 'I *am* Peter Bloggins!' "

OAKHURST: But, my dear colonel, I—

STARBOTTLE: (*Loftily.*) Say no more, sir! I accept the —er—position. Let us see! The gentleman will, on recognition, probably make a personal attack. You are armed. Ah, no? Umph! On reflection I would not permit him to strike a single blow; I would anticipate it. It would provoke the challenge from him, leaving *you*, sir, the—er—choice of weapons.

OAKHURST: Hush! he is moving! Take your stand here, in this alcove. Remember, as a gentleman and a man of honor, Colonel Starbottle, I trust you not to interfere between the injured man and—justice! (*Pushes Col. Starbottle into alcove behind couch and approaches Sandy.*)

SANDY: (*Waking slowly—and incoherently.*) Hush, Silky! Hush! Eh? Oh, hush yourself! (*Sings.*)

Oh, yer's yer Sandy Morton,
  Drink him down!

Eh! Oh! (*Half sits up on couch.*) Where the devil am I?

OAKHURST: (*Advancing and leaning over Sandy's couch.*) In the house of your father, Alexander Morton.

SANDY: (*Recoiling in astonishment.*) His voice, John Oakhurst! What—ah! (*Rises, and rushes towards Oakhurst with uplifted hand.*)

STARBOTTLE: (*Gesticulating in whisper.*) A blow! a single blow would be sufficient.

SANDY: (*Looking at Oakhurst, who regards him calmly.*) I—eh! I—eh! Ha, ha! I'm glad to see—old pard! I'm glad to see ye! (*Col. Starbottle lifts his hand in amazement.*)

OAKHURST: (*Declining his hand.*) Do you understand me, Sandy Morton? Listen. I am John Oakhurst—the man who has deceived your father, who has deceived you.

SANDY: (*Without heeding his words, but regarding him affectionately.*) To think of it—Jack Oakhurst! It's like him, like Jack. He was allers onsartain, the darned little cuss! Jack! Look at him, will ye, boys? look at him! Growed too, and dressed to kill, and sittin' in this yer house as natril as a jay-bird! (*Looking around.*) Nasty, ain't it, Jack? And this yer's your house—the old man's house—eh? Why, this is—this is where she came. Jack! Jack! (*Eagerly.*) Tell me, pard—where is she?

STARBOTTLE: (*Aside, rubbing his hands.*) We shall have it now!

OAKHURST: She has gone—gone! But hear me! She had deceived you as she has me. She has gone—gone with her first husband, Henry Pritchard.

SANDY: (*Stupefied.*) Gone! Her first husband! Pritchard!

OAKHURST: Ay, your wife!

SANDY: Oh, damn my wife! I'm talking of Mary—Miss Mary—the little school-ma'am, Jack; the little rose of Poker Flat. Oh! I see—ye didn't know her, Jack—the pertiest, sweetest little—

OAKHURST: (*Turnign away coldly.*) Ay, ay! She is here!

SANDY: (*Looking after him affectionately.*) Look at him, boys! Allers the same—high-toned, cold, even to his pardner! That's him—Jack Oakhurst! But Jack, Jack, you're goin' to shake hands, ain't ye? (*Extends his hand after a pause. Oakhurst takes it gloomily.*)

STARBOTTLE: (*Who has been regarding interview with visible scorn and disgust, advancing to Oakhurst.*) You will—er—pardon me if, under the—er—circumstances, I withdraw from this—er—disgraceful proceeding. The condonation, by that man, of two of the most tremendous offenses to society and to the code, without apology or satisfaction, Ged, sir, is—er—er—of itself an insult to the spectator. I go, sir—

OAKHURST: But, Colonel Starbottle—

STARBOTTLE: Permit me to say, sir, that I hold myself for this, sir, responsible, sir —personally responsible. (*Exit Starbottle, glancing furiously at Sandy, who sinks on sofa laughing.*)

OAKHURST: (*Aside.*) He will change his mind in half an hour. But, in the meantime, time is precious. (*Aloud.*) Sandy, come!

SANDY: (*Rising with alacrity.*) Yes, Jack, I'm ready.

OAKHURST: We are going (*Slowly and solemnly.*)—we are going to see your father.

SANDY: (*Dropping back with bashful embarrassment and struggling to release his arm from Oakhurst.*) No, Jack! Not just yet, Jack; in a little while, ol' boy! In about six months, or mebbe—a year, Jack. Not now, not now! I ain't feelin' exactly well, Jack—I ain't.

OAKHURST: Nonsense, Sandy! Consider your duty and my honor.

SANDY: (*Regaining his seat.*) That's all very well, Jack, but ye see, pard, you've known the old man for night on a year, and it's twenty-five since I met him. No, Jack; you don't play any ol' man on to me tonight, Jack. No, you and me'll just drop out for a *pasear*—Jack, eh? (*Taking Oakhurst's arm.*) Come!

OAKHURST: Impossible! Hush! (*Listening.*) It is *he* passing through the corridor. (*Goes to wing and listens.*)

SANDY: (*Crowding hastily behind Oakhurst in alarm.*) But, I say, Jack! he won't come in here? He's goin' to bed, you know. Eh? It ain't right for a man o' his years—and he must be goin' on ninety, Jack—to be up like this. It ain't healthy.

OAKHURST: You know him not. He seems to need no rest. (*Sadly.*) Night after night, long after the servants are abed, and the house is still, I hear that step slowly pacing the corridor. It is the last sound as I close my eyes, the first challenge of the morning.

SANDY: The ol' scound— (*Checking himself.*)—I mean, Jack, the ol' man has suthin' on his mind. But, Jack (*In great alarm.*), he don't waltz in upon ye, Jack? He don't p'int them feet in yer, Jack? Ye ain't got to put up with that, Jack, along o' yer other trials?

OAKHURST: He often seeks me here. Ah—yes—he is coming this way now.

SANDY: (*In ludicrous terror.*) Jack, pard, quick! hide me somewhere, Jack!

OAKHURST: (*Opening door.*) In there, quick! Not a sound, as you value your future! (*Exit Sandy hurriedly.*)

SCENE 2: *The same. Enter Old Morton, in dressing-gown with candle.*

OLD MORTON: Not abed yet, Alexander? Well, well, I don't blame you, my son; it has been for you a trying, trying night. Yes, I see: like me, you are a little nervous and wakeful. (*Slowly takes chair and comfortably composes himself.*)

OAKHURST: (*Aside.*) He is in for a midnight gossip. How shall I dispose of Sandy?

OLD MORTON: Ay. I heard voices, and saw a light in your window. I came to tell you, Alexander, Capper has explained all about—about the decoy! More; he has told me of your courage and your invaluable assistance. For a moment, sir—I don't mind telling you now in confidence—I doubted *you*—

OAKHURST: (*In feigned deprecation.*) Oh, sir!

OLD MORTON: Only for a moment. You will find, Alexander, that even that doubt shall have full apology when the year of your probation has expired. Besides, sir, I know all.

OAKHURST: (*Starting.*) All!

OLD MORTON: Yes, the story about the Duchess and your child. You are surprised. Colonel Starbottle told me all. I forgive you, Alexander, for the sake of your boy.

OAKHURST: My boy, sir!

OLD MORTON: Yes, your boy. And let me tell you, sir, he's a fine young fellow. Looks like you—looks as you did when *you* were a boy. He's a Morton too, every inch of him, there's no denying that. No, sir. *You* may have changed, but he—he—is the living image of my little Alexander. He took to me, too—lifted his little arms—and—and—(*Becomes affected and leans his head in his hands.*)

OAKHURST: (*Rising.*) You are not well, sir. Let me lead you to your room.

OLD MORTON: No! It is nothing: a glass of water, Alexander.

OAKHURST: (*Aside.*) He is very pale. The agitation of the night has overcome him. (*Goes to table.*) A little spirits will revive him. (*Pours from decanter in glass and returns to Morton.*)

OLD MORTON: (*After drinking.*) There was spirits in that water, Alexander. Five years ago, I vowed at your mother's grave to abandon the use of intoxicating liquors.

OAKHURST: Believe me, sir, my mother will forgive you.

OLD MORTON: Doubtless. It has revived me. I am getting to be an old man, Aleck. (*Holds out his glass half unconciously and Oakhurst replenishes it from decanter.*) Yes, an old man, Aleck, but the boy—ah, I live again in him. The little rascal! He asked me, Aleck, for a "chaw tobacker"[34] and wanted to know if I was the "ol' duffer." Ha, ha! He did. Ha, ha! Come, come, don't be despondent. I was like you once, damn it—ahem—it's all for the best, my boy, all for the best. I'll take the young rascal—(*Aside.*) damn it, he's already taken me—(*Aloud.*) on equal terms. There, Aleck, what do you say?

OAKHURST: Really, sir, this forbearance—this kindness—(*Aside.*) I see a ray of light.

OLD MORTON: Nonsense! I'll take the boy, I tell you, and do well for him—the little rascal!—as if he were the legal heir. But, I say, Aleck (*Laughing.*), ha, ha!—what about—ha, ha!—what about Dona Jovita, eh? And what about Don Jose Castro, eh? (*Poking Oakhurst in the ribs.*) What will the Don say to the family succession? Ha, ha!

OAKHURST: (*Proudly.*) Really, sir, I care but little.

OLD MORTON: (*Aside.*) Oh, ho! I'll sound him. (*Aloud.*) Look ye, Alexander, I have given my word to you and Don Jose Castro, and I'll keep it. But if you can do any better, eh—if—eh?—the schoolma'am's a mightly pretty girl and a bright one, eh, Aleck? And it's all in the family—eh? And she thinks well of you, and I will say, for a girl brought up as she's been, and knowin' your relations with the Duchess and the boy, to say a kind word for ye, Aleck, is a good sign—you follow me, Aleck—if you think—why, old Don Jose might whistle for a son-in-law, eh?

OAKHURST: (*Interrupting indignantly.*) Sir! (*Aside.*) Stop! (*Aloud.*) Do you mean to say, sir, that if I should consent to this—suggestion—that, if the lady were willing, *you* would offer no impediment?

OLD MORTON: Impediment, my dear boy! you should have my blessing.

OAKHURST: Pardon me a moment. You have in the last year, sir, taught me the importance of business formality in all the relations of life. Following that idea, the conditions of my engagement with Jovita Castro were drawn up with your hand. Are you willing to make this recantation as formal, this new contract as business-like and valid?

OLD MORTON: (*Eagerly.*) I am.

OAKHURST: Then sit here and write at my dictation. (*Pointing to table. Old Morton takes seat at table.*) "In view of the evident preferences of my son Alexander Morton, and of certain family interests, I hereby revoke my consent to his marriage with the Dona Jovita Castro, and accord him full permission to woo and win his cousin, Miss Mary Morris, promising him the same aid and assistance previously offered in his suit with Miss Castro."

OLD MORTON: (*Signing.*) Alexander Morton, Sr. There, Aleck! You have forgotten one legal formality. We have no witness. Ha, ha!

OAKHURST: (*Significantly.*) *I* will be a sufficient witness.

OLD MORTON: Ha, ha! (*Fills glass from decanter, after which Oakhurst quietly removes decanter beyond his reach.*) Very good! Aleck, I've been thinking of a plan—I've been thinking of retiring from the bank. I'm getting old, and my ways are not the popular ways of business here. I've been thinking of you, you dog—of leaving the bank to you—to you, sir—eh—the day you marry the schoolma'am—eh. I'll stay home and take care of the boy—eh—hic! The little rascal!—lifted his arms to me—did, Aleck! by God! (*Incoherently.*) Eh!

OAKHURST: Hush! (*Aside.*) Sandy will overhear him, and appear.

OLD MORTON: (*Greatly affected by liquor.*) Hush! eh!—of course—shoo! shoo! (*The actor will here endeavor to reproduce in Old Morton's drunken behavior, without exactly imitating him, the general characteristics of his son's intoxication.*) Eh—I say, Aleck, old boy! what will the Don say? Eh? Ha, ha, ha! And Jovita, that firebrand, how will she—hic—like it, eh? (*Laughs immoderately.*)

OAKHURST: Hush! We will be overheard! The servants, sir!

OLD MORTON: Damn the servants! Don't I—hic—pay them wages—eh?

OAKHURST: Let me lead you to your own room. You are nervously excited. A little rest, sir, will do you good. (*Taking his arm.*)

OLD MORTON: No, shir, no shir, 'm nerrer goin' to bed any more. Bed's bad habit! —hic—drunken habit. Lesh stay up all ni', Aleck! You and me! Lesh nev'r—go—bed any more! Whar's whiskey—eh? (*Staggers to the table for decanter, as Oakhurst seizes him, struggles up stage, and then Old Morton, in struggle, falls helplessly on sofa, in same attitude as Sandy was discovered.*)

(*Enter Sandy cautiously.*)

SANDY: (*To Oakhurst.*) Jack! Eh, Jack—
OAKHURST: Hush! Go! I will follow you in a moment! (*Pushes him back to door.*)
SANDY: (*Catching sight of Old Morton.*) Hallo! What's up?
OAKHURST: Nothing. He was overtaken with a sudden faintness. He will revive presently: go!
SANDY: (*Hesitating.*) I say, Jack, he wasn't taken sick along o'me, eh, Jack?
OAKHURST: No! No! But go. (*Pushing him toward door.*)
SANDY: Hold on: I'm going. But, Jack, I've got a kind of faintness yer, too. (*Goes to side-table and takes up decanter.*) And thar's nothing reaches that faintness like whiskey. (*Fills glass.*)
OLD MORTON: (*Drunkenly and half consciously from couch.*) Whiskey—who shed —whiskey—eh? Eh—O—gim'me some, Aleck—Aleck, my son,—my son!— my old prodigal—Old Proddy, my boy—gim'me—whiskey—(*Sings:*)

Oh, yer's yer good old whiskey,
  Drink it down!

Eh? I com—mand you—pass the whiskey!

(*Sandy, at first panic-stricken, and them remorsefully conscious, throws glass down, with gesture of fear and loathing. Oakhurst advances to his side hurriedly.*)

OAKHURST: (*In hurried whisper.*) Give him the whiskey, quick! It will keep him quiet. (*Is about to take decanter, when Sandy seizes it; struggle with Oakhurst.*)
SANDY: (*With feeling.*) No, no, Jack, no! (*Suddenly, with great strength and determination, breaks from him, and throws decanter from window.*) No, never!
OLD MORTON: (*Struggling drunkenly to his feet.*) Eh—who shed never? (*Oakhurst shoves Sandy in room and follows him, closing door.*) Eh, Aleck? (*Groping.*) Eh, where'sh light? All gone. (*Lapses on sofa again, after an ineffectual struggle to get up, and then resumes his old attitude.*)

(*Changes scene quickly.*)

SCENE 3. *Ante-room in Mr. Morton's villa. Front scene. Enter Don Jose Castro and Concho, preceded by servant.*

SERVANT: This way, gentlemen.
DON JOSE: Carry this card to Alexander Morton, Sr.
SERVANT: Beg pardon, sir, but there's only one name here, sir. (*Looking at Concho.*)
DON JOSE: (*Proudly.*) That is my servant, sir. (*Exit servant.*)
DON JOSE: (*Aside.*) I don't half like this business. But my money locked up in his bank, and my daughter's hand bound to his son, demand it. (*Aloud.*) This is no child's play, Concho, you understand.
CONCHO: Ah! I am wise. Believe me, if I have not proofs which shall blanch the cheek of this old man, I am a fool Don Jose!

(*Re-enter Servant.*)

SERVANT: Mr. Morton, Sr. passed a bad night and has left word not to be disturbed this morning. But Mr. Morton, Jr. will attend you, sir.

CONCHO: (*Aside.*) So the impostor will face it out. Well, let him come.

DON JOSE: (*To Servant.*) I await his pleasure. (*Exit Servant.*)

DON JOSE: You hear, Concho? You shall face this man. I shall repeat to him all you have told me. If you fail to make good your charge, on your head rests the consequences.

CONCHO: He will of course deny. He is a desperate man; he will perhaps attack me. Eh! Ah! (*Drawing revolver.*)

DON JOSE: Put up your foolish weapon. The sight of the father he has deceived will be more terrible to him than the pistol of the spy.

(*Enter Col. Starbottle.*)

STARBOTTLE: Mr. Alexander Morton, Jr., will be with you in a moment. (*Takes attitude by door, puts his hand in his breast, and inflates himself.*)

CONCHO: (*To Don Jose, aside.*) It is the bullying lawyer. They will try to outface us, my patron, but we shall triumph. (*Aloud.*) He comes, eh!—Mr. Alexander Morton, gentlemen. I will show you a cheat, an impostor!

(*Enter, in correct, precise morning dress, Sandy Morton. There is in his make-up and manner a suggestion of the father.*)

CONCHO: (*Recoiling, aside.*) Diego! The real son! (*Aloud, furiously.*) It is a trick to defeat justice,—eh!—a miserable trick! But it shall fail!

STARBOTTLE: Permit me, a moment,—a single moment. (*To Concho.*) You have —er—er—characterized my introduction of this—er—gentleman as a "cheat" and an "imposture." Are you prepared to deny that this is Alexander Morton?

DON JOSE: (*Astonished, aside.*) These Americanos are of the Devil! (*Aloud and sternly.*) Answer him, Concho, I command you.

CONCHO: (*In half-insane rage.*) It is Alexander Morton, but it is a trick,—a cowardly trick! Where is the other impostor, this Mr. John Oakhurst?

SANDY: (*Advancing with dignity and something of his father's cold manner.*) He will answer for himself when called for. (*To Don Jose.*) You have asked for me, sir; may I inquire your business?

CONCHO: Eh! It is a trick,—a trick!

DON JOSE: (*To Concho.*) Silence, sir! (*To Sandy, with dignity.*) I know not the meaning of this masquerade. I only know that your are *not* the gentleman hitherto known to me as the son of Alexander Morton. I am here, sir, to demand my rights as a man of property and a father. I have received this morning a check from the house of Morton & Son, for the amount of my deposit with them. So far—in view of this complication—it is well. Who knows? Bueno! But the signature of Morton & Son to the check is not in the handwriting I have known. Look at it, sir. (*To Sandy, handing check.*)

SANDY: (*Examining check.*) It is my handwriting, sir, and was signed this morning. Has it been refused?

DON JOSE: Pardon me, sir. It has not been presented. With this doubt in my mind, I preferred to submit it first to you.

STARBOTTLE: A moment, a single moment, sir. While as a—er—gentleman and a man of honor, I—er—appreciate your motives, permit me to say, sir, as a lawyer, that your visit is premature. On the testimony of your own witness, the identification of Mr. Alexander Morton, Jr., is—er—complete; he has admitted the signature as his own; you have not yet presented the check to the bank.

DON JOSE: Pardon me, Colonel Starbottle. It is not all. (*To Sandy.*) By a written agreement with Alexander Morton, Sr., the hand of my daughter is promised to his son, who now stands before me, as my former servant, dismissed from my service for drunkenness.

SANDY: That agreement is revoked.

DON JOSE: Revoked!

SANDY: (*Handing paper.*) Cast your eyes over that paper. At least you will recognize *that* signature.

DON JOSE: (*Reads.*) "In view of the evident preferences of my son Alexander Morton, and of certain family interests, I hereby revoke my consent to his marriage with the Dona Jovita Castro, and accord him full permission to woo and win his cousin, Miss Mary Morris; promising him the same aid and assistance previously offered in his suit with Miss Castro.—Alexander Morton, Sr."

CONCHO: Ah! Carramba! Do you not see the trick—eh, the conspiracy? It was this man, as Diego, your daughter's groom, helped his friend Mr. Oakhurst to the heiress. Ah, you comprehend! It was an old trick! You shall see, you shall see! Ah! I am wise, I am wise.

DON JOSE: (*Aside.*) Could I have been deceived? But no! This paper that releases *him* gives the impostor no claim.

SANDY: (*Resuming his old easy manner, dropping his formality, and placing his hand on Don Jose's shoulder.*) Look yar, ole man; I didn't allow to ever see ye agin, and this yer ain't none o' *my* seekin'. But since ye're here, I don't mind tellin' ye that but for me that gal of yours would have run away a year ago and married an unknown lover. And I don't mind adding, that hed I known that unknown lover was my friend John Oakhurst, I'd have helped her do it. (*Going.*) Good morning, Don Jose.

DON JOSE: Insolent! I shall expect an account for this from your—father, sir.

SANDY: Adios, Don Jose. (*Exit.*)

CONCHO: It is a trick—I told you. Ah, I am wise. (*Going to Don Jose.*)

DON JOSE: (*Throwing him off.*) Fool! (*Exit Don Jose.*)

CONCHO: (*Infuriated.*) Eh! Fool yourself—dotard! No matter: I will expose all—ah! I will see Jovita—I will revenge myself on this impostor! (*Is about to follow, when Col. Starbottle leaves his position by the door and touches Concho on the shoulder.*)

STARBOTTLE: Excuse me.

CONCHO: Eh?

STARBOTTLE: You have forgotten something.

CONCHO: Something?

STARBOTTLE: An apology, sir. You were good enough to express—er—incredulity —when I presented Mr. Morton; you were kind enough to characterize the conduct of my—er—principal by—an epithet. You have alluded to me, sir,—ME—

CONCHO: (*Wrathfully.*) Bully! (*Aside.*) I have heard that this pomposo, this braggart, is a Yankee trick too; that he has the front of a lion, the liver of a chicken. (*Aloud.*) Yes, I have said, you hear I have said, I, Concho (*striking his breast*), have said you are a—bully!

STARBOTTLE: (*Coolly.*) Then you are prepared to give me satisfaction, sir,—personal satisfaction.

CONCHO: (*Raging.*) Yes, sir, now—you understand, now (*taking out pistol*), anywhere, here! Yes, here. Ah! you start,—yes, here and now! Face to face, you understand, without seconds,—face to face. So! (*Presenting pistol.*)

STARBOTTLE: (*Quietly.*) Permit me to—er—apologize.

CONCHO: Ah! It is too late!

STARBOTTLE: (*Interrupting.*) Excuse me, but I feared you would not honor me so completely and satisfactorily. Ged, sir, I begin to respect you! I accede to all your propositions of time and position. The pistol you hold in your hand is a derringer, I presume, loaded. Ah—er—I am right. The one I now produce (*showing pistol*) is—er—as you will perceive the same size and pattern, and—er—unloaded. We will place them both, so, under the cloth of this table. You shall draw one pistol, I will take the other. I will put that clock at ten minutes to nine, when we will take our positions across this table; as you—er—happily express it, "face to face." As the clock strikes the hour, we will fire on the second stroke.

CONCHO: (*Aside.*) It is a trick, a Yankee trick! (*Aloud.*) I am ready. Now—at once!

STARBOTTLE: (*Gravely.*) Permit me, sir, to thank you. Your conduct, sir, reminds me of singular incident—

CONCHO: (*Angrily interrupting.*) Come, come! It is no child's play. We have much of this talk, eh! It is action, eh, you comprehend—action.

(*Starbottle places pistol under the cloth, and sets clock. Concho draws pistol from cloth; Starbottle takes remaining pistol. Both men assume position, presenting their weapons; Starbottle pompously but seriously, Concho angrily and nervously.*)

STARBOTTLE: (*After a pause.*) One moment, a single moment—

CONCHO: Ah, a trick! Coward! you cannot destroy my aim.

STARBOTTLE: I overlook the—er—epithet. I wished only to ask, if you should be—er—unfortunate, if there was anything I could say to your—er—friends.

CONCHO: You cannot make the fool of me, coward. No!

STARBOTTLE: My object was only precautionary. Owing to the position in which you—er—persist in holding your weapon, in a line with my right eye, I perceive that a ray of light enters the nipple, and—er—illuminates the barrel. I judge from this, that you have been unfortunate enough to draw the—er—er—unloaded pistol.

CONCHO: (*Tremulously lowering weapon.*) Eh! Ah! This is murder! (*Drops pistol.*) Murder!—eh—help (*retreating*), help! (*Exit hurriedly door center, as clock strikes. Col. Starbottle lowers his pistol, and moves with great pomposity to the other side of the table, taking up pistol.*)

STARBOTTLE: (*Examining pistol.*) Ah! (*Lifts it, and discharges it.*) It seems that I am mistaken. (*Going.*) The pistol *was*—er—loaded! (*Exit.*)

SCENE 4: *Front scene. Room in villa. Enter Miss Mary and Jovita.*

MISS MARY: I tell you, you are wrong. You are not only misunderstanding your lover, which is a woman's privilege, but you are abusing my cousin, which, as his relative, I won't put up with.

JOVITA: (*Passionately.*) But hear me, Miss Mary. It is a year since we were betrothed; and such a betrothal! Why, I was signed, sealed, and delivered to him, on conditions, as if I were part of the rancho; and the very night, too, I had engaged to run away with him! And during that year, I have seen the gentleman twice,—yes, twice!

MISS MARY: But he has written?

JOVITA: Mother of God! Yes,—letters delivered by my father, sent to *his care*, read by him first, of course; letters hoping that I was well and obeying my father's commands; letters assuring me of his unaltered devotion; letters that, compared with the ones he used to hide in the confessional of the ruined mission church, were as ice to fire, were as that snow-flower you value so much, Mary, to this mariposa blossom I wear in my hair. And then to think that this man—this John Oakhurst, as I knew him; this man who used to ride twenty miles for a smile from me on the church porch; this Don Juan, who leaped that garden wall (fifteen feet, Mary, if it is an inch), and made old Concho his stepping-stone; this man, who daily periled death for my sake—is changed into this formal, methodical man of business—is—is—I tell you there's a *woman* at the bottom of it! I know it sure!

MISS MARY: (*Aside.*) How can I tell her about the Duchess? I won't! (*Aloud.*) But listen, my dear Jovita. You know he is under probation for you, Jovita. All this is for you. His father is cold, methodical, unsympathetic. *He* looks only to his bond with this son—this son that he treats, even in matters of the heart, as a *business* partner. Remember, on his complete reformation, and subjection to his father's will, depends your hand. Remember the agreement!

JOVITA: The agreement; yes! It is the agreement, always the agreement. May the Devil fly away with the agreement! Look you, Miss Mary, I, Dona Jovita, didn't fall in love with an agreement: it was with a man! Why, I might have married a dozen agreements—yes, of a shorter limitation than this! (*Crossing.*)

MISS MARY: Yes. But what if your lover had failed to keep those promises by which he was to gain your hand? What if he were a man incapable of self-control? What if he were—a—a—drunkard!

JOVITA: (*Musing.*) A drunkard! (*Aside.*) There was Diego; he was a drunkard, but he was faithless. (*Aloud.*) You mean a weak, faithless drunkard?

MISS MARY: No! (*Sadly.*) Faithless only to himself, but devoted—yes, devoted to *you.*

JOVITA: Miss Mary, I have found that one big vice in a man is apt to keep out a great many smaller ones.

MISS MARY: Yes, but if he were a slave to liquor?

JOVITA: My dear, I should try to change his mistress. Oh, give me a man that is capable of a devotion to anything, rather than a cold, calculating average of all the virtues!

MISS MARY: (*Aside.*) I, who aspire to be her teacher, am only her pupil. (*Aloud.*)

But what if, in this very drunkenness, this recklessness, he had once loved and worshipped another woman? What if you discovered all this after—after—he had won your heart?

JOVITA: I should adore him! Ah, Miss Mary! Love differs from all the other contagious diseases: the last time a man is exposed to it, he takes it most readily, and has it the worst! But you, *you*, you cannot sympathize with me. You have some lover, the ideal of the virtues; some man as correct, as well regulated, as calm as—yourself; someone who addresses you in the fixed morality and severe penmanship of the copy-books. He will never precipitate himself over a garden wall or through a window. Your Jacob will wait for you through seven years and receive you from the hands of your cousin and guardian—as a reward of merit! No, you could not love a vagabond.

MISS MARY: (*Very slowly and quietly.*) No?

JOVITA: No! (*Passionately.*) No, it is impossible. Forgive me, Miss Mary: you are good; a better girl than I am. But think of me! A year ago my lover leaped a wall at midnight to fly with me; today, the day that gives me to him, he writes a few cold lines, saying that he has business, *business*—you understand—business, and that he shall not see me until we meet in the presence of—of—of—our fathers.

MISS MARY: Yes, but you will see him at least, perhaps alone. Listen: it is no formal meeting, but one of festivity. My guardian has told me, in his quaint scriptural way, it is the killing of the fatted calf, over his long lost prodigal. Have patience, little one. Ah! Jovita, we are of a different race, but we are of one sex, and as a woman I know how to accept another woman's abuse of her lover. Come, come! (*Exeunt Miss Mary and Jovita.*)

SCENE 5: *The drawing-room of Mr. Morton's villa. Large open arch in center, leading to veranda, looking on distant view of San Francisco; richly furnished— sofas, armchairs, and tete-a-tetes. Enter Col. Starbottle carrying bouquet, preceded by Servant, bowing.*

STARBOTTLE: Take my kyard to Miss Morris. (*Exit Servant.*) Star! This is the momentous epoch of your life! It is a moment for which you—are—I may say alone responsible—personally responsible! She will be naturally gratified by the—er—flowers. She will at once recognize this bouquet as a delicate souvenir of Red Gulch and will appreciate your recollection. And the fact, the crushing fact, that you have overlooked the—er—ungentlemanly conduct of her *own* cousin Sandy, the real Alexander Morton, that you have—er—assisted to restore the ex-vaquero to his rights, will—er—er—at once open the door to—er—mutual confidence and—er—a continuance of that—er—prepossession I have already noticed. Ahem! here she is.

(*Enter Miss Mary in full dress.*)

MISS MARY: You are early, Colonel Starbottle. This promptitude does honor to our poor occasion.

STARBOTTLE: Ged, Miss Mary, promptness with a lady and an adversary is the first duty of—er—gentlemen. I wished that—er—the morning dew might still be—er—fresh in these flowers. I gathered them myself (*presenting bouquet*) at er—er—flower stand in the—er—California market.

MISS MARY: (*Aside.*) Flowers! I needed no such reminder of poor Sandy. (*Aloud.*) I thank you, colonel.

STARBOTTLE: Ged, ma'am, I am repaid doubly. Your conduct, Miss Mary, reminds me of little incident that occurred at Richmond, in '53. Dinner party—came early—but obliged to go—as now—on important business, before dessert—before dessert. Lady sat next to me—beautiful woman—excuse me if I don't mention names—said to me, "Star,"—always called me Star,—"Star, you remind me of the month of May."—Ged, madam,"—I said, "delighted, proud, but why?"—"Because," she said, "you come in with the—er—oysters"—No! Ged, pardon me—ridiculous mistake! I mean—er—"you come in with the —er—flowers, and go before the—er—fruits."

MISS MARY: Ah, colonel! I appreciate her disappointment. Let us hope, however, that some day you may find that happy woman who will be able to keep you through the whole dinner and the whole season, until December and the ices!

STARBOTTLE: Ged! excellent! Capital! (*Seriously.*) Miss Mary! (*Suddenly inflating his chest, striking attitude, and gazing on Miss Mary with languishing eyes.*) There is—er—such a woman!

MISS MARY: (*Aside.*) What can he mean?

STARBOTTLE: (*Taking seat beside her.*) Allow me, Miss Mary, a few moments of confidential—er—confidential disclosure. Today is, as you are aware—the day on which, according to—er—agreement between parties, my friend and client Mr. Morton, Sr., formally accepts his prodigal son. It is my—er—duty to state that—er—the gentleman who has for the past year occupied that position has behaved with great discretion, and—er—fulfilled his part of the—er—agreement. But it would—er—appear that there has been a—er—slight delusion regarding the identity of that prodigal—a delusion shared by all the parties except, perhaps, myself. I have to prepare you for a shock. The gentleman whom you have recently known as Alexander Morton, Jr., is not the prodigal son; is not your—er—cousin; is, in fact, no relation to you. Prepare yourself, Miss Mary, for a little disappointment—for—er—degradation. The genuine son has been—er—discovered in the person of—er—low menial—er—vagabond— "Sandy," the—er—outcast of Red Gulch!

MISS MARY: (*Rising in astonishment.*) Sandy! Then he was right. (*Aside.*) The child is his, and that woman—

STARBOTTLE: Compose yourself, Miss Mary. I know the—er—effect of—er— revelation like this upon—er—proud and aristocratic nature. Ged! My own, I assure you, beats in—er—responsive indignation. You can never consent to remain beneath this roof, and—er—receive a—er—vagabond and—er—menial on equal terms. The—er—necessities of my—er—profession may—er—compel me, but you—er—never! Holding myself—er—er—responsible for having introduced you here, it is my—er—duty to provide you with—another home! It is my—er—duty to protect—

MISS MARY: (*Aside.*) Sandy here and beneath this roof! Why has he not sought me? Ah, I know too well: he dare not face me with his child!

STARBOTTLE: (*Aside.*) She turns away! It is maiden coyness. (*Aloud.*) If, Miss

Mary, the—er—devotion of a lifetime; if the—er—chivalrous and respectful adoration of a man—er—whose record is—er—not unknown in the Court of Honor (*dropping on one knee with excessive gallantry*); if the—er—measure—

MISS MARY: (*Oblivious of Col. Starbottle.*) I *will*—I *must* see him! Ah! (*looking left*) he is coming!

(*Enter Sandy.*)

STARBOTTLE: (*Rising with great readiness and tact.*) I have found it. (*Presenting flower.*) It had fallen beneath the sofa.

SANDY: (*To Miss Mary, stopping short in embarrassment.*) I did not know you—I —I thought there was no one here.

MISS MARY: (*To Starbottle.*) May I ask you to excuse me for a moment? I have a few words to say to—to my *cousin!*

(*Starbottle bows gallantly to Miss Mary, and stiffly to Sandy, and exits. A long pause; Miss Mary remains seated, pulling flowers; Sandy remains standing by wing, foolish and embarrassed. Business.*)

MISS MARY: (*Impatiently.*) Well?

SANDY: (*Slowly.*) I axes your pardon, miss, but you have told *that* gentleman you had a few words—to say to me.

MISS MARY: (*Passionately, aside.*) Fool! (*Aloud.*) I had, but I am waiting to first answer your inquiries about your—your—child. I have fulfilled my trust, sir.

SANDY: You have, Miss Mary, and I thank you.

MISS MARY: I might perhaps have expected that this revelation of our kinship would have come from other lips than a stranger's, but—no matter! I wish you joy, sir, of your heritage. (*Going.*) You have found a home, sir, at last, for yourself and—and—your child. Good-day, sir.

SANDY: Miss Mary!

MISS MARY: I must make ready to receive your father's guests. It is his orders; I am only his poor relation. Good-by, sir. (*Exit.*)

SANDY: (*Watching her.*) She is gone!—gone! No! She has dropped on the sofa in the ante-room and is crying. Crying! I promised Jack I wouldn't speak until the time came. I'll go back. (*Hesitating and looking toward left.*) Poor girl! How she must hate me! I might just say a word, one word to thank her for her kindness to Johnny—only one word, and then go away. I—I—can keep from liquor. I swore I would to Jack, that night I saw the old man—drunk,—and I have. But—I can't keep—from—her! No—damn it! (*Going toward left.*) No!—I'll go! (*Exit.*)

(*Enter hurriedly and excitedly Jovita, followed by Manuela.*)

JOVITA: Where is she? Where is *he?*—the traitor!

MANUELA: (*Entreatingly.*) Compose yourself, Dona Jovita, for the love of God! This is madness; believe me, there is some mistake. It is some trick of an enemy

—of that ingrate, that coyote, Concho, who hates the Don Alexandro.

JOVITA: A trick! Call you this a trick? Look at this paper, put into my hands by my father a moment ago. Read it. Ah! listen. (*Reads.*) "In view of the *evident preferences* of my son Alexander Morton, I hereby revoke my consent to his marriage with the Dona Jovita Castro, and accord him full permission to woo and win his cousin, Miss Mary Morris!" Call you this a trick, eh? No, it is their perfidy! This is why *she* was brought here on the eve of my betrothal. This accounts for his silence, his absence. Oh, I shall go mad!

MANUELA: Compose yourself, miss. If I am not deceived, there is one here who will aid us—who will expose this deceit. Listen: an hour ago, as I passed through the hall, I saw Diego, our old Diego—your friend and confidant, Diego.

JOVITA: The drunkard—the faithless Diego!

MANUELA: Never, Miss Jovita; not drunken! For as he passed before me, he was straight, as upright, as fine as your lover. Come, miss, we will seek him.

JOVITA: Never! He, too, is a traitor.

MANUELA: Believe me, no! Come, Miss Jovita. (*Looking toward left.*) See, he is there. Someone is with him.

JOVITA: (*Looking.*) You are right, and it is she—she, Miss Mary! What? he is kissing her hand! And she—she, the double traitress—drops her head upon his shoulder! Oh, this is infamy!

MANUELA: Hush! Someone is coming. The guests are arriving. They must not see you thus. This way, Miss Jovita—this way. After a little, a little, the mystery will be explained. (*Taking Jovita's hand, and leading her right.*)

JOVITA: (*Going.*) And this was the correct schoolmistress, the preceptress and example of all the virtues! ha! (*laughing hysterically*) ha! (*Exeunt Jovita and Manuela.*)

SCENE 6: *The same. Enter Servant; opens folding doors, revealing veranda, and view of distant city beyond. Stage, fog*[35] *effect from without. Enter Starbottle and Oakhurst in full evening dress.*

STARBOTTLE: (*Walking towards veranda.*) A foggy evening for our anniversary.

OAKHURST: Yes. (*Aside.*) It was such a night as this I first stepped into Sandy's place; I first met the old man. Well, it will be soon over. (*Aloud.*) You have the papers and transfers all ready?

STARBOTTLE: In my—er—pocket. Mr. Morton, Sr., should be here to receive his guests.

OAKHURST: He will be here presently; until then the duty devolves on me. He has secluded himself even from me! (*Aside.*) Perhaps it is in very shame for his recent weakness.

(*Enter Servant.*)

SERVANT: Don Jose Castro, Miss Castro, and Miss Morris.

(*Enter Don Jose with Jovita and Miss Mary on either arm. All formally salute Mr.*

Oakhurst, except Miss Jovita, who turns coldly away, taking seat remotely on sofa. Col. Starbottle gallantly approaches Miss Mary and takes seat beside her.)

OAKHURST: (*Aside.*) They are here to see my punishment. There is no sympathy even in her eyes.

(*Enter Servant.*)

SERVANT: Mr. Concepcion Garcia and Mr. Capper.
CONCHO: (*Approaching Oakhurst, rubbing his hands.*) I wish you joy, Mr. Alexander Morton!
OAKHURST: (*Excitedly, aside.*) Shall I throw him from the window! The dog!—even he!
CAPPER: (*Approaching Mr. Oakhurst.*) You have done well. Be bold. *I* will see you through. As for *that* man (*pointing to Concho*), leave him to *me*! (*Lays his hand on Concho's shoulder, and leads him to sofa. Oakhurst takes seat in chair, as Sandy enters quietly from door and stands leaning upon his chair.*)
STARBOTTLE: (*Rising.*) Ladies and gentlemen, we are waiting only for the presence of Mr. Alexander Morton, Sr. I regret to say that for the last twenty-four hours—he has been—er—exceedingly preoccupied with the momentous cares of the—er—occasion. You who know the austere habits of my friend and—er—client will probably understand that he may be at this very moment engaged in prayerful and Christian meditation, invoking the Throne of Grace, previous to the solemn duties of—er—er—tonight.

(*Enter Servant.*)

SERVANT: Mr. Alexander Morton, Sr.

(*Enter Old Morton, drunk, in evening costume, cravat awry, coat half buttoned up, and half surly, half idiotic manner. All rise in astonishment. Sandy starts forward. Oakhurst pulls him back.*)

MORTON: (*Thickly.*) Don't rishe! Don't rishe! We'll all sit down! How do you do, sir? I wish ye well, miss. (*Goes around and laboriously shakes hands with everybody.*) Now lesh all take a drink! lesh you take a drink, and you take a drink, and you take a drink!
STARBOTTLE: Permit me, ladies and gentlemen, to—er—explain: our friend is—er—evidently laboring under—er—er—accident of hospitality! In a moment he will be himself.
MORTON: Hush up! Dry up—yourself—old turkey-cock! Eh!
SANDY: (*Despairingly.*) He will not understand us! (*To Starbottle.*) He will not know me! What is to be done?
MORTON: Give me some whishkey. Lesh all take a drink! (*Enter Servant with decanter and glasses. Morton starting forward.*) Lesh all take a drink!
SANDY: Stop!
MORTON: (*Recovering himself slightly.*) Who says stop? Who dares countermand

my ordersh?

CONCHO: (*Coming forward.*) Who? I will tell you: eh! eh! Diego—dismissed from the rancho of Don Jose for drunkenness! Sandy—the vagabond of Red Gulch!

SANDY: (*Passionately seizing Old Morton's arm.*) Yes, Diego—Sandy—the outcast —but, God help me! no longer the drunkard. I forbid you to touch that glass!— I, your son, Alexander Morton! Yes, look at me, father: I, with drunkenness in my blood, planted by you, fostered by you—I whom you sought to save—I—I, stand here to save you! Go! (*To Servant.*) Go! While he is thus, I—I, am master here!

MORTON: (*Cowed and frightened.*) That voice! (*Passing his hand over his forehead.*) Am I dreaming? Aleck, where are you? Alexander, speak, I command you: is this the truth?[36]

OAKHURST: (*Slowly.*) It is!

STARBOTTLE: One moment—a single moment: permit me to—er—er—explain. The gentleman who has just—er—dismissed the refreshment is, to the best of my legal knowledge, your son. The gentleman who for the past year has so admirably filled the functions of that office is—er—prepared to admit this. The proofs are—er—conclusive. It is with the—er—intention of offering them, and —er—returning your lawful heir, that we—er—are here tonight.

MORTON: (*Rising to his feet.*) And I renounce you both! Out of my house, out of my sight, out of my heart, forever! Go! liars, swindlers, confederates! Drunk—

OAKHURST: (*Retiring slowly with Sandy.*) We are going, sir!

MORTON: Go! open the doors there *wide*, wide enough for such a breadth of infamy! Do you hear me? *I* am master here!

(*Stands erect, as Oakhurst and Sandy, hand in hand, slowly retreat backward to center,—then suddenly utters a cry, and falls back heavily on sofa. Both pause: Oakhurst remains quiet and motionless; Sandy, after a moment's hesitation, rushes forward, and falls at his feet.*)

SANDY: Father, forgive me!

MORTON: (*Putting his hand round Sandy's neck, and motioning him to door.*) Go! both of you, both of you! (*Resisting Sandy's attempt to rise.*) Did you hear me? Go!

STARBOTTLE: Permit me to—explain. Your conduct, Mr. Morton, remind me of sing'lar incident in '47—

MORTON: Silence!

OAKHURST: One word, Mr. Morton! Shamed and disgraced as I am, I leave this roof more gladly than I entered it. How I came here, you best know. How I yielded madly to the temptation, the promise of a better life; how I fell, through the hope of reformation,—no one should know better than you, sir, the reformer. I do not ask your pardon. You know that I did my duty to you as your presumed son. Your real son will bear witness that, from the hour I knew of his existence, I did my duty equally to him. Colonel Starbottle has all the legal transfers and papers necessary to make the restoration of your son—the integrity of your business name—complete. I take nothing out of this life that I did not bring in it,—except my self-respect! I go—as I came—alone!

JOVITA: (*Rushing towards him.*) No! no! You shall take *me*! I have wronged you, Jack, cruelly; I have doubted you, but you shall not go alone. I care not for this contract! You are more to me, by your own right, Jack, than by any kinship with such as these!

OAKHURST: (*Raising her gently.*) I thank you, darling. But it is too late now. To be more worthy of you, to win *you*, I waived the title I had to you in my own manhood, to borrow another's more legal claim. I, who would not win you as a gambler, cannot make you now the wife of a convicted impostor. No! Hear me, darling! do not make my disgrace greater than it is. In the years to come, Jovita, think of me as one who loved you well enough to go through shame to win you, but too well to ask you to share with him that shame. Farewell, darling, farewell! (*Releases himself from Jovita's arms, who falls beside him.*)

CONCHO: (*Rubbing his hands, and standing before him.*) Oho! Mr. John Oakhurst—eh—was it for this, eh—you leaped the garden wall, eh? Was it for this you struck me down, eh? You are not wise, eh? You should have run away with the Dona when you could—ah, ah, impostor!

SANDY: (*Leaping to his feet.*) Jack, you shall not go! I will go with you!

OAKHURST: No! Your place is there. (*Pointing to Old Morton, whose head has sunk drunkenly on his breast.*) Heed not this man; his tongue carries only the borrowed lash of his master.

CONCHO: Eh! you are bold now—bold, but I said I would have revenge—ah, revenge!

SANDY: (*Rushing towards him.*) Coward!

DON JOSE: Hold your hand, sir! Hold! I allow no one to correct my menials but myself. Concho, order my carriage!

CONCHO: It is ready, sir.

DON JOSE: Then lead the way to it, for my daughter and her husband, John Oakhurst.—Goodnight, Mr. Morton. I can sympathize with you, for we have both found a son. I am willing to exchange my dismissed servant for your dismissed *partner.*

STARBOTTLE: (*Advancing.*) Ged, sir, I respect you! Ged, sir, permit me, sir, to grasp that honorable hand!

MORTON: (*Excitedly.*) He is right, my partner. What have I done! The house of Morton & Son dissolved. The man known as my partner—a fugitive! No, Alexander!

STARBOTTLE: One moment—a single momet! As a lawyer, permit me to say, sir, that the whole complication may be settled, sir, by the—er—addition of—er—single letter! The house of Morton & Son shall hereafter read Morton & Sons. The papers for the legal adoption of Mr. Oakhurst are—er—in my pocket.

MORTON: (*More soberly.*) Have it your own way, sir! Morton & Sons be it. Hark ye, Don Jose! We are equal at last. But—hark ye, Aleck! How about the boy, eh?—my grandson, eh? Is this one of the sons by adoption?

SANDY: (*Embarrassedly.*) It is my own, sir.

CAPPER: (*Advancing.*) He can with safety claim it, for the mother is on her way to Australia with her husband.

MORTON: And the schoolma'am, eh?

MISS MARY: She will claim the usual year of probation for your prodigal, and then—
SANDY: God bless ye, Miss Mary!
MORTON: I am in a dream! But the world—my friends—my patrons—how can I explain?
STARBOTTLE: I will—er—explain. (*Advancing slowly to front—to audience.*) One moment—er—a single moment! If anything that has—er—transpired this evening—might seem to you, ladies and gentlemen—er—morally or—er—legally—or honorably to require—er—apology or—er—explanation!—permit me to say—that I—Colonel Culpepper Starbottle, hold myself responsible—er—personally responsible.

(*Curtain.*)

END

FOOTNOTES

[1] *Vaquero*: horseman or cowboy.

[2] *Semper*: always.

[3] *Manta*: shawl.

[4] *Saya y manta*: skirt and shawl.

[5] *Solus*: alone.

[6] *Serape*: blanket, cloak, poncho; worn over the shoulder or shoulders.

[7] *Greasers*: American slang for Mexicans, suggested by the supposedly more oily complexions of the Hispanics, compared with the dry-skinned Yankees.

[8] *No sabe*: I don't know.

[9] *Caballero*: gentleman, swain, horseman.

[10] *Pass his hash!*: leave it alone; forget it!

[11] *I looks toward ye*: Here's looking at you; your health; a toast.

[12] *Surcle*: colloquial for cinch, the strap which holds the saddle on the mount.

[13] *Cayotes*: coyotes; an insult.

[14] *You're blowed upon*: you're given away; your secret is known; your cover is blown.

[15] *Er—er*: Harte's method of indicating that Col. Starbottle stammers, intended as a comic effect.

[16] *Muchacho*: boy.

[17] *Sembi Canca*: a dance of the period; related to the Can Can.

[18]*Glass*: a glass-eye, regarded as comical—and undesirable in a prospective mate; red hair was also thought unattractive and was long worn by comic characters.

[19]*No shabe likoquize*: stage-dialect Chinese for: *No sabe* recognize; *no sabe* meaning "I don't know."

[20]*Alle same, John*: They're all the same man, to John; here, Hop Sing uses an American slang designation for Chinese: "Chinaman John."

[21]*Shabbee*: dialect for *sabe*; colloquial: savvy; meaning, "Do you understand?"

[22]*Poco tiempo*: In a little while.

[23]*Madre de Dios*: Mother of God!

[24]*Manzanita*: literally "little apple," a Western shrub with gnarled branches and tiny blossoms from which bees make aromatic honey.

[25]*'Frisco*: slang for San Francisco; San Francisco newspaper columnist Herb Caen has insisted: "Don't call it 'Frisco."

[26]*If*: the meaning is "Even if . . ."

[27]*Natril*: dialect for natural.

[28]*A single question*: from what follows, it's clear that there are *two* questions; an oversight by playwright Harte.

[29]*Upper Stanislaus*: the Stanislaus River, which had some prosperous placer mines on or near it.

[30]*Pasear*: a walk, a promenade, but here in the sense of having a night out.

[31]*Three years*: since Sandy's son, Tommy, has earlier been described as a pupil of Miss Mary's at the Red Gulch School, this sudden reduction in the boy's age appears a device to elicit audience sympathy; it may have been an awkward expedient in the stage-production, but Bret Harte permitted it to remain in all printings of his *Collected Works*. Tots of three didn't go to school, though they might begin as early as five years.

[32]*Ez white a man ez they is*: "He's as white a man as there is"; a colloquial compliment similar to the 19th century British and American: "You've behaved like a white man!" and "That's mighty white of you!"

[33]*Ekal*: equal.

[34]*Chaw tobacker*: a chew of tobacco; chewing-tobacco.

[35]*Fog*: a distinctive attribute of San Francisco's climate, then as now.

[36]*Is this the truth*: considering the slovenly drunk-scene obviously intended for comic effect immediately preceding, this rapid recovery of self-possession and speech clarity to facilitate the denouement seems improbable.

A BRIEF CHRONOLOGY OF CALIFORNIA HISTORY

1542 — Spanish expedition under Cabrillo.

1579 — Sir Francis Drake explores the California Coast.

1768 — Spanish colonization of California—for fear of British and Russian en-
croachments—through the efforts of Padre Junipero Serra in founding the Mis-
sions; Franciscan fathers converted native Indians and taught them to work on
the Mission lands and build the Mission-churches and compexes; the Spanish also
established *presidios*—military stations—and *pueblos*—civilian towns. Early
pueblos in California were those of Nuestra Senora de Los Angeles and Yerba
Buena (San Francisco), among others.

1812 — Russians establish Fort Ross on the California coast above San Francisco Bay;
they are engaged in the fur trade.

1822 — Spanish domination of Mexico ends; Mexican self-rule begins, including what
will one day be the State of California.

1826 — Jedediah Smith and a group of trappers make the first overland entry by white
men into California; whaling-men and sea-born fur traders from the Eastern
United States are also becoming familiar with the area; some begin to settle.

1833 — Mexico secularizes the Mission lands, making generous land-grants from them
and other areas occupied only by Indians; some grants give title to as many as
50,000 acres.

1841 — The first overland settlers arrive from the East.

1842-45 — Exploratory expeditions by U.S. General John C. Fremont.

1846 — (14 June) "Bear Flag Revolt" in Sonoma; William Ide and other feisty American
settlers—alleging a Mexican threat to drive them from their homes and ranches—
capture the astonished local Mexican authorities and declare a California

Republic, with the distinctive bear emblem that is later to become the state flag. The U.S. Navy is conveniently close in Monterey.

1848 — (24 January) At Sutter's Mill in Coloma, on the South Fork of the American River, James Marshall discovers the first important gold nugget, triggering the great Gold Rush to California.

1848 — (2 February) Under the Treaty of Guadelupe Hidalgo, the Mexican government, defeated in a war with the United States, cedes California and other valuable western territories, including what will become the State of Nevada; in 1859, the fabulous Comstock Lode in Virginia City begins to produce $300 million in gold and silver in just two decades.

1849 — The year of the great Gold Rush; Monterey is the California capital.

1850 — (9 September) California becomes the 31st state in the union; it's admitted as a "free state," in the controversy between North and South regarding slavery. The Nevada lands are made part of the Utah Territory; only in 1861, as a result of Comstock wealth, will they become the Nevada Territory, with statehood in 1864, through Civil War pressures.

1851 — San Francisco has its first Vigilance Committee, in which irate citizens, angered at crime and corruption, take the law into their own hands.

1853 — Gold-bearing quartz ore is discovered in Grass Valley, California, giving new life to the northern goldfields, seemingly exhausted by placer mining; this signals the era of "hard-rock" mining, with experienced miners brought from Cornwall ("Cousin Jacks") and from Wales.

1854 — Sacramento becomes the new state capital.

1856 — San Francisco has a new group of vigilantes, who lynch their prey, Cora and Casey, among other extra-legal activities.

1857 — The Butterfield Overland Mail is inaugurated.

1858 — With the amazing number of quartz-gold strikes being made, there are now some 280 quartz-mills in California, used for crushing the ore so that gold particles can be separated from it.

1860 — The Pony Express begins its services.

1861 — The transcontinental telegraph is completed.

1869 — With the driving of the Golden Spike at Promontory, Utah, the transcontinental railroad is finished, linking California with the East—and promoting even more theatrical trouping from the East than before had been possible by sea and overland.

1882 — Concerned by the presence of so many Chinese immigrants in California, brought first by the lure of gold and work, and later imported as cheap labor to build the railroads, Western lawmakers succeed in getting the Senate and the House of Representatives to pass the (Oriental) Exclusion Act.

BIBLIOGRAPHY
Selected Works

Ashley, Celeste. *Gold Rush Theatre in Nevada City, California.* Unpublished M.A. Thesis, Stanford University, 1957.

Delano, Alonzo ("Old Block"). *A Live Woman in the Mines; or, Pike County Ahead!.* New York: Samuel French, 1857.

Foster, Lois M. *Annals of the San Francisco Stage—1850-1880.* Unpublished Federal Theatre/WPA Project Manuscript, San Francisco, 1937.

Gaer, Joseph. *The Theatre of the Gold Rush Decade in San Francisco.* New York: Burt Franklin, 1970.

Gagey, Edmond M. *The San Francisco Stage.* New York: Columbia University Press, 1950.

Goldberg, Isaac. *Queen of Hearts: the Passionate Pilgrimage of Lola Montez.* New York: The John Day Co., 1936.

Harte, Bret. *Two Men of Sandy Bar.* Boston: J. R. Osgood, 1876. Also in Harte's *Collected Works.*

Howe, Charles E. B. *Joaquin Murieta de Castillo, the Celebrated California Bandit.* San Francisco: Commercial Book and Job Steam Printing Establishment, 1858.

Hyde, Stuart Wallace. *The Representation of the West in American Drama from 1849 to 1917.* Unpublished Ph.D. Dissertation, Stanford University, 1954.

Leman, Walter. *Memories of an Old Actor.* San Francisco: A. Roman & Co., 1886.

MacMinn, George R. *The Theatre in the Golden Era in California.* Caldwell, Idaho: Caxton Printers, 1941.

McElhaney, John. *The Professional Theatre in San Francisco, 1880-1889.* Unpublished Ph.D. Dissertation, Stanford University, 1972.

Phillips, Levi Damon. *Arthur McKee Rankin's Touring Production of Joaquin Miller's "The Danites."* Unpublished Ph.D. Dissertation, University of California at Davis, 1981.

Robinson, Dr. D. G. *Comic Songs; Or, Hits at San Francisco.* San Francisco: Commercial Book and Job Office, 1853.

Rourke, Constance. *Troupers of the Gold Coast; or, The Rise of Lotta Crabtree.* New York: Harcourt, Brace & Co., 1928.

San Francisco Theatre Research. 1st Series, edited by Lawrence Estavan. San Francisco: Mimeographed monographs, prepared for the Federal Theatre under WPA Project 8386, 1938.